Italy al Dente

ALSO BY BIBA CAGGIANO:

From Biba's Italian Kitchen
Trattoria Cooking
Modern Italian Cooking
Northern Italian Cooking

ITALY
al Dente

PASTA, RISOTTO, GNOCCHI,
POLENTA, SOUP

BIBA CAGGIANO

WILLIAM MORROW AND COMPANY, INC. / NEW YORK

It is the policy of William Morrow and Company, Inc., and its imprints and affiliates, recognizing the importance of preserving what has been written, to print the books we publish on acid-free paper, and we exert our best efforts to that end.

Library of Congress Cataloging-in-Publication Data has been applied for.

ISBN 0-688-14877-8

Printed in the United States of America

First Edition

2   3   4   5   6   7   8   9   10

BOOK DESIGN BY JOANN METSCH

www.williammorrow.com

To my family,
Vincent, Carla, Paola, Brian, Tim, Luise, Larry, Frank, and Marissa
with love

Acknowledgments

Thank you to all the following people for their help, support, and encouragement.

To Vincent, my husband and best friend, for sharing with me the daily grind of writing a book, and for being my official "tester."

To my immensely gifted kitchen staff—Don Brown, John Eichhorn, T. K. Kodsuntie, Pam Barton, and Tony Sanguinetti—for the food preparation and retesting of recipes. You all made my job so much easier.

To Glenn Stewart, my invaluable assistant, for retesting recipes and keeping my schedule straight.

To Maureen and Eric Lasher, my agents, for their friendship and for steering me toward great career choices.

To Ann Bramson, Gail Kinn, and Pam Hoenig, some of the most talented editors in the business, for giving me so much space and so many choices.

To Ellen Silverman for her mouthwatering photographs, Anne Disrude and Betty Alfenito for making the food look so incredibly appetizing, and to Carol Jillot for her drawings.

Then, of course, there is Italy, for which I have so much to thank: Great beauty, a glorious culinary heritage and passionate cooks; open markets and wondrous specialty stores, great restaurants, *trattorie* and *osterie*, and generous cooks all over who so willingly shared their culinary traditions with me. Thank you.

Contents

Introduction

There is an old Italian saying, *A tavola non s'invecchia*, or "At the table one never grows old!" That is probably one of the reasons why Italians spend such a great deal of time around the dinner table. The other reason is perhaps quite obvious to everyone: Italians love food. They don't intellectualize about food. They celebrate it!

Some of the best and fondest memories of my childhood and young adulthood in Italy are of events that have taken place around the table. Simple family dinners, special events, celebrations, and even mourning—all found our family gathered around our large kitchen table. What I remember most and what is embedded deep within me is the aroma of the food. The slow-simmering broth that would wake me up on Sunday mornings. The nutmeg that was used for the passatelli, a soft bread dough riced into soup. The hearty Bolognese meat ragù that would be served over homemade tagliatelle. The aroma of food was everywhere. Walking up the stairs of our apartment building around lunchtime, I could smell what each family was preparing for the *pranzo*, the noon meal. The aromas were comfortable and familiar. They spoke of regional culture and family traditions. That is probably why most Italians are instinctive cooks. They have been nurtured and lulled by those strong gastronomical traditions.

Even though I believe that good Italian cooking should be rooted in strong regional traditions, I also believe that one should not follow rules slavishly because, like language, music, or art, food adapts itself to new modes. My philosophy, which is shared by most Italian cooks, is that flexibility in the kitchen is essential, that quality of ingredients is everything, and that simplicity of execution is a must. Another important prerequisite of the Italian cook is *fantasia*, or imagination and creativity.

Italian culinary creativity is unparalleled. And it reaches its peak with the kind of food that is close to my heart: pasta, risotto, gnocchi, soups, and polenta, the first courses in a traditional Italian meal. This is the heart of Italian cooking; it's soul food. These are the dishes that every Italian wants when he or she sits down at the table.

That Italians are passionately in love with their first courses, especially pasta, is evident. Just walk into an Italian *trattoria* or restaurant and you will see people resolutely twirling their pasta perfectly around the fork, in anticipation of the mouthful to come. This is all quite natural, since pasta has been basic to the Italian diet for centuries. No Italian in his or her right mind would ever voluntarily give up their pasta. With my own family in Bologna, pasta—homemade or factory made—is almost always the dish of choice.

While pasta is the food that unites Italians regardless of regional background, status, age, or sex, other splendid dishes—such as risotto, gnocchi, soups, and polenta—highlight the Italian genius with food. These dishes are more popular than ever because they can be as simple or as elaborate as one wishes. Just imagine what a velvety seafood risotto or a steaming bowl of potato gnocchi with a long-simmered meat ragù can do for your soul. This is food that nourishes and satisfies. It is food that you want to share with family and friends. It makes you want to celebrate life.

Today, when most women are working outside the home and the demands of contemporary life have changed the way the Italian family eats its daily meals, dishes such as pasta, risotto, gnocchi, and soups have grown even more important. Often the daily meal is composed of one of these dishes, a salad, and some cheese, while the traditional Italian meal, with its sequence of small courses, is reserved for the weekend and special occasions.

When I was given the contract for this new book, I was so excited and eager to start that I immediately went into the kitchen and began testing dishes, one after the other. After a few weeks of that intense routine, I realized I had to slow down. So I settled into a comfortable pace of testing one dish a day. And every day, like clockwork, after lunch had been served at my restaurant, I would go into the kitchen to test the chosen dish. Then as I was ready to put the food on the plates, I would call my staff so we all could taste it and comment. It got to the point that we all looked forward to what had become a ritual: sharing good food during a few minutes of spontaneous, lighthearted pleasure and relaxation.

This is a book I have wanted to do for years because it is the food I passionately love, and love to cook. Here, I have gathered a compendium of traditional and contemporary recipes. As always, Italy with its unbelievably rich culinary flair has been my inspiration. Consider the recipes in this book your passport to Italian cooking. With the exception of a few dishes in the chapter on fresh pasta, most of the recipes are quite straightforward and simple to prepare. And often I have given tips on preparing the dish ahead, which will allow you as much flexibility as possible.

Keep in mind that for a true Italian flavor, you must try to secure the ingredients listed in the recipe, even if that means going the extra mile. Even though the Italian attitude toward food is surprisingly more relaxed than it used to be, thankfully we still don't do fusion cooking!

To simplify these already simple dishes, do a bit of preparation ahead. First, read the recipe carefully, so you will be aware of the ingredients needed and the length of the preparation. Chop the onion, parsley, or garlic, peel the tomatoes, peel the shrimp, and so on. Line up all your ingredients on a tray in the order in which you are going to use them (cooking professionals do that all the time) so that you can concentrate on what is happening in the skillet, and you can carry on a conversation with your friends as well. If a dish is a bit more involved, try it on your family first before doing it for company, so that you can smooth out any rough edges. Please don't be intimidated. Just think that this is *only food* and not brain surgery. If you make a mistake, you can always start over again. Also, keep in mind that just as no two people cook alike, no recipe ever comes out tasting the same. Much depends on the mood of the moment, our senses, the ingredients at hand, the appeal of the dish, and so many other things.

I hope these dishes will draw you into the kitchen. I hope that their flavors will linger on your palate and will find a secure place in your sensory memory, so that you too will be able to cook like Italians do. With a sense of tradition, exuberance, and *fantasia*.

The
Basics

Ingredients

In the mid-seventies and early eighties, when Italian cooking was highly stereotyped, the availability of authentic Italian ingredients was almost nonexistent. That was about the time when I embarked on my newfound career as a teacher of Italian cooking. (What timing!) Thankfully Corti Brothers, the lone Italian specialty store in Sacramento, and Molinari in San Francisco, were ahead of the pack, and could provide me with the most basic ingredients, which I often carried with me to other cities when I was teaching a class. What a change twenty years have made! And what a joy for people like me, who rely entirely on authentic Italian ingredients to produce uncompromisingly Italian dishes. If you have watched me on The Learning Channel, you know the importance I give to ingredients, because without them there would not be any Italian cooking to speak of.

Even though Italian cooking is one of immediacy, made with the freshest ingredients available, it also relies heavily on basic staples that can and should always be available in an Italian pantry. For this reason, I have divided the Basic Italian Ingredients into two categories: the dry ingredients, which are stored in the pantry; and other ingredients that need to be stored in the refrigerator. The ingredients in the pantry can be kept for months. The ingredients in the refrigerator—cheeses, herbs, hams, and so on—should be purchased and used when needed. Just keep in mind that these ingredients are the key to the success of your Italian dishes.

THE DRY PANTRY

Dried pasta: Spaghetti, linguine, bucatini, penne, rigatoni, and shells, just to mention a few, are vital to the Italian pantry. Choose a good brand of factory-made pasta imported from Italy, made with 100 percent semolina flour (durum wheat). See page 149 for some of my favorite brands.

Rice: In order to make risotto, one of greatest dishes of northern Italy, you need the correct rice. Arborio, Vialone Nano, and Carnaroli are excellent and are widely available in Italian markets and specialty food stores. See page 236 for a short explanation of these rice varieties.

Beans: The Italian table uses a rich variety of fresh or dried legumes. The following dried beans can be kept in the pantry for several months: Cannellini and borlotti beans, brown lentils, fava beans, green peas, chick-peas. Dried beans are economical and nutritious and, when properly cooked, are far superior to the canned variety.

Dried porcini mushrooms: Porcini are wild Italian mushrooms that grow under chestnut trees in spring and fall. Dried porcini, which are available all year, have a musky, highly concentrated flavor that can enrich pasta sauces, ragùs, soups, stews, or game dishes. Dried porcini are used extensively by the Italian cook because they can be stored in the pantry for several months. Dried porcini, which are generally sold in small transparent packages, should have a light creamy color.

Canned plum tomatoes: The best imported Italian canned tomatoes are the San Marzano variety. In these cans you will find only whole, peeled, firm-fleshed plum tomatoes with some of their juices. No tomato paste, no herbs, no chunks of anything else. Good canned tomatoes can be transformed into a great tomato sauce with little or no effort at all. Search for these tomatoes as if you were searching for truffles. If unavailable, try other canned tomatoes until you find one that is acceptable to you.

Tomato paste: Very useful for quick sauces, or to add color and taste to soups, stews, and braised meats or body to thin tomato sauces. It should be used with moderation.

Yellow cornmeal: Use for making polenta. Cornmeal can be fine grained or coarse. In this book I use a mixture of the two, which gives my polenta a perfect texture. Cornmeal can be kept tightly sealed in the pantry for several months, or it can be frozen.

Flour: Use unbleached all-purpose for pasta, pastry, and bread.

Bread crumbs: Bread crumbs can be used in a number of surprising ways in Italian cuisine. They are essential to a variety of fried dishes and a revelation when they toasted in oil and paired with garlic, anchovies, and hot pepper and tossed with pasta.

Anchovies: Anchovies are available packed in oil, in salt, or as a paste. If you are using canned anchovies, store leftovers in a small bowl, cover with oil, and refrigerate until ready to use again. Anchovies packed in salt are a good alternative. I do not recommend anchovy paste in a tube, even though it is convenient to use; it will rob you of true anchovy flavor.

Olives: In my recipes I use black and green, preferably packed in brine and imported from Italy. Pair them with oil, anchovies, capers, and garlic for a great southern Italian sauce for spaghetti. Olives can be stored in unopened cans up to two years, and, once opened, can be refrigerated in their own liquid in a glass container for two weeks.

Olive paste: Imported from Italy. Extra-virgin olive oil, garlic, and a bit of olive paste make a great, quick appetizing sauce for pasta.

Sun-dried tomatoes: The best sun-dried tomatoes come from Liguria. Use them to enrich a pasta sauce when winter tomatoes are bland. To rehydrate dried tomatoes, cover them with extra-virgin olive oil and leave at room temperature overnight.

Capers: Capers are the unopened buds of a wild Mediterranean plant. Capers come in two sizes: the small nonpareil, which are usually pickled in vinegar, and the larger, which are packed in salt and used liberally in Sicilian and Sardinian cooking. Pickled capers are quite convenient, since they can be kept for a long time; rinse these thoroughly before using to get rid of the strong vinegar taste. I prefer the larger capers because they are meatier. Before using, soak salted capers in a bowl of cold water for a few minutes, then rinse them thoroughly to remove as much salt as possible. Use capers in moderation; their pleasant but assertive taste can over take a dish.

Olive oil: Olive oil unites all Italian cooking. Olive oil comes in several grades. Extra-virgin olive oil is the best and purest of all the oils, with less than 1 percent acidity. This oil is produced without chemical means by stone crushing and cold pressing hand-picked olives. Virgin olive oil has a higher degree of acidity, up to 4 percent; it's made of riper olives that have fallen to the ground. And pure olive oil, in spite of its label, is an oil that has been deodorized, deacidified, and decolorized by chemical means. Extra-virgin olive oil is a bit more expensive than regular oil but well worth it. There are many great varieties on the market; to choose your favorite, try a selection until you find the one that appeals to your palate. I prefer oils that are not too aggressive, with a pale golden color and a smooth, light, round flavor because they pair well with many dishes. Store olive oil in a cool, dark corner of your pantry, away from heat.

Balsamic vinegar: Balsamic, an aromatic vinegar from Modena, is made from the boiled-down, sweet juices (must) of white Trebbiano grapes, following a centuries-old tradition. The juices are aged for decades in a series of barrels of different woods until the vinegar has acquired its distinctive thick, velvety, and aromatic quality. The older the vinegar, the more flavorful and the more expensive it is. A few drops of balsamic added to a grilled steak or a lamb or veal chop will impart the dish with incredible flavor. It is also marvelous over fresh strawberries and over chunks of Parmigiano-Reggiano cheese. True balsamic should bear the mark of *Aceto Balsamico Tradizionale di Modena.* If you can find a ten-, fifteen-, or twenty-year-old balsamic, and if money is no object, buy it and use it sparingly and wisely. Unfortunately, most balsamic vinegar available in this country is commercially produced and bears very little resemblance to the traditional artisan product.

Fine and coarse sea salt: Choose this salt; it's the purest, with a mild, clean taste.

Pine nuts: Pine nuts form the basis for pesto and other sauces. Toasted pine nuts or walnuts and almonds add crunch and depth of flavor when sprinkled over a creamy pasta or salads.

Spices: Spices are power culinary tools. They give individuality to dishes. Nutmeg adds a subtle sweetness to pasta stuffing. Red pepper flakes and whole dried hot red pepper kick up flavor and give edge to spicy southern Italian dishes. Saffron adds flavor and a great golden color to risotto.

Dried herbs: For those few months of the year when you can't get fresh herbs, keep oregano, rosemary, sage, thyme, and marjoram at hand. But remember, dry herbs get old, too. Don't keep them on the shelf for five years and expect them to retain their original aroma. Dried herbs give personality as well as taste. But you need to use them with moderation because they can be quite overpowering.

Garlic: Even though garlic is available all year, it is at its best in spring when its flavor is more restrained. As garlic ages, its flavor becomes sharper and more pronounced. Choose a firm, compact head of garlic with clear white skin and use it in moderation. Go easy on the garlic, please. A heavy hand with garlic doesn't make a dish "Italian." Always use fresh garlic. Never use garlic flakes or garlic powder. Garlic keeps best if stored out of the refrigerator.

THE REFRIGERATED PANTRY

The Cheeses

Parmigiano-Reggiano: This is the king of Italian cheeses; it is impossible to imaging Italian cooking without it. Parmigiano is a low-fat cheese with a high protein content produced from the best possible milk, following a centuries-old cheese-making tradition. This noble cheese is produced under strict regulations in the provinces of Parma, Reggio, Modena, Mantua, and Bologna. By law, Parmigiano-Reggiano is aged a minimum of one year. In buying Parmigiano, look for the words *Parmigiano-Reggiano* etched in tiny dots on the rind of the cheese. Its color should be somewhere between a very pale yellow to creamy. Its texture should be moist and a bit crumbly. Its taste should be nutty and just a bit salty. Parmigiano-Reggiano can never be too salty or too assertive; that is why it complements so well a large variety of dishes. Parmigiano is an expensive cheese, but a little goes a long way. Grate the cheese as needed, then wrap it tightly in plastic wrap, then again in foil and refrigerate it. It will keep well for several weeks. Domestic "parmesan" has absolutely no relation to Parmigiano-Reggiano.

Mozzarella: The best mozzarella is made from water buffalo milk. (Yes, there are water buffalo in southern Italy.) *Mozzarella di buffala* has a creamy, delicate consistency and a savory taste. Unfortunately, 100 percent buffalo milk mozzarella might become a thing of the past since in southern Italy the number of domesticated water buffalo are rapidly shrinking. What we find today is mozzarella made with a percentage of buffalo milk and a percentage of cow's milk, and *Fior di latte,* a whole-milk mozzarella. Both these mozzarellas are quite good and can be found in Italian markets and specialty food stores across the country. Mozzarella is quite perishable and it should be consumed within a day or two of its purchase. Do not substitute the rubbery mozzarella found on supermarket shelves.

Ricotta: A soft, delicious, delicately sweet cheese, ricotta is made from the whey, or the watery part of the cow's milk. Ricotta is great for pasta filling and desserts. Again, check your local Italian markets for the best product available.

Mascarpone: A sinfully delicious imported double cream cheese, mascarpone is used for cooking, for desserts, or as a table cheese served with fruit. My favorite way of using mascarpone is to simmer it with butter and cream and serve it over homemade fettuccine. Yum.

Fontina: Fontina is a sweet, delicate table cheese from the Val d'Aosta. Because of its soft, melting quality, fontina cheese is ideal for cooking. Fontina is also terrific in baked pasta dishes.

The Meats

Prosciutto: Prosciutto is unsmoked, salted, air-cured ham. *Prosciutto di Parma,* which is produced in the hills of Langhirano just outside Parma, is perhaps the best and most well-known prosciutto. Its outstanding quality derives from the best-quality pigs fed with a special high-protein diet. The curing process of prosciutto ranges from ten months to two years. During that time, the moisture in the meat is slowly drawn out by the salt. The end result is a prosciutto that is fragrant, sweet, moist, and totally unforgettable. Luckily, *prosciutto di Parma* is now available in this country. Look for the Parma crown branded on the side of the ham; its color should be a rich rose with a very light marbling of fat. Try to use it as soon as you can. Sliced prosciutto, tightly wrapped in plastic, can be kept for a day or two in the refrigerator. After that it will dry out and lose a considerable amount of its fragrance. American-made prosciutto such as Volpi, Danieli, and Citterio are good substitutes.

Pancetta: Pancetta is unsmoked Italian bacon that is cured in salt and spices and aged for several months. It has approximately the same amount of fat as it has of lean meat. Pancetta is rolled up like a salami. Its unique, savory taste is essential to many Italian dishes. (My mother would send us children to school with delicious *panini con la pancetta,* or pancetta sandwiches.) Because Italian pancetta is still not imported into the United States, check with your Italian specialty store for a good American-made brand. Volpi is my favorite national brand. If you are in San Francisco, go to Molinari in North Beach. This little Italian deli makes the best pancetta this side of the Atlantic Ocean.

Speck: Speck is smoked Italian ham from the Alto Adige region. I love the smoky flavor of speck, especially when paired with cabbage or Brussels sprouts and tossed with buckwheat noodles (page 131).

Bresaola: Bresaola is cured dried beef that is often served as a component of an *antipasto misto.* Bresaola is also delicious as a component of a pasta sauce. Speck and bresaola are available in Italian markets and specialty food stores.

How To

How do I peel tomatoes or peppers? Why do the dried beans break apart as they cook? Why are the eggplants bitter? Should I wash dirty mushrooms? Once there were knowledgeable mothers or grandmothers in the kitchen to answer these questions. Today most beginning cooks have to rely on cookbooks and cooking shows to learn these "secrets." Sometimes, with just a bit of good common sense, we can figure out the solution all by ourselves. Other times we need someone to show us exactly how to do it.

Some basic cooking techniques are essential in the kitchen, because they enable us to work faster and more efficiently, and make our time in the kitchen much more enjoyable.

HOW TO PEEL TOMATOES

Cut a cross at the bottom end of the tomatoes and drop them into boiling water. Boil the tomatoes until their skins begin to split, 1 to 3 minutes. (The cooking time varies depending on the ripeness of the tomatoes and the thickness of their skins.) Transfer tomatoes to a bowl of ice water. As soon as you can handle them, remove their skins, which will peel off effortlessly. Seed, dice, mince, or chop the tomatoes as needed.

HOW TO CLEAN BABY ARTICHOKES

These small artichokes are perfect in sauces and salads because they are easy and quick to clean.

Remove the green leaves of the artichokes by snapping them off at the base. Stop when the leaves closer to the base are pale yellow and the tips are pale green. Slice off the green tops. Cut the stem off at the base and trim off the remaining green part at the base. Place the artichokes in a bowl of cold water with the juice of a lemon to prevent discoloring.

Drop the artichokes in salted boiling water and cook, uncovered, until tender—7 to 10 minutes, depending on size. Drain artichokes when tender, pat dry, and slice into wedges. Put the artichokes in a bowl, cover tightly, and refrigerate until ready to use. They can be kept for a few days.

HOW TO PURGE EGGPLANT

Because eggplants have an underlying bitter flavor, which will affect the taste of a dish if not removed, they need to be purged by steeping in salt. The salt draws out the bitter juices.

Trim and peel the eggplant, and cut into ½-inch-thick rounds. Put the slices on a large baking sheet, sprinkle liberally with salt, and let stand 30 to 40 minutes. Pat the slices well with paper towels to remove the salt and excess juices, and use as instructed in the recipe.

HOW TO RECONSTITUTE DRIED PORCINI MUSHROOMS

Dried porcini mushrooms, with their musky, earthy flavor, are a vital component of innumerable sauces. Before you use dried mushrooms, they must be reconstituted to their original soft texture.

Soak the porcini in lukewarm water for 20 to 30 minutes. Drain the porcini mushrooms and reserve the soaking water. Rinse the mushrooms well under cold running water. Mince or chop as needed and use as instructed in your recipe.

Strain the soaking water through a few layers of paper towels over a small bowl to get rid of the sandy deposit. Use the water as instructed in the recipe.

HOW TO CLEAN FRESH MUSHROOMS

The ideal way of cleaning mushrooms is with a soft mushroom brush; in lieu of that, a moist kitchen towel will do. If mushrooms are very dirty, rinse them quickly, a few at a time, under cold running water, lay them on a large kitchen cloth, and dry them thoroughly with another towel. Never slice the mushrooms before washing them.

HOW TO ROAST PEPPERS

Peppers roasted directly on an open flame have the most delicious flavor. However, peppers are also delicious if they are roasted under the broiler. No matter what method you choose, this is what you do:

Roast the peppers until they are charred on one side. Turn them with long tongs to char and blister the skin all over. Place the peppers in a plastic bag and secure it tightly. Leave the peppers in the bag to cool and soften for about 30 minutes.

Peel off the blistered skin. Open the peppers wide and remove the seeds. Use the peppers as instructed in your recipe

HOW TO PEEL FRESH FAVA BEANS

The season for fresh fava beans is spring. When the beans are very small, young, and fresh, their skin doesn't need to be removed. When the beans are large, their skin is tougher and needs to be peeled off.

Shell the beans and discard the pods. Drop the beans in a pot of boiling salted water and cook for about 1 minute. Drain the beans and place them in a bowl of iced water. When cool, drain again. Pinch the skin of each bean, breaking it at one end, and squeeze the bean out of its skin. Use the beans as instructed in individual recipes.

Five pounds of fresh fava beans in their pods give approximately 2 pounds shelled beans. Two pounds of shelled beans give approximately 1½ pounds peeled beans.

For dried fava beans, follow instructions given for Dried Beans.

HOW TO COOK DRIED BEANS

Before cooking dried beans, they must be soaked in cold water for at least 12 hours. These basic soaking and cooking guidelines apply to all types of dried beans. Lentils do not need to be presoaked.

Pick the beans over and place them in a large bowl. Cover the beans generously with cold water and let them soak overnight at room temperature.

Drain the beans and rinse them under cold running water. Put the beans in a large pot and cover them with cold water by 3 to 4 inches. Cover the pot partially and bring the water to a gentle simmer. Simmer the beans over low heat, stirring occasionally, until they are tender, 45 minutes to 1 hour. Add salt only at the end of cooking or the beans' skin will crack as they cook.

If you are not using the beans right away, transfer them to a bowl with their liquid and cool. Cover and refrigerate for a day or two.

Two cups of dried beans is approximately 1 pound. Two cups of dried beans give approximately 4 cups cooked beans.

HOW TO CLEAN MUSSELS AND CLAMS

Mussels: Soak the mussels in a large bowl of cold salted water for 30 minutes. (Salt will help draw out the sand from the mollusks.) Remove the mussel's beard by pulling it off. Scrub mussels well under cold running water to remove all dirt and slime. Discard any mussels that won't close shut as they are handled. After they are thoroughly cleaned, place the mussels in a large bowl, cover with a wet towel, and refrigerate them until ready to use.

Clams: Soak and scrub clams as indicated above.

HOW TO CLEAN SQUID

If you are squeamish about cleaning squid, you should know that many fish markets sell squid already cleaned. If you are interested in learning how to do it, follow these instructions:

Put the squid in a bowl of cold water and let it soak for about 1 hour. Hold the squid body with one hand and pull away the tentacles. Cut the tentacles just above the eyes. Squeeze off the little beak inside the tentacles. Discard the head. Remove the long cartilage from the squid body. Clean the squid body under cold running water, pulling out any matter that remains inside. Wash and peel away any grayish skin from the body and the tentacles and discard it. (If you can't remove the skin completely from the tentacles, it is okay.) Cut the squid body into ¼-inch rings. Use the squid as instructed in your recipe.

HOW TO POWDER SAFFRON STRANDS

Saffron comes in powder and in strands; the powdered is somewhat more expensive and not as readily available as the strands. If you are using saffron strands, put the strands in a small resealable plastic bag, seal it, and press the saffron with a large spoon or a small rolling pin to break it into a powder.

AND, DID YOU KNOW . . .

- That Italians don't generally add grated cheese to garlic-oil-anchovy dishes or other seafood preparations? The cheese overpowers the taste of the fish.
- That putting the pasta in the skillet with the sauce will allow the sauce to thicken and coat the pasta perfectly. It also gets the pasta to the table piping hot.
- That ripe, red, meaty imported canned tomatoes from San Marzano are a much better choice than the fresh, truck-refrigerated summer tomatoes found in most supermarkets.

- That in Italy leftover pan juices from roasts and braised meats become a sauce for pasta.
- That if a wine is good for drinking, it is also perfect for cooking.
- That adding a bit of butter to a sauce just before tossing it with the pasta will make the sauce creamier and denser so that it will cling to the pasta.
- That if you eat food that is too garlicky, you should munch on some fresh parsley to clean your mouth of the strong garlic taste.
- That fresh herbs added to a sauce at the very last moment retain their bright green color and distinctive flavor.
- That by blanching vegetables in boiling salted water and dropping them immediately into ice water, they will retain their bright green color and will stop cooking instantly.
- That, not surprisingly, Italians consume more pasta per capita (28 kilograms) than any other nation on earth?
- That Italy, next to Greece and Spain, consumes more olive oil than any other nation?
- That if you remove the small green sprout from the center of the garlic clove, you will have a gentler flavor.
- That if you chop garlic with a bit of salt, it will not stick to the knife or cutting board.
- That if you want to be sure to remove all possible small insects from the leaves of vegetables or lettuce, add vinegar to a large bowl of water and soak the greens for 10 to 15 minutes.

Soups

Basic Meat Broth

Basic Chicken Broth

Basic Fish Broth

Vegetable Broth

Quick Broth

Mushroom and Bean Soup

Mixed Mushroom and Bread Soup

Fava Bean and Potato Soup Neapolitan Style

Sicilian Fresh Fava Bean Soup

Bean, Cabbage, and Rice Soup

Pasta and Bean Soup Neapolitan Style

Bean and Mussel Soup

Mixed Bean Soup

The Tomato and Bread Soup of Siena

Minestrone of Green Vegetables

Mushroom, Potato, and Smoked Ham Soup

Lentil Soup

Zucchini and Fresh Tomato Soup

Cabbage, Pea, and Rice Soup

Baked Cabbage and Bread Soup

Vegetable Minestrone with Rice

Royal Soup

Pea and Zucchini Soup with Pesto

Zucchini Soup

Lentil and Escarole Soup

Roasted Butternut Squash Soup

Asparagus and Rice Soup

Zucchini and Cabbage Soup

Squash and Potato Soup

Tuscan Onion Soup

Escarole Soup

Barley and Porcini Mushroom Soup

Chick-pea and Clam Soup

Tuscan Chick-pea and Pasta Soup

Artichoke, Leek, and Rice Soup

Fava Bean and Artichoke Soup

Angel Hair in Broth

Parmesan, Egg, and Nutmeg Soup

Rice, Egg, and Parmesan Soup

oups are the best kept secret of Italian cooking. There are regions in Italy where soup, not pasta, appears on the table daily and is considered the most important element of the meal. Every time I think about my father I see him slowly savoring a bowl of hot soup. Never mind the great tagliatelle, tortellini, and lasagne that my mother would routinely prepare; father was happiest when dining on a bowl of perfectly clear, fragrant, homemade meat broth in which swam golden, thin taglioline.

Italian soups are multifaceted and regional in their particulars. In my region of Emilia-Romagna, as well as in several other northern Italian regions, the soups are generally prepared with a flavorful, homemade meat broth and often have the addition of homemade pasta or rice. The soups of Tuscany and Umbria are fortified with beans or bread. The soups of the Italian Riviera and the South are fragrant with herbs, garlic, and tomatoes, while the soups of the high mountain ranges have big, full flavors and a dense consistency.

In addition to all these great traditional soups there are the soups of *fantasia,* or imagination, which tell the story of a people, place, and circumstance. These dishes are often the product of necessity or of a creative mood. For example, after the Second World War, when good ingredients were scarce or unaffordable, my mother would prepare a bean soup without the traditional base of pancetta and fresh herbs. Instead, she would make the soup with a base of chopped onion and parsley; water would replace the homemade broth. The pasta was omitted in favor of a larger amount of beans and a few potatoes. And even though that soup was not fancy, it was thick and delicious.

Another soup my mother used to make, especially in leaner times, was *pancotto,* literally translated "cooked bread." This was made with a few days'-old bread cooked in a bit of broth or water, and seasoned with olive oil, salt, and pepper. Occasionally she would add butter and Parmigiano-Reggiano, or fresh sage. *Pancotto* was as thick as a porridge, velvety and very appetizing—a major feat considering the few, humble ingredients that were used to make it.

But perhaps one of the best examples of Italian imagination and resourcefulness is *ribollita,* a traditional Tuscan soup in which a bit of leftover minestrone is stretched to feed many by the addition of bread and then *reboiled* into a new thick and delicious soup. Today this simple peasant dish is celebrated as one of the greatest soups of Italy.

In Italy, soups are called with many names: *minestra in brodo, minestrina, minestrone, zuppa, passato.* All these names indicate a style of preparation and identify the soups as thick and hearty or a clear broth with the addition of pasta or pastina, and so on. For instance, thick and hearty soups generally begin with a base of *soffritto,* an array of savory ingredients that are first chopped or minced, then slowly sautéed together. This sautéing is perhaps the most important step in making such a soup, for it creates the rich, flavorful taste. On the other hand, clear soups rely primarily on top-quality homemade broth.

In this chapter, you will find some pretty outstanding soups that are amazingly easy to prepare. The beautiful thing about soups is that you don't need to be a slave to the recipe. If the recipe tells you to use white cultivated mushrooms and you come across some great wild mushrooms, use them. If you can't find fresh mint, use fresh parsley. If you hate anchovies, omit them. The important thing, however—and with all Italian cooking in general—is to keep a balance of flavors. Too much garlic or chili pepper will obliterate the flavors of the other ingredients.

You probably will have noticed that in many recipes I say to "let the soup rest for 20 to 30 minutes after it is done." This is because the short rest brings together the separate flavors of the ingredients and also thickens it. That is why minestrone, bean, or lentil soups are even better the day after they are made.

Most of the time a soup can be prepared ahead and left at room temperature for a few hours or refrigerated for a few days. And, of course, many can be frozen for future use. When holding over the soup calls for a different procedure, I've noted that at the end of the recipe.

I urge you to get into the kitchen and do yourself and your family a favor.

Cook a soup. In this chapter you will find some delicious recipes. Try the Fava Bean and Potato Soup Neapolitan Style or the Bean and Mussels Soup, or the Mixed Mushroom and Bread Soup. These soups will make you forget the pasta, at least for a while!

THE IMPORTANCE OF HOMEMADE BROTH

In many Italian regions, soups made with a clear homemade broth were ritually made on Sundays. In my region of Emilia-Romagna, this ritual was perhaps more heartfelt than anywhere else in Italy. Early on Sunday mornings my mother (as well as any other mother or grandmother of the region) would get up earlier than usual in order to *mettere su la pentola,* or put the large pot with all the meats on the stove for the long, slow cooking that would produce a great aromatic meat broth.

On Sunday, we children were allowed to sleep late, perhaps so that my mother would have the chance to cook undisturbed for a few hours. What routinely would awake us was the tempting aroma of the broth that permeated the house. The meats that would produce the much desired broth were basically always the same: beef, veal, chicken, or capon, plus bones and a few vegetables. The cooking of the broth, done at the barest of a simmer, would take about 4 hours. During the long, slow cooking, the broth would be skimmed and allowed to reduce to a little more than half its original amount. Its aroma would become more pronounced, its color would turn to a light golden, and its taste would send shivers down your spine.

At the end of the cooking, the broth would be strained and skimmed of the fat, and freshly prepared tagliolini, quadrucci, or tortellini would be added and cooked. And that soup would become the first course of our traditional Sunday meal. Any leftover broth was used throughout the week in myriad ways. It gave character to sauces, stews, and braised meats. It was used for risotto and minestrone. Without any doubt, homemade broth was—and still is—one of the most important foods in the Italian kitchen.

BASIC MEAT BROTH
Brodo di Carne

❧

MAKES APPROXIMATELY 2 QUARTS

It is amazing how many people confuse the Italian *brodo,* or broth, with the French stock. Stock is made by browning assorted bones in the oven and simmering those bones with vegetables and water on top of the stove. Stock has a rich, dense flavor. Italian *brodo,* in contrast, is made by placing a variety of meat pieces or meat scraps and bones in a large pot with vegetables, covering them with cold water, and bringing it to a gentle simmer. The result is a light, flavorful broth that is used for soups and risotto, and for cooking in general. *Brodo* uses a variety of meats or meat scraps, such as beef, veal, chicken, and bones, especially knuckle bones or bones with marrow. Lamb or pork are generally not used in a *brodo* because of their assertive flavor. A good homemade *brodo* is essential to Italian cooking, yet making a *brodo* is quite simple. Make a large batch and freeze it in several containers. It will enrich your cooking tremendously, and it will also save you quite a bit of money.

5 pounds bones and meat
    scraps from beef, veal, and
    chicken
A few sprigs fresh parsley
2 carrots, cut into pieces
2 celery stalks, cut into pieces
1 small yellow onion, peeled
    and quartered
2 small ripe tomatoes,
    quartered
Salt to taste

Put all the ingredients except the salt in a large stockpot and cover by 3 to 4 inches with cold water. Set the cover askew on the pot and bring the liquid to a gentle boil over medium heat. Reduce the heat to low so that the liquid will simmer at a very slow pace. Skim off all the foam and scum that comes to the surface of the water with a slotted spoon or a skimmer. Partially cover the pot and simmer about 3 hours. Because broth reduces considerably during cooking, its flavor will become more accentuated. Therefore, season with salt during the last 10 to 15 minutes of cooking.

Line a large wire strainer with paper towels and strain the broth, a few ladles at a time, directly into a large bowl. Cool the broth, uncovered, at room temperature, then refrigerate it overnight. The next day remove the fat that has solidified on the surface. The broth is now fat free, ready to use or to freeze.

BASIC CHICKEN BROTH
Brodo di Gallina

MAKES APPROXIMATELY 3 QUARTS

This preparation is basically the same as for a meat broth. The only change is that a whole chicken is added to the bones and vegetables. Older chickens are generally best for this broth, for they impart a greater depth of flavor, especially if used whole, with the neck, feet, and giblets. Some cooks prefer to use capons instead of chickens, which give the broth a more aromatic flavor. In any event, this basic broth is easy to prepare, easy to store, economical to make, and great to have at hand (see Keeping Broth, above). There is the added bonus of the boiled chicken, which can be served in a variety of interesting ways.

3 pounds bones and meat
    scraps from veal and chicken
A few sprigs fresh parsley
2 carrots, cut into pieces
2 celery stalks, cut into pieces
1 small yellow onion, peeled
    and quartered

2 small ripe tomatoes,
    quartered
1 large, plump chicken
    (3 to 4 pounds)
Salt to taste

CONTINUED

Put all the ingredients except the whole chicken and the salt in a large stock-pot and cover by 5 to 6 inches with cold water. Set the cover askew on the pot and bring the liquid to a gentle boil over medium heat. Reduce the heat to low so that the liquid will simmer at a very slow pace. Skim off all the foam and scum that comes to the surface of the water with a slotted spoon or a skimmer. Partially cover the pot and simmer 1½ hours.

Add the chicken to the simmering broth and partially cover the pot. Simmer 1½ hours longer. Skim any foam that comes to the surface of the water. Season lightly with salt during the last minutes of cooking.

Remove the chicken from the pot and set it aside. Line a large wire strainer with paper towels and strain the broth, a few ladles at a time, directly into a large bowl. Cool the broth, uncovered, at room temperature, then refrigerate it overnight. The next day remove the fat that has solidified on the surface. The broth is now fat free, ready to use or freeze.

CHICKEN THE NEXT DAY

The broth can also make a light soup out of which you can prepare two courses the next day. Cut the chicken or capon into serving pieces and place in the cooled broth. Cover the bowl and refrigerate it overnight. Remove the fat and place the broth and the chicken in a large pot. Bring the broth to a gentle simmer. Transfer the chicken from the hot broth to a large platter, cover with foil, and keep warm in a low heated oven. Add your favorite noodles (mine are tagliolini) to the hot broth and cook until tender for a delicious bowl of soup. Serve the moist chicken—which remains so for having sat overnight in the broth—as a second course served with warm mashed potatoes.

BASIC FISH BROTH
Brodo di Pesce

❧

MAKES APPROXIMATELY 8 CUPS OF BROTH

3 pounds fish frames (see Note, below)

1 large onion, coarsely chopped

2 medium celery stalks, cut into pieces

2 small carrots, cut into pieces

3 to 4 sprigs fresh parsley

2 cups dry white wine

3 quarts cold water

Salt to taste

Rinse the fish frames under cold running water. Combine all the ingredients in a large saucepan and bring to a boil over medium heat. Reduce the heat to medium-low. With a slotted spoon or a skimmer, skim the scum that comes to the surface of the water. Simmer, uncovered, about 1 hour.

Line a strainer with a few layers of paper towels and strain the broth into a bowl. If you are not planning to use the broth right away, cool it to room temperature. It can be refrigerated for a few days or it can be frozen.

❧

NOTE

"Fish frames" are a mixture of fish bones, heads, scales, etc., available in fish markets, sold for the purpose of making fish broth. You can assemble your own fish frames by freezing any odd pieces of fish you have left over from other preparations.

VEGETABLE BROTH
Brodo Vegetale

❧

MAKES APPROXIMATELY 2 ½ QUARTS

A nice, light vegetable broth is flavorful and simple to prepare. It can be used for risotto and soups, instead of meat or chicken broths. Basically any fresh seasonal vegetables can be used, as well as vegetables that are always in season.

2 pounds mixed fresh vegetables, such as potatoes, carrots, leeks, onions, zucchini, peas, celery, tomatoes, asparagus

Salt to taste

Wash, peel, shell the vegetables, and cut them into medium pieces. Put all the vegetables in a medium pot and cover by 3 inches of cold water. Set the cover askew on the pot and bring the liquid to a gentle boil over medium heat. Reduce the heat to low and simmer 1½ hours. Season with salt. Skim off the foam that comes to the surface of the water.

Line a wire strainer with paper towels and strain the broth, a few ladles at a time, directly into a large bowl. The broth is now ready to use, or refrigerate or freeze.

QUICK BROTH
Brodo Veloce

❧

MAKES 6 CUPS BROTH

Because we cannot prepare homemade broth on the spur of the moment, it is useful to keep a small supply of low-sodium canned broth in the pantry. A simple way to prepare a quick broth is to mix canned broth with water and vegetables and simmer it for about half an hour. The result is an acceptable product that will allow you to prepare a soup or a risotto in a short amount of time.

4 cans (14 to 16 ounces each) low-sodium chicken broth
2 cups water
1 medium yellow onion, peeled and quartered

1 carrot, cut into 1-inch pieces
1 celery stalk, cut into 1-inch pieces
Several sprigs fresh parsley

Pour the broth and the water into a medium saucepan and skim off the solid fat. Add the vegetables and parsley and bring the broth to a boil over medium heat. Reduce the heat to low and partially cover the pot. Simmer 20 to 25 minutes. Strain the broth. It is now ready to use, refrigerate, or freeze.

MAMMA'S WAY

My mother would "stretch" a few cups of homemade broth into enough broth to feed a family of five. She mixed the flavorful broth with water and vegetables, and simmered it until the vegetables imparted their own aroma to the thin broth.

MUSHROOM AND BEAN SOUP
Zuppa di Funghi e Fagioli

❦

SERVES 4 TO 6

Most Tuscan soups are basic, uncomplicated, and thick. Bread and beans, two favorite Tuscan staples, are used exuberantly to thicken these soups because they satisfy hunger. In this dish, white cannellini beans are paired with mushrooms and a handful of other savory ingredients to impart a richer, fragrant taste.

1 cup (½ pound) dried white cannellini beans, soaked overnight in cold water to cover generously

2 quarts water

⅓ to ½ cup extra-virgin olive oil

1 cup finely minced yellow onion

2 pounds white cultivated mushrooms, wiped clean and finely sliced

2 garlic cloves, minced

4 anchovy fillets, minced

Chopped fresh red chili pepper or hot red pepper flakes to taste

2 cups canned Italian plum tomatoes with their juice, put through a food mill to remove seeds

4 cups Basic Chicken Broth (page 21) or low-sodium canned broth

Salt to taste

8 to 10 fresh basil leaves, shredded, or 1 to 2 tablespoons chopped fresh parsley

Drain the beans and rinse under cold running water. Put them in a large pot, add the water, and cook as instructed on page 11. Drain and set beans aside.

Heat the oil in a large pot over medium heat. Add the onion and cook, stirring, until pale yellow and soft, 4 to 5 minutes. Raise the heat to high and add the mushrooms. Cook, stirring, for 2 to 3 minutes. Add the garlic, anchovies, and hot pepper and stir for a minute or two. Add the tomatoes and simmer for 5 to 6 minutes, then add the beans. Stir the beans well into the sauce. Add the broth and season with salt. Bring the liquid to a boil. Reduce the heat to medium-low and simmer, uncovered, for 15 to 20 minutes, stirring occasionally. (The soup can be prepared to this point several hours ahead and left at room temperature, or it can be refrigerated for 2 days or frozen up to a month. Reheat gently before proceeding.)

When ready to serve, stir in the basil or parsley, taste, and adjust the seasoning. Turn the heat off under the pot and let rest for 20 to 30 minutes. Serve hot.

MIXED MUSHROOM AND BREAD SOUP
Zuppa di Funghi Misti e Pane

❧

SERVES 8

This is a soup of *fantasia,* or improvisation. One rainy Sunday I wanted to make a quick soup. Besides all the basic staples I had in the house, olive oil, garlic, parsley, and canned tomatoes, I found some white cultivated mushrooms and a loaf of day-old bread. I followed the traditional method of sautéing the mushrooms, the garlic, and the parsley and adding broth, and, in no time at all, a lovely, fragrant soup was slowly bubbling in the pot. But it was the simple addition of the bread, which thickened the soup, giving it a somewhat velvety texture, that changed this simple soup into a satisfying meal. For another splendid variation, use a combination of wild mushrooms, and just before serving, stir in a small handful of finely shredded fresh mint.

⅓ to ½ cup extra-virgin olive oil

2 pounds mixed mushrooms, such as white cultivated mushrooms, chanterelles, shiitake, brown mushrooms, or oyster mushrooms, wiped clean and finely sliced

2 garlic cloves, minced

2 tablespoons chopped fresh parsley

2 cups canned Italian plum tomatoes with their juice, put through a food mill to remove seeds

6 cups Vegetable Broth (page 24) or low-sodium canned chicken broth

Salt and freshly ground black pepper to taste

6 cups cubed stale Italian bread, crusts removed

8 to 10 fresh mint leaves, shredded, or 1 tablespoon additional chopped fresh parsley

Heat the oil in a large pot over high heat. Add the mushrooms and cook, stirring, for 2 to 3 minutes. Add the garlic and the parsley, and stir for about 1 minute. Add the tomatoes and the broth, then season with salt and pepper. Bring the liquid to a boil and add the bread. Stir a few times, then reduce the heat to medium-low and simmer, uncovered, for 35 to 40 minutes, stirring occasionally.

CONTINUED

Taste and adjust the seasoning. Turn the heat off under the pot and let the soup rest for 20 to 30 minutes.

Just before serving, stir in the mint or the parsley. Serve hot.

FAVA BEAN AND POTATO SOUP NEAPOLITAN STYLE

Zuppa di Fave e Patate alla Napoletana

SERVES 6

In Rome and Naples, fava beans were generally cooked with a savory base of *guanciale* (pork jowl) or *lardo,* a very fatty piece of pork. Today, with Italians more in tune with healthy food, they opt for olive oil and perhaps just a bit of pancetta or prosciutto to add taste to their soups or vegetables.

Make a double batch of this thick, flavorful soup, and later on when you are ready to serve the leftover, grill or toast a few slices of Italian bread, break it into pieces, and add it to the soup with a generous sprinkling of Parmigiano-Reggiano cheese. You will have a whole, wonderful meal in a bowl.

⅓ cup extra-virgin olive oil
1 cup finely minced yellow
    onion
1 thick slice prosciutto
    (2 to 3 ounces), finely diced
2 garlic cloves, minced
2 medium russet potatoes,
    peeled and diced
5 pounds fresh fava beans,
    shelled, blanched, and peeled
    (page 11)

6 cups Vegetable Broth
    (page 24) or low-sodium
    canned chicken broth or
    water
Salt and freshly ground black
    pepper to taste
2 tablespoons chopped fresh
    parsley
Extra-virgin olive oil to taste

Heat the oil in a large pot over medium heat. Add the onion, prosciutto, and garlic and cook, stirring, until onion is pale yellow and soft, 4 to 5 minutes. Add the potatoes and beans, and stir for a few minutes. Add the broth or water and bring to a gentle simmer. Cover the pot partially and cook, stirring occasionally, until the potatoes and beans are very tender, 20 to 30 minutes. Season with salt and pepper.

Puree half the beans and potatoes in a food processor or through a food mill and return to the pot. Simmer the soup 5 to 6 minutes longer. Stir in the parsley, taste and adjust the seasoning, and turn the heat off under the pot. Let the soup rest for 20 to 30 minutes. Serve hot or at room temperature with a few drops of olive oil drizzled over each serving.

SICILIAN FRESH FAVA BEAN SOUP

Zuppa di Fave alla Siciliana

❦

SERVES 8

Italians love fresh fava beans. One of the most popular ways to eat them is to dip them raw in a bowl of salt. Another is to turn them into a thick, satisfying soup. Because the season for fresh fava beans is short—from late Spring to early Summer—this soup can also be made with dried fava beans (see Fava Bean and Artichoke Soup, page 70).

⅓ cup extra-virgin olive oil
1 cup finely minced yellow
    onion
3 ounces pancetta, chopped
2 tablespoons chopped fresh
    parsley
2 cups canned Italian plum
    tomatoes with their juice, put
    through a food mill to
    remove seeds

Salt and freshly ground black
    pepper to taste
5 pounds fresh fava beans,
    shelled, blanched, and peeled
    (page 11)
2 quarts Vegetable Broth
    (page 24) or water
Extra-virgin olive oil to taste

Heat the oil in a large pot over medium heat. Add the onion, pancetta, and parsley and cook, stirring, until the onion is soft and the pancetta is lightly golden, 5 to 6 minutes. Add the tomatoes and season with salt and pepper. Simmer, uncovered, 8 to 10 minutes. Add the fava beans to the sauce and simmer for a minute or two. Add the broth or water and bring to a gentle boil. Cover the pot partially and cook until beans are tender, 20 to 30 minutes.

Puree half the beans in a food processor or through a food mill and return to the pot. Simmer the soup 5 to 6 minutes longer. Taste and adjust the seasoning, then turn the heat off under the pot and let the soup rest for 20 to 25 minutes. Serve hot or at room temperature with a few drops of olive oil drizzled over each serving.

BEAN, CABBAGE, AND RICE SOUP
Zuppa di Fagioli, Cavolo, e Riso

SERVES 8

This is the kind of peasant soup that an Italian *nonna,* grandmother, would make. The ingredients are humble—beans, cabbage, onion, carrots, garlic, and olive oil—and yet, as they simmer together, they are transformed into a richly aromatic, thick, and substantial soup—a meal in itself.

1 cup (½ pound) dried cannellini beans, soaked overnight in cold water to cover generously

2 quarts plus ½ to ¾ cup Basic Chicken Broth (page 21) or low-sodium canned chicken broth

1 pound Savoy cabbage

⅓ cup extra-virgin olive oil

1 cup finely minced red onion

1 cup finely minced carrots

2 tablespoons chopped fresh parsley

2 garlic cloves, minced

Salt and freshly ground black pepper to taste

1 cup imported Arborio rice

Extra-virgin olive oil to taste

Drain and rinse the beans under cold running water, put them in a large pot, and add 2 quarts of the broth. Cook as instructed on page 11. Puree half the beans in a food processor or through a food mill and return to the pot. Turn the heat off under the pot.

Remove and discard any bruised outer leaves of the cabbage. Slice the cabbage in half and remove the core. Cut the cabbage into thin strips and chop the strips roughly.

Heat the oil in a medium saucepan over medium heat. Add the onion, carrots, parsley, and garlic and cook, stirring, until the vegetables are soft, about 8 minutes. Add the cabbage and stir for a minute or two. Add ½ cup of the broth and stir a few times, then cover the pan partially and reduce the heat to low. Simmer until the cabbage begins to soften, 8 to 10 minutes, adding a bit more broth if needed. Season with salt and pepper, stir well, then add to the beans.

Put the soup over medium-low heat and simmer 8 to 10 minutes. Add the rice and cook, stirring occasionally, making sure that the rice does not stick to the bottom of the pot, until the rice is tender but still a bit firm to the bite, 10 to 12 minutes.

Taste and adjust the seasoning. If the soup is too thick, simply add a bit more broth or water. Turn the heat off under the pot and let the soup rest for a few minutes. Serve hot or at room temperature with a dash of fragrant olive oil atop each serving.

PASTA AND BEAN SOUP
NEAPOLITAN STYLE
Pasta e Fagioli alla Napoletana

❧

SERVES 8

There is no doubt that *pasta e fagioli* is the most famous and most loved soup of Italy. Every region, city, town, and hamlet has its own version. In Bologna prosciutto rind and the hard crust of Parmigiano-Reggiano are added for additional flavor and the pasta of choice is *maltagliati,* a homemade pasta that is cut in odd pieces. In Tuscany the soup often has the addition of cabbage or some other vegetables and bread. The bean soups of Lombardy and the Veneto are usually enriched with rice, while in Naples and in the other cities of the Campania region the pasta of choice is generally spaghetti, which has been broken into smaller pieces.

This Neapolitan soup is thick, delicious, and immensely appetizing. Try to eat it at room temperature to fully enjoy its flavor.

2 cups (1 pound) dried cranberry beans or red kidney beans, soaked overnight in cold water to cover generously

2 quarts water

1 thick slice prosciutto (2 to 3 ounces), cut into 3 or 4 pieces

⅓ cup extra-virgin olive oil

1 cup finely minced yellow onion

2 tablespoons chopped fresh parsley

3 garlic cloves, minced

1 pound ripe plum tomatoes, halved, seeded, and finely minced

Chopped fresh red chili pepper or hot red pepper flakes to taste

Salt to taste

6 ounces spaghetti, broken into small pieces

Extra-virgin olive oil to taste

Drain and rinse the beans under cold running water. Put them in a large pot, add the water and the prosciutto, and cook as instructed on page 11. Turn the heat off under the pot and set aside until ready to use.

With a slotted spoon, scoop up the pieces of prosciutto from the beans and cut them into small pieces. Heat the oil in a medium saucepan over medium heat. Add the onion, parsley, and garlic. Cook, stirring, until the onion is pale yellow and soft, about 5 minutes. Add the tomatoes, prosciutto pieces and the hot pepper, then season with salt. Simmer, uncovered, until the tomatoes are soft, 10 to 12 minutes. If the tomatoes are not very ripe, and the mixture looks dry, add a few tablespoons of the bean cooking water.

Puree half of the beans in a food processor or food mill and return to the pot. Add the tomato mixture to the beans and put the pot back on medium heat. Simmer the soup 4 to 5 minutes longer. Add the pasta and cook, stirring occasionally, until it is tender but still firm to the bite. Turn the heat off under the pot and let the soup rest for a few minutes. Serve hot or at room temperature with a dash of fragrant olive oil on each serving.

A COOL SOUP FOR A HOT DAY

If you prefer to eat the soup at room temperature, like most Italians do in summer, leave the soup out for several hours. Cook the pasta separately in salted boiling water, drain it, and add it to the soup just before serving.

BEAN AND MUSSEL SOUP
Passato di Fagioli con le Cozze

❧

SERVES 8

This classic bean soup from southern Italy has plump, fragrant fresh mussels instead of the traditional pasta. I found this combination absolutely irresistible. If you let the soup rest for 20 to 30 minutes after it is done, it will become denser and more flavorful. If you prefer, clams can be substituted for mussels.

2 cups (1 pound) dried cannellini beans, soaked overnight in cold water to cover generously

2 quarts cold water

⅓ cup extra-virgin olive oil

1 cup finely minced yellow onion

3 garlic cloves, minced

6 to 8 fresh sage leaves, chopped, or 2 to 3 dried sage leaves

2 cups canned Italian plum tomatoes with their juice, put through a food mill to remove seeds

Salt and chopped fresh chili pepper or hot red pepper flakes to taste

1 cup water

2 tablespoons extra-virgin olive oil

4 pounds mussels (1 pound shelled), soaked and scrubbed (page 11)

2 tablespoons chopped fresh parsley

Extra-virgin olive oil to taste

Drain and rinse the beans under cold running water, put them in a large pot, and add the water. Cook as instructed on page 11. (The beans can be prepared a day ahead. Refrigerate tightly covered.)

Heat the oil in a small saucepan over medium heat. Add the onion, garlic, and sage. Cook, stirring, until the onion is pale yellow and soft, 5 to 6 minutes. Add the tomatoes and season with salt and hot pepper. Reduce the heat to low and simmer, uncovered, 10 to 12 minutes.

Puree all the beans with some broth in a few batches in a food processor until smooth. Return pureed beans to the pot, then add the tomato mixture. Put the pot back on medium-low heat and simmer 5 to 6 minutes. Let the soup rest for 20 minutes or so.

Put the water and oil in a large, deep pan and place over medium heat. Add the mussels and cover the pan, cooking just until the mussels open. With a slotted spoon, transfer them to a bowl as they open. Line a strainer with paper towels and strain the liquid into a bowl to get rid of the sandy deposits. Detach the meat from the shells. Cut the mussels into two or three pieces and add them to the bowl with the liquid.

Stir the mussels, their juices, and the parsley into the soup and leave for 4 to 5 minutes. Taste, adjust the seasoning, and serve with a dash of olive oil atop each serving.

MIXED BEAN SOUP
Zuppa di Fagioli Misti

❧

SERVES 8

This big, full-flavor bean soup can be made with as many types of beans as you like. Keep in mind, however, that different beans have different cooking times. So make sure to cook the beans until they are all quite soft.

2 cups assorted dried beans (cannellini, cranberry, kidney beans, black-eyed peas), soaked overnight in cold water to cover generously

2 quarts cold water

⅓ cup extra-virgin olive oil

1 cup finely minced yellow onion

1 cup finely minced carrot

1 cup finely minced celery

2 garlic cloves, minced

2 cups Vegetable Broth (page 24) or low-sodium canned beef broth

Salt and freshly ground black pepper to taste

2 tablespoons minced fresh basil

2 tablespoons chopped fresh parsley

¼ cup minced chives

Extra-virgin olive oil to taste

Drain and rinse the beans under cold running water, put them in a large pot, and add the water. Cook as instructed on page 11. Puree half of the beans in a food processor or through a food mill and return them to the pot. Turn the heat off under the pot.

Heat the oil in a medium saucepan over medium heat. Add the onion, carrot, celery, and garlic and cook, stirring, until the vegetables are soft, about 8 minutes. Add the broth, season with salt and pepper, and bring to a simmer. Cook, uncovered, stirring occasionally, for 10 to 12 minutes. Add a bit more broth or water if mixture reduces too much.

Add the vegetable mixture to the beans, then put the pot back on medium-low heat and simmer 10 to 15 minutes longer. Turn the heat off under the pot and let the soup rest 20 to 30 minutes.

Stir the basil, parsley, and chives into the soup. Taste and adjust the seasoning. Serve hot or at room temperature with a few drops of olive oil over each serving.

THE TOMATO AND
BREAD SOUP OF SIENA
La Pappa al Pomodoro e
Pane di Siena

※

SERVES 8

Bread and tomato soups are popular throughout Tuscany. The best known is perhaps the famous *pappa al pomodoro* of Florence. However, the beautiful city of Siena south of Florence also boasts a great traditional *pappa al pomodoro*. This version has the addition of finely minced sautéed vegetables and herbs, which become the savory base of this delightful soup. To make this absolutely outstanding, you need three basic ingredients: fresh, ripe plum tomatoes; fresh, fragrant basil; and extra-virgin olive oil. Don't settle for anything else.

⅓ to ½ cup extra-virgin
   olive oil
1 cup finely minced yellow onion
1 cup finely minced carrot
1 cup finely minced celery
2 tablespoons chopped fresh
   parsley
2 garlic cloves, minced
6 cups cubed stale Italian
   bread, crusts removed

2½ pounds ripe plum tomatoes,
   peeled, seeded, and minced
   (page 9)
6 cups Vegetable Broth
   (page 24) or low-sodium
   canned chicken broth
Salt to taste
8 to 10 fresh basil leaves,
   shredded
Extra-virgin olive oil to taste

Heat the oil in a large pot over medium heat. Add the onion, carrot, celery, parsley, and garlic. Cook, stirring, until vegetables are soft, 7 to 8 minutes. Add the bread and stir for a minute or so until well coated with the savory vegetable base. Add the tomatoes, stir for a few minutes, then add the broth. Bring the broth to a gentle boil, season with salt, and reduce the heat to medium-low. Simmer, uncovered, stirring occasionally until the bread is completely soft and becomes an integral part of the soup, 45 to 50 minutes. At this point if there are still some large pieces of bread floating in the soup, beat the soup with a wire wisk until everything is blended into a creamy, thick mixture. Turn the heat off under the pot and let the soup rest for 20 to 30 minutes.

Just before serving, stir in the basil, then serve hot or at room temperature with a few drops of olive oil over each serving.

MINESTRONE OF GREEN VEGETABLES
Minestrone Verde

❧

SERVES 8 TO 10

T his is a lovely, easy-to-make minestrone that uses only green vegetables. Don't be afraid to make it a day or two ahead because its flavor intensifies as it sits and when it reheats.

⅓ cup extra-virgin olive oil
1 cup finely minced long green
   onions, white part only
2 tablespoons fresh parsley
1 cup finely minced celery
2 ounces prosciutto, cut in
   1 thick slice and finely diced
3 pounds assorted green
   vegetables (zucchini, string
   beans, asparagus, peas,
   spinach, artichokes, etc.),
   washed and diced

2½ quarts Vegetable Broth
   (page 24) or low-sodium
   canned chicken broth
Salt to taste
½ cup freshly grated
   Parmigiano-Reggiano cheese

Heat the oil in a large pot over medium heat. Add the green onions, parsley, celery, and prosciutto. Cook, stirring, until the onion is pale yellow and soft, 4 to 5 minutes. Add all the vegetables and cook, stirring constantly for a few minutes, until vegetables are thoroughly coated with the savory onion base.

Add the broth and bring to a gentle boil. Season with salt and reduce the heat to medium-low. Simmer, stirring occasionally, until the vegetables are tender and the soup has a medium-thick consistency, 30 to 40 minutes.

Turn the heat off under the pot and let the soup rest 20 to 30 minutes. Serve hot or at room temperature with a sprinkling of grated Parmigiano.

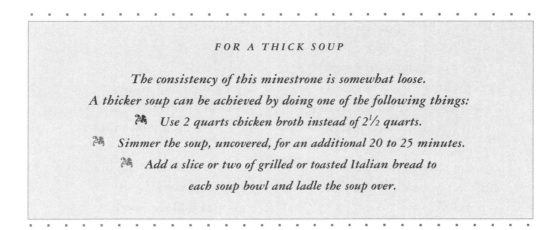

FOR A THICK SOUP

The consistency of this minestrone is somewhat loose.
A thicker soup can be achieved by doing one of the following things:
Use 2 quarts chicken broth instead of 2½ quarts.
Simmer the soup, uncovered, for an additional 20 to 25 minutes.
Add a slice or two of grilled or toasted Italian bread to
each soup bowl and ladle the soup over.

MUSHROOM, POTATO, AND SMOKED HAM SOUP

Zuppa di Funghi, Patate, e Speck

❦

SERVES 8

The soups of the northeastern regions of Trentino–Alto Adige and Friuli–Venezia Giulia have one thing in common—they're substantial. This full-flavored soup, which uses dried porcini and white cultivated mushrooms, also has potatoes, which add body and thickness.

2 ounces dried porcini
    mushrooms, soaked
    in 2 cups lukewarm water
¼ cup extra-virgin olive oil
2 tablespoons unsalted butter
½ cup finely minced yellow
    onion
2 garlic cloves, minced
2 tablespoons chopped fresh
    parsley
2 ounces speck, cut in 1 thick
    slice and finely diced
1½ pounds white cultivated
    mushrooms, wiped clean and
    thinly sliced

3 medium russet potatoes
    (1½ pounds), peeled
    and diced
1 cup canned Italian plum
    tomatoes with their juices,
    put through a food mill to
    remove seeds
Salt and freshly ground black
    pepper to taste
6 cups Basic Meat Broth
    (page 20) or low-sodium
    canned beef broth or water
½ cup freshly grated
    Parmigiano-Reggiano cheese

Drain the porcini mushrooms and mince. Strain and reserve their soaking water.

Heat the oil and butter in a large saucepan over medium heat. Add the onion, garlic, parsley, and speck. Cook, stirring, until the onion is pale yellow and soft, 4 to 5 minutes. Raise the heat to high and add the cultivated mushrooms and porcini. Cook, stirring, for 2 to 3 minutes. Add the potatoes, reserved porcini soaking water, and tomatoes. Season with salt and pepper. Bring the sauce to a gentle simmer and cook, uncovered, 10 to 12 minutes.

Add the broth or water to the saucepan and bring to a boil, then reduce the heat to low and simmer, uncovered, 35 to 40 minutes. Stir a few times during the cooking.

Puree half of the soup in a food processor or food mill and return to the pan. Simmer the soup 5 to 6 minutes longer, then taste and adjust the seasoning. Turn the heat off under the pot and let the soup rest for 20 to 30 minutes. Serve hot with a sprinkling of grated Parmigiano.

LENTIL SOUP
Zuppa di Lenticchie

❧

SERVES 8

This is a great winter soup—thick, hearty, and very easy to prepare. You can also use beans or chick-peas. All these legumes are high in vitamins, minerals, and soluble fiber. How nice it is to eat a dish that is not only very good but also good for you.

FOR THE BREAD

⅓ cup olive oil
2 cups cubed stale Italian bread
  (1-inch pieces), crusts
  removed

FOR THE SOUP

⅓ cup extra-virgin olive oil
1 cup finely minced yellow
  onion
¼ pound pancetta, finely
  chopped
1 pound ripe plum tomatoes,
  seeded and diced

2 tablespoons tomato paste
  diluted in ½ cup beef broth
  or water
Salt and freshly ground black
  pepper to taste
2 cups dried brown lentils
  (about ¾ pound), washed in
  several changes of cold water
2 quarts Basic Meat Broth
  (page 20) or low-sodium
  canned beef broth
1 to 2 tablespoons chopped
  fresh parsley
⅓ to ½ cup freshly grated
  Parmigiano-Reggiano cheese

CONTINUED

Prepare the bread: Heat the oil in a medium skillet over medium heat. Add the bread cubes and cook until they are golden on all sides. Transfer to paper towels to drain and set aside until ready to use.

Prepare the soup: Heat the oil in a large saucepan over medium heat. Add the onion and pancetta and cook, stirring, until lightly golden, about 5 minutes. Add the tomatoes, stir a few times, then add the diluted tomato paste. Season lightly with salt and pepper. Cook, uncovered, for 10 to 12 minutes, stirring occasionally.

Add the lentils to the pan and stir well. Add the broth, bring it to a boil, and reduce the heat to low. Cover the pot partially and simmer, stirring from time to time, until the lentils are tender, 45 minutes to 1 hour.

When the soup is done, stir in the parsley and adjust the seasoning. Turn the heat off under the pot and let the soup rest 20 to 30 minutes. Immediately before serving, put some bread cubes into each soup bowl and ladle the soup over the bread. Serve with a sprinkling of grated Parmigiano.

ZUCCHINI AND FRESH
TOMATO SOUP
Zuppa di Zucchine e Pomodori

❧

This is a soup that screams summer! You won't believe how good it looks and how great it tastes until you try it. Because the ingredients are so few, they must be very fresh and of the best quality. Look for sweet onions, very ripe, juicy tomatoes, and fresh basil. And to fully appreciate the lightness and freshness of this soup, serve it at room temperature.

⅓ to ½ cup extra-virgin olive oil

2 cups finely minced yellow
  onion

2 pounds small zucchini, ends
  removed and diced into small
  pieces

2 pounds plum tomatoes,
  seeded and diced

2 quarts Vegetable Broth
  (page 24) or low-sodium
  canned chicken broth

Salt to taste

8 to 10 fresh basil leaves, finely
  shredded, or 1 to 2
  tablespoons minced fresh
  chives

Heat the oil in a large pot over medium-high heat. Add the onion and cook, stirring, until onion has a nice golden color, 6 to 7 minutes.

Raise the heat to high and add the zucchini. Cook and stir until zucchini begins to color, about 5 minutes. Add the tomatoes, stir for a few minutes, then add the broth. Season with salt and bring the broth to a boil. Reduce the heat to low and simmer the soup, uncovered, for 30 to 40 minutes, stirring from time to time. Turn the heat off under the pot and let the soup rest for 20 to 30 minutes.

When you are ready to serve, stir the basil or the chives into the soup, adjust the seasoning, and serve.

CABBAGE, PEA, AND RICE SOUP
Minestra di Verza, Piselli, e Riso

❧

SERVES 8

Here's a wholesome and delicious soup that uses the simplest ingredients. And like most other soups, it is quite versatile. If I make it in spring or summer, I reduce the amount of cabbage and increase the amount of fresh peas. In winter, I do the opposite and use small frozen peas since fresh peas are not available.

Occasionally I omit the rice in favor of grilled or fried slices of bread, which I put in the bowl and cover with the soup. But keep two things in mind: good homemade broth will make your soup sing; and do not let the rice sit in the soup too long or it will become soggy. *Buon appetito!*

4 tablespoons unsalted butter
1 cup finely minced yellow onion
½ a large head Savoy cabbage (about 2½ pounds), core removed and leaves thinly sliced
Salt and freshly ground black pepper to taste

2 quarts Basic Chicken Broth (page 21) or low-sodium canned chicken broth
1 cup imported Arborio rice
2 pounds fresh peas in their pods, shelled, or 1 cup frozen peas, thawed
⅓ to ½ cup freshly grated Parmigiano-Reggiano cheese

Heat the butter in a large pot over medium heat. Add the onion and cook, stirring, until it is lightly golden, about 5 minutes. Add the cabbage, season lightly with salt and generously with pepper, and stir for a few minutes. Add 1 cup of the broth, then cover the pot and reduce the heat to low. Let the cabbage stew slowly, stirring occasionally, until it is completely soft and almost wilted, 15 to 20 minutes.

Add the remaining broth to the cabbage and bring to a gentle boil over medium heat. Add the rice and, if using fresh peas, add them at this point. Reduce the heat to medium-low and cook the rice, uncovered, until tender but still firm to the bite, stirring occasionally. If using frozen peas, add them to the soup at this time. Let the soup rest for a few minutes, then adjust the seasoning and serve with a generous sprinkle of grated Parmigiano.

BAKED CABBAGE AND BREAD SOUP

Zuppa di Verza e Pane al Forno

❦

SERVES 8 TO 10

Cabbage is a glorious ingredient that gives flavor, body, and lots of vitamins to a soup. The people of the high mountain regions of Italy know this quite well because they use cabbage in soups, stews, and side dishes. And if they could get away with it, I bet they would sneak it also into desserts! They also know that cabbage and pork is a perfect combination.

This is one of the most appetizing, thick, and filling soups of this chapter. It screams out for cold, cold weather. (People in Arizona or California—don't make this soup.) This thick soup is ladled over slices of grilled bread, laced generously with Parmigiano-Reggiano cheese, and baked for a short amount of time.

4 tablespoons unsalted butter
¼ pound pancetta, chopped
½ a large head Savoy or regular cabbage (2½ to 3 pounds), core removed and leaves thinly sliced
Salt and freshly ground black pepper to taste

6 cups Basic Chicken Broth (page 21) or low-sodium canned chicken broth
20 to 24 slices Italian bread, toasted or grilled
1 cup freshly grated Parmigiano-Reggiano cheese

CONTINUED

Heat the butter in a large pot over medium heat. Add the pancetta and cook, stirring, until it is lightly golden, 2 to 3 minutes. Add the cabbage, then season with salt and generously with pepper. Stir for a few minutes. Add 1 cup of the broth, cover the pot, and reduce the heat to low. Let the cabbage stew slowly, stirring occasionally, for about 15 minutes. Add the remaining broth and bring to a gentle boil. Simmer, uncovered, until the cabbage is very soft, 15 to 20 minutes longer. Let the soup sit for a few minutes.

Preheat the oven to 400° F. Butter an ovenproof 2-quart casserole or deep baking dish. Layer the bottom of the dish with slices of bread. Spoon half of the cabbage and broth over the bread and sprinkle generously with about half of the Parmigiano. Top with another layer of bread, soup, and Parmigiano. Put the dish on the middle rack of the oven and bake until the top of the bread has a rich golden color, 10 to 15 minutes.

Remove casserole from the oven, let the soup rest for a few minutes, then serve.

FOR A THINNER SOUP

During baking the bread will absorb the broth almost completely. In essence what you have are slices of golden, very moist bread laced with melted cheese. If you want a thinner soup, just add a few cups additional broth.

VEGETABLE MINESTRONE
WITH RICE
Minestrone con Riso

✦

SERVES 8 TO 10

Northern Italian minestroni are rich and thick. They contain a large variety of vegetables and are often enriched by rice or pasta. Potatoes and beans are frequently the thickening agent, while a *soffritto* of prosciutto, pancetta, or lard chopped together with parsley, garlic, or onion is the savory base. In summer, serve this minestrone at room temperature.

2 tablespoons unsalted butter

3 tablespoons extra-virgin olive oil

1 cup minced yellow onion

1 cup minced carrot

1 cup minced celery

2 garlic cloves, minced

¼ pound pancetta, chopped

4 fresh sage leaves, shredded

¼ pound fresh green beans, trimmed and diced

2 cups peeled and diced potatoes

2 cups diced fresh tomatoes, or 2 cups minced canned tomatoes

1 cup fresh or thawed frozen small green peas

2 medium zucchini, diced

¼ pound white cultivated mushrooms, wiped clean and thinly sliced

Salt and freshly ground black pepper to taste

Crust from a small piece of Parmigiano-Reggiano cheese, scraped clean (optional)

2 quarts Vegetable Broth (page 24) or Basic Chicken Broth (page 21) or low-sodium canned chicken broth

½ cup imported Arborio rice

⅓ to ½ cup freshly grated Parmigiano-Reggiano cheese

CONTINUED

Heat the butter and oil in a large pot over medium heat. Add the onion, carrot, celery, garlic, and pancetta. Cook, stirring, until the vegetables and pancetta are lightly golden, 5 to 6 minutes. Add the sage and stir for a few minutes. Add all the vegetables and season lightly with salt and pepper. Stir for a few minutes. Add the Parmigiano crust, if using, and the broth. Bring to a gentle boil, reduce the heat to low, and simmer, uncovered, 40 to 50 minutes, stirring occasionally.

Add the rice and cook for 12 to 15 minutes. Turn the heat off under the pot and let the soup rest for a few minutes. Remove the cheese crust, adjust the seasoning, and serve with a sprinkle of grated Parmigiano.

WASTE NOT

In the old Italian tradition that nothing goes to waste, the crust of Parmigiano-Reggiano is scraped clean with a knife and added to the soup. The flavor of the cheese crust comes through once it is cooked, and it enlivens the soup considerably.

ROYAL SOUP

Minestra di Pasta Reale

🌱

There was a time several decades ago when this soup was always part of an important, multicourse dinner, for it was light, delicious, and quite elegant. Even though the origin of this soup is French, many northern Italian regions—and in particular my region of Emilia-Romagna—consider it their own. The most important element is the quality of the broth, which must be homemade. And the great secret is that making a batch of delicious homemade broth is really a simple task. Elegance needn't be difficult.

1 cup cold water

3 tablespoons unsalted butter

Salt to taste

½ cup all-purpose flour

⅔ cup freshly grated
    Parmigiano-Reggiano cheese

1 large egg, lightly beaten

5 cups Basic Meat Broth
    (page 20)

Preheat the oven to 325° F. Butter and flour a cookie sheet.

In a small pan, place the water, butter, and salt and put it over medium heat. When the butter is melted and the water comes short of a boil, remove the pan from the heat and add the flour and ⅓ cup of the Parmigiano. Mix quickly and energetically with a wooden spoon, then put the pan back over medium heat. Cook, stirring constantly, until the mixture gathers together, detaching itself from the bottom and sides of the pan, 2 to 3 minutes. Place the mixture in a bowl and cool it slightly. Add the egg and mix quickly until the egg is completely incorporated and the mixture is smooth and velvety.

Place the dough in a pastry bag fitted with a medium round tip. Pipe small, grape-size rounds on the cookie sheet, leaving about 1 inch between them. Bake 8 to 10 minutes or until the puffs are golden and have doubled in size. Transfer the puffs to a large platter and let them cool, uncovered, several hours. You should have approximately 50 puffs. (The recipe can be prepared ahead to this point 2 hours ahead.)

In a medium saucepan, bring the broth to a boil over medium heat. Add the puffs and cook about 1 minute. Ladle the soup into individual bowls, sprinkle with the remaining grated Parmigiano, and serve.

PEA AND ZUCCHINI SOUP
WITH PESTO

Minestra di Piselli e Zucchine al Pesto

❧

The cooking of Liguria is simple, fresh, and aromatic. Somehow it seems that the vegetables and the herbs of this region, which is known as the "Italian Riviera," smell and taste better than any other place in Italy.

This soup employs fresh, sweet spring peas, small zucchini, prosciutto, and homemade broth. It is generally served at room temperature, with a dollop of fresh pesto.

FOR THE LIGURIAN PESTO

2 cups loosely packed fresh
   basil leaves
⅓ to ½ cup olive oil
¼ cup pine nuts
2 garlic cloves, peeled
Salt and freshly ground black
   pepper to taste
⅓ cup freshly grated
   Parmigiano-Reggiano cheese
2 tablespoons freshly grated
   pecorino Romano cheese, or
   2 additional tablespoons of
   Parmigiano

FOR THE SOUP

⅓ cup extra-virgin olive oil
1 cup finely minced yellow
   onion
¼ pound prosciutto, cut in
   1 thick slice and finely
   minced
2 pounds zucchini, ends
   removed and cut into small
   dice
2 pounds fresh peas in their
   pods, shelled, or 1 cup frozen
   peas, thawed
6 cups Vegetable Broth (page
   24) or Basic Chicken Broth
   (page 21) or low-sodium
   canned chicken broth

Prepare the pesto: Put all the pesto ingredients except the cheeses in the bowl of a food processor and process until smooth. Pour the sauce into a small bowl and stir in the Parmigiano and the pecorino cheeses. Taste and adjust the seasoning. Set aside 2 to 3 tablespoons of pesto, then cover the bowl with plastic wrap and freeze or refrigerate the remainder for another time. (Pesto can be kept in the refrigerator quite well for several days.)

Prepare the soup: Heat the oil in a large pot over medium heat. Add the onion and cook, stirring, until the onion is lightly golden, about 5 minutes. Add the prosciutto and stir for a minute or two. Raise the heat to high and add the zucchini. Stir to coat the zucchini with the savory base. Add the fresh peas if using, stir for a few minutes, then add the broth. Season with salt and pepper and bring the broth to a gentle simmer. Reduce the heat to low and simmer the soup, uncovered, 30 to 35 minutes. If using frozen peas, add them at this point. Turn the heat off under the pot and let the soup rest for a while.

When you are ready to serve, adjust the seasoning. Ladle the soup into individual bowls, spoon about a teaspoon of pesto into each bowl, and serve.

ZUCCHINI SOUP

Minestra di Zucchine

❦

SERVES 4 TO 6

Italian cooks rely on this type of soup when time is limited. Some fresh vegetables and herbs, extra-virgin olive oil, a bit of garlic, and *pronto*—a lovely soup is ready to be served. And you still thought that Italian women spent the whole day in the kitchen, right?

⅓ cup extra-virgin olive oil
3 garlic cloves, minced
2 tablespoons chopped fresh
    parsley
3 pounds zucchini, ends
    removed and cut into
    small dice
1 cup canned Italian plum
    tomatoes with their juice,
    put through a food mill to
    remove seeds

Salt and freshly ground black
    pepper to taste
5 cups Vegetable Broth (page
    24) or Basic Chicken Broth
    (page 21) or low-sodium
    canned chicken broth
5 or 6 fresh basil leaves, roughly
    chopped

Heat the oil in a large pot over medium heat. Add the garlic and parsley, and cook, stirring, until the garlic begins to color, about 1 minute. Raise the heat to high and add the zucchini. Stir for a minute or two, until zucchini is well coated with oil and garlic. Add the tomatoes and season with salt and pepper. Add the broth and bring to a gentle simmer. Reduce the heat to low and simmer the soup, uncovered, 30 to 35 minutes. Stir a few times during cooking. Turn the heat off under the pot and let the soup rest for a while.

When ready to serve, stir in the basil, adjust the seasoning, and serve.

LENTIL AND ESCAROLE SOUP
Zuppa di Lenticchie e Scarola

❧

SERVES 8 TO 10

Escarole is a mildly bitter, dark green, bushy type of chicory that is much loved by southern Italians. The regions of Puglia, Basilicata, and Campania adore escarole and use it in simple vegetable and soup preparations. This is one of the wonderful soups of Puglia.

⅓ cup extra-virgin olive oil

2 garlic cloves, minced

2 cups canned Italian plum tomatoes with their juice, put through a food mill to remove seeds

2 cups (about ¾ pound) dried brown lentils, washed in several changes of cold water

2 quarts cold water

Salt and freshly ground black pepper to taste

1 head escarole (about 1¼ pound)

Additional extra-virgin olive oil to taste

Heat the oil in a large saucepan over medium heat. Add the garlic and cook until it is lightly golden. Add the tomatoes and bring to a gentle simmer. Cook, stirring occasionally, for 6 to 8 minutes. Add the lentils and stir well. Add the water, bring to a gentle boil, season with salt and pepper, reduce the heat to low, and simmer, uncovered, for 20 minutes.

While the lentils are cooking, detach the leaves from the root end of the escarole, discarding any that are bruised or wilted. Wash the leaves well under cold running water. Drain and cut into 1-inch strips.

Add the escarole to the lentils, cover the pot, and continue cooking at a low simmer until the lentils and escarole are tender, 25 to 30 minutes. Stir the soup from time to time and add a bit more water if it becomes too thick. Turn the heat off under the pot and let the soup rest for 20 to 30 minutes.

Ladle the soup into individual bowls, drizzle a little fresh olive oil over each bowl, and sprinkle with a bit of black pepper. Serve hot.

ROASTED BUTTERNUT SQUASH SOUP
Passato di Zucca

❧

SERVES 6

It is a fact that northern Italians love squash. This sweet orange vegetable is forged into delicious pasta fillings by creative cooks, or transformed into glorious, melt-in-your-mouth gnocchi and delicate, creamy soups.

In this preparation, the squash is roasted instead of boiled, then mixed with creamy shallots and stirred into a flavorful broth, preferably homemade. A light, flavorful homemade broth will make this soup sing. Toasted almonds, chives, and Parmigiano-Reggiano are added to the soup at the time of serving.

3 pounds butternut squash	1 to 2 tablespoons minced
3 tablespoons unsalted butter	chives
½ cup finely minced shallots	⅓ to ½ cup lightly toasted,
Salt to taste	thinly sliced almonds
6 to 7 cups Basic Chicken Broth	⅓ to ½ cup freshly grated
(page 21) or low-sodium	Parmigiano-Reggiano cheese
canned chicken broth	

Preheat the oven to 400° F. Cut the squash lengthwise, and with a tablespoon, scoop out the seeds. Wrap the squash in foil, put it on a cookie sheet, and place in the oven. Bake 1½ hours or until squash is very tender when pierced with a long, thin knife. Cool the squash, then unwrap it. Scoop the pulp out from the shell with a tablespoon and place in a bowl. Set aside until ready to use. (Makes about 4 cups cooked squash pulp.)

Heat the butter in a medium saucepan over medium heat. Add the shallots and cook, stirring, until translucent, 6 to 7 minutes. Add the squash pulp, season with salt, and stir well. Add the broth and mix energetically with a wooden spoon or a wire whisk. Bring the broth to a boil, then reduce the heat to low and simmer, uncovered, for 30 to 35 minutes. Stir occasionally during cooking.

Puree the soup through a food mill or in a food processor until smooth and return to the pan. Bring the soup back to a very gentle simmer and cook 5 to 6 minutes longer. Turn the heat off under the pan, adjust the seasoning, and let the soup sit for a few minutes.

Ladle the soup into individual bowls. Sprinkle some chives, almonds, and grated Parmigiano on each serving and serve hot.

ASPARAGUS AND RICE SOUP

Minestrina di Asparagi e Riso

❧

SERVES 6

Minestrone means "big soup," while minestrina means "little soup." A *minestrina* generally is light, flavorful, and not elaborate—which is just the case here. These are soups that Italians love to have for supper because they are satisfying but not overly filling.

3 pounds thin fresh asparagus
3 tablespoons unsalted butter
½ cup finely minced yellow onion
2 ounces prosciutto, cut in 1 thick slice and finely minced
1 tablespoon tomato paste diluted with 1 cup chicken broth

Salt and freshly ground black pepper to taste
6 cups Basic Meat Broth (page 20) or Basic Chicken Broth (page 21) or low-sodium canned chicken broth
1 cup imported Arborio rice
⅓ to ½ cup freshly grated Parmigiano-Reggiano cheese

Cut off the asparagus tips from the spears (3 pounds asparagus yield approximately ½ pound tips) and wash the tips well under cold running water. Reserve the spears for other use. You should have about 8 ounces asparagus tips.

CONTINUED

Heat the butter in a medium saucepan over medium heat. When the butter begins to foam, add the onion and cook, stirring, until lightly golden and soft, 6 to 7 minutes. Add the prosciutto and stir for a minute or two. Add the asparagus tips and diluted tomato paste and bring the liquid to a gentle simmer. Season with salt and pepper. Simmer, uncovered, 6 to 7 minutes, stirring occasionally. Turn the heat off under the pan.

Heat the broth in a large pot over medium heat. When the broth begins to simmer, add the rice and cook 5 to 6 minutes. Stir the asparagus mixture into the broth and cook until the rice is tender but still a bit firm to the bite. Taste and adjust the seasoning. Turn the heat off under the pot and let the soup rest for a few minutes.

Ladle the soup into individual bowls, sprinkle with grated Parmigiano, and serve.

ZUCCHINI AND CABBAGE SOUP
Minestra di Zucchine
e Cavolo

❦

SERVES 8 TO 10

Soups were peasant cooking's legacy to the Italian table. The peasants used humble ingredients with imagination and inventiveness, so that every day they could put something different on the table. In this version of a traditional Neapolitan soup, broth replaces the water and pancetta is used instead of lard.

⅓ cup extra-virgin olive oil
¼ pound pancetta, finely
    chopped
2 garlic cloves, minced
2 pounds zucchini, ends
    removed and roughly diced
½ a large head Savoy or regular
    cabbage (2½ to 3 pounds),
    core removed and leaves
    thinly sliced
Salt and freshly ground black
    pepper to taste
2 quarts Vegetable Broth
    (page 24) or Basic Chicken
    Broth (page 21) or
    low-sodium canned
    chicken broth

6 or 7 fresh basil leaves,
    roughly shredded, or
    1 to 2 tablespoons
    chopped fresh parsley
8 to 10 small slices crusty
    Italian bread, toasted, grilled,
    or fried
⅓ to ½ cup freshly grated
    Parmigiano-Reggiano cheese

Heat the oil in a large pot over medium heat. Add the pancetta and the garlic, and cook, stirring, until the pancetta is lightly golden, 2 to 3 minutes. Add the zucchini and stir for a minute or two. Add the cabbage, season lightly with salt and pepper, and stir for a few minutes. Add 1 cup of the broth, then cover the pot and reduce the heat to low. Let the cabbage and zucchini stew slowly so they can release their juices, and cook, stirring occasionally, until the vegetables are soft, 15 to 20 minutes.

CONTINUED

Add the remaining broth to the pot and bring to a gentle boil over medium heat. Reduce the heat to low and simmer, uncovered, 15 to 20 minutes longer. Taste, adjust the seasoning, and turn the heat off under the pot. Let the soup rest for 20 to 30 minutes.

Just before serving, stir the basil or parsley into the soup. Place a slice of bread into each soup bowl and ladle the soup over the bread. Sprinkle generously with Parmigiano and serve.

A THINNER SOUP

Always have a little more broth at hand because this type of soup thickens as it sits. If you prefer your soup a bit thinner, just add a little more broth.

SQUASH AND POTATO SOUP
Minestra di Zucca e Patate

❧

This simplest water-based soup is prepared without even the benefit of a savory base. The only flight of fancy here is the bread, which is fried, not grilled. Don't pass this soup up, you will be surprised by its great flavor.

2 medium leeks (about
  12 ounces)
2 pounds boiling potatoes,
  peeled and cubed
1 medium butternut squash
  (2 to 2½ pounds), peeled,
  seeded, and cut into
  1- to 2-inch pieces
2½ to 3 quarts cold water
Salt and freshly ground black
  pepper to taste

½ cup olive oil
4 cups cubed stale Italian bread
  (½-inch cubes), with crusts
  removed
1 to 2 tablespoons chopped
  fresh parsley
⅓ to ½ cup freshly grated
  Parmigiano-Reggiano cheese

Cut the roots off the leeks and remove one third of the green stalks. Cut the leeks in half lengthwise, then slice them into 1-inch pieces. Place the leeks in a colander and wash them well under cold running water, making sure to remove all dirt. Put leeks, potatoes, and squash into a large pot. Add enough cold water to cover the vegetables by 1 to 2 inches and bring the water to a boil over medium heat. Reduce the heat to low and cook, uncovered, until all vegetables are tender, 50 to 60 minutes.

Puree the vegetables with their cooking water through a food mill or in a food processor and return to the pot. Season with salt and pepper. Bring the soup back to a very gentle simmer and cook 5 to 6 minutes longer. Turn the heat off under the pot, adjust the seasoning, and let the soup rest for several minutes.

Meanwhile, heat the oil in a medium skillet over medium heat. Add the bread cubes and cook until they are golden on all sides. (Keep your eyes on the bread because the cubes will turn golden in no time at all.) Transfer to paper towels to drain.

Just before serving, stir the parsley into the soup. Ladle the soup into individual soup bowls, add some bread cubes, sprinkle with grated Parmigiano, and serve.

TUSCAN ONION SOUP
Cipollata

❧

SERVES 6

Of the many versions of Tuscan onion soups, this is perhaps my favorite. Here the onions are cooked slowly for a long time until they become meltingly soft and sweet. Then tomatoes, herbs, and broth are added and the soup is simmered until fairly thick and very flavorful. Some Tuscan *trattorie* serve this soup with slices of grilled bread, while others stir in a couple of beaten raw eggs to make it more nourishing. For me, the soup is perfect just the way it is here.

½ cup extra-virgin olive oil
2 large garlic cloves, peeled and
  lightly crushed
2½ to 3 pounds red onions,
  thinly sliced
1 cup canned Italian plum
  tomatoes with their juice, put
  through a food mill to
  remove seeds

½ cup loosely packed, finely
  shredded fresh basil,
  thyme, and oregano,
  or 2 tablespoons chopped
  fresh parsley
Salt and freshly ground
  black pepper to taste
6 cups cold water
⅓ to ½ cup freshly grated
  Parmigiano-Reggiano cheese

Heat the oil in a medium pot over medium heat. Add the garlic and cook until golden on all sides. Discard the garlic, reduce the heat to medium-low, and add the onions. Cook, stirring, until the onions are pale yellow and soft, about 12 minutes.

Raise the heat to high and add the tomatoes and the herbs. Season with salt and several grinds of pepper, and stir until the mixture begins to simmer. Add the water, bring to a gentle boil, reduce the heat to low, and simmer, uncovered, for about 1 hour, stirring occasionally.

Turn the heat off under the pot and let the soup rest for 20 to 30 minutes. Serve hot with a sprinkle of grated Parmigiano.

ESCAROLE SOUP

Zuppa di Scarola

❧

SERVES 6

In the region of Campania, this soup is made with escarole, or a type of bitter chicory. Minced pancetta and sausage are browned in oil, then the bitter greens are added and cooked in broth to form a thick, vitamin-loaded soup. And as with most rustic or peasant dishes, grilled bread slices are added, turning the soup into a substantial meal.

2 heads escarole (about
 1½ pounds each)
Salt to taste
⅓ cup extra-virgin olive oil
¼ pound pancetta, chopped
¼ pound mild Italian sausage,
 casings removed and finely
 chopped

6 cups Vegetable Broth
 (page 24) or Basic Chicken
 Broth (page 21) or low-
 sodium canned chicken
 broth
6 slices crusty Italian bread,
 toasted, grilled, or fried
⅓ to ½ cup freshly grated
 Parmigiano-Reggiano cheese

Detach the leaves from the root end of the escarole and discard any leaves that are bruised or wilted. Wash the leaves well under cold running water, drain, and cut roughly into 1-inch strips.

Bring a medium pot of water to a boil. Add a pinch of salt and the escarole. Bring the water back to a boil, blanch the escarole for a minute or two, then drain and squeeze out some of the water by pressing the leaves with a large spoon. Set aside.

Heat the oil in a large pot over medium heat. Add the pancetta and sausage, and cook for a minute or two. Add the escarole and mix well. Add the broth and season with salt. Bring to a gentle boil, then cover the pot partially and simmer the soup until the escarole is meltingly tender, about 1 hour. Stir and check the consistency of the soup several times during cooking.

Taste, adjust the seasoning, and turn the heat off under the pot. Let the soup rest for 20 to 30 minutes.

Just before serving, place a slice of bread into each soup bowl and ladle the soup over the bread. Sprinkle generously with grated Parmigiano and serve.

MEATLESS ZUPPA

If you want a meatless soup, omit the pancetta and sausage, and in its place sauté 1 cup of minced onion or leek and 1 chopped garlic clove in oil until soft. Then proceed as instructed in the recipe.

BARLEY AND PORCINI MUSHROOM SOUP

Zuppa di Orzo e Funghi Porcini

✤

SERVES 8 TO 10

This barley soup is typical of the Trentino–Alto Adige and Friuli–Venezia Giulia regions. Its appeal is its uncompromising rusticity. This version has dried porcini mushrooms, which add another layer of flavor to an already delicious soup.

2 ounces dried porcini mushrooms, soaked in 2 cups lukewarm water

2 tablespoons unsalted butter

2 tablespoons extra-virgin olive oil

1 cup finely minced yellow onion

½ cup finely minced celery

½ cup finely minced carrot

2 tablespoons chopped fresh parsley

¼ pound speck or prosciutto, cut in 1 thick slice and diced

1½ cups (about ¾ pound) pearl barley, picked over

2 to 2½ quarts water

Salt and freshly ground black pepper to taste

⅓ to ½ cup freshly grated Parmigiano-Reggiano cheese

Drain the porcini mushrooms and mince; set aside. Reserve 1 cup of the soaking water.

Heat the butter and oil in a large pot over medium heat. Add the onion, celery, carrot, and parsley and cook, stirring, until vegetables are soft, 6 to 7 minutes. Add the speck or prosciutto and the porcini mushrooms, and stir for a few minutes. Add the reserved mushroom water and bring to a gentle simmer. Add the barley and mix well. Stir in the water and bring to a boil. Season with salt and pepper, reduce the heat to low, and partially cover the pot. Simmer, stirring occasionally, until barley is tender, about 1 hour.

Taste, adjust the seasoning, and turn the heat off under the pot. Let the soup rest 20 to 30 minutes.

Ladle the soup into individual bowls, sprinkle with grated Parmigiano, and serve.

❧

PREPARING AHEAD

When a barley soup is prepared several hours ahead, it absorbs the liquid and becomes so thick you could almost eat it with a fork. As you reheat the soup, simply add more water or broth to give it the consistency you like.

CHICK-PEA AND CLAM SOUP
Passato di Ceci con Vongole

❦

SERVES 4 TO 6

Puglia is an intensely beautiful southern Italian region at the heel of the boot, which is touched by two great seas—the Adriatic and the Ionian. Puglia also boasts a great *cucina* that is intensely regional and relies heavily on local ingredients—grains, seafood, and vegetables. These ingredients especially shine when they are used in glorious, flavorful pasta dishes and, of course, this great and yet-so-simple soup.

2 cups (1 pound) dried chick-peas (garbanzo beans), picked over and soaked overnight in cold water to cover generously

6 cups cold water

Salt to taste

1 cup dry white wine mixed with ½ cup water

3 pounds manilla clams (or the smallest you can get), soaked and scrubbed (page 11)

¼ cup extra-virgin olive oil

2 garlic cloves, minced

4 anchovy fillets, chopped

Chopped fresh chili pepper or hot red pepper flakes to taste

1 to 2 tablespoons chopped fresh parsley

Additional extra-virgin olive oil to taste

Drain and rinse the chick-peas under cold running water. Put them in a large pot and add the water. Cook as instructed on page 11. When the chick-peas are tender, puree them through a food mill or in a food processor and return to the pot. Season with salt and turn the heat off under the pot. (The pureed chick-peas can be prepared a day ahead. Refrigerate tightly covered.)

Put the wine and water in a large deep pan and place over medium heat. Add the clams and cover the pan. Cook just until the clams open. With a slotted spoon, transfer them to a bowl. Detach the meat from the shells. If the clams are large, cut them into 2 to 3 pieces; if they are small, leave them as they are.

Line a strainer with paper towels and strain the clam liquid into a bowl to get rid of sandy deposits. Wipe the pan in which the clams have cooked with paper towels and put it back over medium heat. Add the oil, garlic, anchovies, and chili pepper and cook, stirring, until the garlic begins to color, about 1 minute. Add the strained clam liquid, season lightly with salt, and simmer until the liquid is reduced to about half its original amount. Pour the liquid over the clams.

Put the pot with the pureed chick-peas back over medium heat and when the mixture begins to simmer, stir the clams, juices, and parsley into the soup just before serving. Turn the heat off under the pot and let the soup rest for 4 to 5 minutes. Taste, adjust the seasoning, and serve with a dash of olive oil over each serving.

TUSCAN CHICK-PEA AND PASTA SOUP

Minestra di Ceci e Pasta alla Toscana

%

SERVES 4 TO 6

Traditionally the liquid used to cook this Tuscan peasant soup was water, not broth. However, cooks today often use broth to add another dimension of flavor. Almost any kind of hard wheat pasta can be used for this soup; my preference is for ditalini or spaghettini. If using spaghettini, break them into small pieces. And if you prefer bread, omit the pasta and add a slice of grilled or toasted Italian bread to each bowl as you serve the soup.

2 cups (1 pound) dried chick-peas (garbanzo beans), picked over and soaked overnight in cold water to cover generously

6 cups Vegetable Broth (page 24) or Basic Chicken Broth (page 21) or water

⅓ cup extra-virgin olive oil

1 cup finely minced red onion

2 garlic cloves, minced

¼ pound sliced prosciutto, chopped

2 tablespoons tomato paste diluted with 1 cup chicken broth or water

Salt and freshly ground black pepper to taste

3 ounces pasta, such as spaghettini or ditalini

CONTINUED

Drain and rinse the chick-peas under cold running water, put them in a large pot, and add the broth or water. Cook as instructed on page 11.

While the chick-peas are cooking, heat the oil in a medium saucepan over medium heat. Add the onion and garlic, and cook, stirring, until the onion is lightly golden, 5 to 6 minutes. Add the prosciutto and stir for a minute or two. Add the diluted tomato paste, season with salt and pepper, and reduce the heat to low. Simmer, uncovered, 6 to 8 minutes.

Add the tomato mixture to the cooked chick-peas and mix well. Simmer the soup a few minutes longer.

Raise the heat to medium-high and add the pasta. Cook, uncovered, until the pasta is tender but still firm to the bite. Stir several times during cooking. Taste, adjust the seasoning, and serve.

MAKE MORE BEANS

When I prepare bean, chick-pea, or lentil soups, I generally cook double the amount of beans and reserve half to use in salads.

OPEN THE CAN

You can use canned chick-peas in a pinch. Drain, rinse, and add them to the tomato mixture along with the broth or water and simmer for 15 to 20 minutes. Add the pasta, cook, and serve.

ARTICHOKE, LEEK, AND RICE SOUP
Minestra di Carciofi, Porri, e Riso

⁂

SERVES 8

This is a thick soup made even thicker and more wholesome with the addition of rice. If you prefer a lighter, more liquid soup, add two additional cups of liquid and omit the rice. Then serve it, not with Parmigiano, but with a dash of wonderfully aromatic extra-virgin olive oil.

4 pounds baby artichokes, cleaned (page 9)
Juice of 1 lemon
¼ cup extra-virgin olive oil
2 medium leeks (1½ pounds)
½ cup finely minced yellow onion
½ cup finely minced celery

2 quarts Vegetable Broth (page 24) or Basic Chicken Broth (page 21) or low-sodium canned chicken broth
Salt to taste
½ cup imported Arborio rice
⅓ to ½ cup freshly grated Parmigiano-Reggiano cheese

Cut the artichokes into thin wedges. Place the wedges in a bowl of cold water with the lemon juice until ready to use.

Heat the oil in a large pot over medium heat. Add the leeks, onion, and celery and cook, stirring, until the vegetables are very soft, 6 to 8 minutes. Add the artichokes, stir them with the other vegetables for a few minutes, then add the broth. Season lightly with salt and bring the broth to a gentle boil. Cover the pot partially and reduce the heat to low. Simmer 45 minutes to 1 hour or until artichokes are tender.

Add the rice to the soup and cook, uncovered, stirring a few times, until the rice is tender but still firm to the bite, about 10 to 12 minutes. Serve hot or at room temperature with a sprinkle of grated Parmigiano.

FAVA BEAN AND ARTICHOKE SOUP

Zuppa di Fave e Carciofi

❧

SERVES 10 TO 12

Fava beans, artichokes, chicory, and escarole are some of the Puglia region's basic staples. They appear in endless preparations, either alone or in interesting combinations. This soup, typical of Puglia, has a fresh-tasting flavor if made with fresh fava beans, but becomes more wholesome and satisfying when it is made with dried fava beans, as in this recipe.

Nevio, one of the top waiters at my restaurant in Sacramento, is from Trieste and is an avid vegetarian. After devouring two large bowls of this soup, he said: "This is the best soup I have ever had in all my life!" Well, perhaps he went a little overboard, but I hope you will try it. And if you serve it at room temperature, it tastes even better. If you have trouble finding dried fava beans at your local supermarket, try health food stores. But do not substitute lima beans.

2 cups dried fava beans (¾ pound), soaked overnight in cold water to cover generously (4 cups soaked)

4 pounds baby artichokes, cleaned (page 9)

Juice of 1 lemon

⅓ cup extra-virgin olive oil

1 cup finely minced yellow onion

2 garlic cloves, minced

2 tablespoons chopped fresh parsley

2¼ quarts Vegetable Broth (page 24) or Basic Chicken Broth (page 21) or low-sodium canned chicken broth or water

Salt and freshly ground black pepper to taste

Drain and rinse the beans under cold running water, put them in a large pot, cover with water, and boil for 3 to 5 minutes. Drain the beans and peel them, following the instructions on page 11.

Cut the artichokes into thin wedges. Place the wedges in a bowl of cold water with the lemon juice until ready to use.

Heat the oil in a large pot over medium heat. Add the onion, garlic, and parsley and cook, stirring, until the onion is pale yellow and soft, about 5 minutes. Add the artichokes and the fava beans, and stir them with the other ingredients for a few minutes. Add the broth or the water and bring to a gentle boil. Cover the pot partially and reduce the heat to low. Simmer, stirring occasionally, until the artichokes and beans are tender, 45 minutes to 1 hour. Season with salt and pepper. Turn the heat off under the pot and let the soup rest 20 to 30 minutes. Serve warm or at room temperature.

ANGEL HAIR IN BROTH
Capelli d'Angelo in Brodo

SERVES 4

If you are in Emilia-Romagna, Piedmont, or Lombardy and you are lucky enough to find a restaurant or *trattoria* that serves traditional local food, chances are you will see this dish. And if you do, order it because in its simplicity this dish is a small masterpiece. The waiter will come to your table with a large chunk of very fresh Parmigiano, which he will grate over your soup. Now, as you begin to eat, just think that one reason we Italians hold dear to traditions is because of food that tastes like this.

6 cups Basic Meat Broth (page 20) or Basic Chicken Broth (page 21)

6 ounces homemade or store-bought angel hair or tagliolini pasta

⅓ cup freshly grated Parmigiano-Reggiano cheese

Bring the broth to a boil in a medium pot over high heat. Add the pasta, and when the broth comes back to a rolling boil, reduce the heat a little and cook, uncovered, stirring occasionally with a long fork until the pasta is tender. Turn the heat off under the pot and let the soup rest for a few minutes to allow the pasta to absorb the flavorful broth.

Ladle the soup into individual soup bowls and serve hot with a sprinkle of grated Parmigiano.

ACCEPT NO SUBSTITUTES

This dish needs three ingredients to be outstanding: homemade broth, homemade pasta, and Parmigiano-Reggiano cheese. While homemade pasta can be substituted with a good brand of imported angel hair or tagliolini, canned broth and supermarket Parmesan are not acceptable alternatives.

PARMESAN, EGG, AND
NUTMEG SOUP
Passatelli

❧

SERVES 4 TO 6

Passatelli are made with an unusual dough of Parmigiano-Reggiano cheese, eggs, nutmeg, and bread crumbs. The dough is riced into an aromatic hot broth, and as it cooks, it forms small golden strands. The result is a soup that is both delicate and intensely flavorful. This traditional soup of Emilia-Romagna should be made only with good homemade meat broth.

6 cups Basic Meat Broth
   (page 20)
2 medium eggs
½ teaspoon freshly grated
   nutmeg

¾ cup freshly grated
   Parmigiano-Reggiano cheese
⅓ cup fine, plain bread crumbs

Put the broth in a medium pot and bring it to a gentle boil over medium heat.

Meanwhile, beat the eggs in a medium bowl with a fork. Always using a fork, mix in the nutmeg, Parmigiano, and bread crumbs. Mix all the ingredients thoroughly and work into a soft dough. Place the dough on a pastry board and give it a brief kneading, adding a bit more cheese and bread crumbs if it is too soft or moist. At this point you should have a somewhat firm, granular dough. (The dough can be made an hour or so ahead and set aside, covered, until ready to use.)

When the broth begins to boil, put half the dough into a potato ricer or food mill fitted with the large hole disk and rice the dough directly into the simmering broth. Repeat with the remaining dough. Reduce the heat to medium-low and cook the *passatelli* for about 1 minute.

Turn the heat off under the pot and let the soup rest for about 5 minutes. Ladle the soup into individual bowls and serve hot with a sprinkle of a little extra grated Parmigiano.

RICE, EGG, AND PARMESAN SOUP
Minestra del Paradiso

❦

SERVES 4 TO 6

*M*inestra del paradiso means "heavenly soup." And heavenly it certainly is, provided fragrant homemade broth is used to prepare this wonderful, easy soup, which is typical of the Emilia-Romagna region. Even though it is traditionally served at Easter, my mother would serve it throughout the year as the beginning of a light supper because it was so delicious and very quick to prepare.

6 cups Basic Meat Broth (page 20) or Basic Chicken Broth (page 21)
1 cup imported Arborio rice
3 large eggs
¼ cup freshly grated Parmigiano-Reggiano cheese

¼ teaspoon freshly grated nutmeg
1 tablespoon chopped fresh parsley
Salt to taste

Bring the broth to a boil in a medium pot over high heat. Add the rice, reduce the heat to medium, and cook until rice is tender but still a bit firm to the bite, 12 to 14 minutes (see Preparing Ahead, below).

While the rice is cooking, beat the eggs, Parmigiano, nutmeg, and parsley in a bowl and season with salt.

When the rice is cooked, turn the heat off under the pot and stir in the egg mixture. Mix well with a spoon or a wire whisk until the eggs begin to solidify and form small strands. Ladle the soup into individual soup bowls, sprinkle with a little extra Parmigiano, and serve.

❦

PREPARING AHEAD

This soup needs to be made at the last moment or the rice will become soft and mushy. However, you can prepare the broth, keeping it warm, and beat the eggs with the other ingredients 1 hour or so ahead. Fifteen minutes before you are ready to serve, cook the rice, then stir in the eggs.

Fresh Pasta

STUFFED PASTAS

Cappellacci Filled with Squash

Ravioli with White Fish

Ravioli with Salmon

Roasted Red Beet Ravioli with Lemon-Sage Butter Sauce

Tortelli with Radicchio, Ricotta, and Goat Cheese

Tortelli with Ricotta, Mascarpone, and Swiss Chard

Eggplant–Goat Cheese Tortelli with Fresh Tomatoes and Black Olives

Agnolotti with Four Cheeses

Tortelloni with Swiss Chard, Spinach, Ham, and Ricotta

Lasagne with Eggplant, Mozzarella, and Tomatoes

Lasagne with Walnut Pesto and Ricotta

Lasagne with Speck and Mixed Mushrooms

Spinach Lasagne with Enriched Bolognese Meat Ragù

Cannelloni with Shrimp Stuffing

Spinach Cannelloni with Duck and Wild Mushroom Stuffing

STRING PASTAS

Tonnarelli with Spicy Scallop Sauce

*Yellow and Green Noodles with Mortadella, Peas,
and Mushrooms*

Red Tagliatelle with Bresaola and Porcini Mushrooms

Chestnut Flour Tagliatelle with Cabbage and Fontina Cheese

Spinach Tagliatelle with Clams and Scallops

Tagliatelle with Fresh Porcini Mushrooms

Buckwheat Noodles with Brussels Sprouts and Speck

Pappardelle with Rabbit Ragù

Pappardelle with Pietro's Meat Ragù

Tagliolini with Zucchini, Shrimp, and Saffron

Tagliolini with Lobster and Fresh Tomatoes

Tagliolini with Butter and Cream

Fettuccine with Lamb Ragù

Fettuccine with Chanterelles, Prosciutto, Tomatoes, and Cream

Fettuccine with Pancetta, Plum Tomatoes, and Peas

For Italians, pasta is as essential to life as water—and the love of it is deeply woven into everyday family life. In a steaming plate of pasta there are family histories, childhood memories, and local traditions. Pasta speaks a language all its own. It is colorful, ebullient, and gregarious in the south; rustic and straightforward in central Italy; and refined, restrained, and more complex in the north. Fettuccine, tagliatelle, spaghetti, bucatini, rigatoni, cannelloni, tortellini, lasagne, ziti, fusilli, ravioli, orecchiette; string pasta, stuffed pasta, baked pasta. Without pasta Italian cooking would not be known and enjoyed as it is throughout the world.

Although regional differences determine the choice of pasta, the basic ingredients for pasta making are unequivocally two: egg and flour for homemade pasta, and flour and water for factory-made pasta. Both types of pasta when properly made are excellent and one is not better than the other. Since homemade and factory-made pasta are two entirely different products, I discuss each in separate chapters. This chapter is devoted to homemade pasta and dishes that use it.

In most northern Italian regions the pasta is homemade. In Emilia-Romagna—the region that sets a standard of excellence for pasta making—the pasta is made only with all-purpose unbleached flour and eggs. No salt or oil are ever used in the dough. These ingredients, plus the expert hands of the pasta maker, produce a delicate pasta that is layered into delicate lasagne, wrapped around voluptuous fillings, and shaped into golden tagliatelle.

Years ago, the only tools one needed to make fresh pasta at home were a large wooden board for the dough, your hands to knead it, and a long rolling pin to roll it out. My mother would make fresh pasta several times a week. She kneaded the large dough with impressive, short strokes until it was smooth and silky, like a baby's bottom. Then she stretched the dough with a long rolling pin until it was enormously large, round, and transparent. It was a sight to behold!

Making pasta entirely by hand is not as easy as some cookbooks tell you. It boils down to individual skill, time, and commitment. If you love making bread or rolling out delicate pastries, you will find pasta making quite attainable and thoroughly enjoyable. If you have problems boiling water, you are better off using one of the alternate methods suggested here, which are quite simple and nonthreatening. Just keep in mind that the only way to learn how to do something new is to go ahead and try it.

Pasta Made by Hand

The ingredients are simple: unbleached all-purpose flour and eggs. See individual recipes for the proportions. You'll need the following equipment:

- A large wooden board. A Formica or marble board can also be used.
- A fork to mix the flour with the eggs.
- A long Italian rolling pin for pasta. Check with your local gourmet cooking store, or use a regular rolling pin.
- A dough scraper to clean the board of sticky pieces of dough.
- A scalloped pastry wheel to cut the pasta into the desired shapes.

MAKING THE DOUGH

Heap the flour onto a large wooden board or other surface. With your fingers, make a hollow, round well in the center of the flour. Break the eggs into the well. Stir the eggs briefly with a fork, then begin to draw some of the flour from inside the well over the eggs. Add the flour a little at a time, always mixing with the fork. When you reach the point where a soft paste begins to form, switch to a dough scraper.

With the dough scraper, push all the remaining flour to one side of the board and scrape off and discard the bits and pieces attached to the board. Add to the paste some of the flour you have pushed aside and begin kneading the dough gently at first. As you keep incorporating more flour, your kneading will become more energetic. Do not add all the flour too hastily because you might not need to use it all.

The moment you have a soft, manageable dough, clean the board again of sticky pieces and wash your hands. Knead the dough more energetically now, pushing the dough with the palms of your hands away from you and folding half of the dough back toward you. Keep turning the dough as you knead it. Push, fold over, and turn. Knead the dough about 8 minutes, adding a bit more flour if it sticks to the board and to your hands.

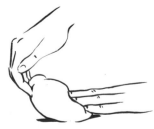

Push a finger into the center of the dough. If it comes out barely moist, the dough is ready to be rolled out. If the dough is sticky, knead it a little longer, adding a bit more flour. At the end of the kneading time, the dough should be compact, pliable, and smooth. Keep in mind that a good dough is vital to good pasta. Do not skimp on the kneading.

If you are planning to roll out the dough with a pasta machine, the dough can be used immediately. If you are planning to roll out the dough with a rolling pin, wrap the dough in plastic wrap and set it aside to *rest* for 15 to 20 minutes. Do not refrigerate the dough. After that time, the gluten in the dough will be more relaxed, and it will be easier to roll out by hand. If the dough should be too soft and limp when you remove the plastic wrap, give it a light kneading to regain a firmer consistency.

ROLLING OUT THE DOUGH

After the dough has rested, dust a large wooden board or work surface very lightly with flour. Flatten the dough with your hands and start rolling from the center of the dough forward and away from you, toward the edges. Rotate the dough slightly and roll out again from the center toward the edges. Keep rolling and turning the dough to produce a circular sheet of dough. If the dough sticks to the work surface, wrap it loosely around the rolling pin, lift the rolling pin, and dust the working surface lightly with more flour.

Once you have a nice, round circle of dough—about the size of an individual pizza—wrap the far edges of the pasta sheet around the rolling pin. Hold the dough at the bottom while you push the rolling pin gently away from you, stretching the dough. Repeat a few more times, trying to keep a circular shape if possible by rotating the dough. Dust your hands and the pasta sheet very lightly if the dough sticks to the board or the rolling pin. (Do not use too much flour or the dough will dry out.)

When the sheet of dough has doubled in size, wrap the far edges of the pasta sheet snugly around the pin, rolling only half of the pasta sheet toward you. Put the palms of your hands in the center of the rolling pin and gently roll the pin back and forth while stretching the dough forward. While you are doing this, your hands should never remain in the same position, but rather move from the center to the sides in a continuous motion. This action will stretch the dough sideways as well as forward. Keep stretching the dough this way, trying to work as fast as you can or the pasta will dry out and it will be impossible to stretch. Once you are experienced, it should not take longer than 8 to 10 minutes to roll out a small batch of dough. The dough is done when it is thin, almost transparent.

CUTTING THE PASTA

If you are using the hand-rolled dough for stuffed pasta, cut and stuff it immediately, while it is still moist, so that it can seal properly. See individual recipes. Keep the remaining strips of dough covered with plastic wrap so they won't dry out. Repeat with remaining dough.

If you are using the dough for string pasta such as tagliatelle or fettuccine, the sheet of pasta should be allowed to dry until it is no longer sticky to the touch. To do this, place the sheet of dough on a lightly floured tablecloth and let it dry 6 to 7 minutes, depending on the room's temperature. Turn the sheet gently to dry on the other side. If the sheet of pasta is too dry, it will crack and break.

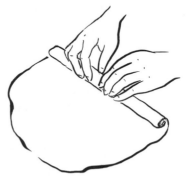

When the pasta sheet is no longer sticky, fold it loosely into a flat roll about 2 inches across. With a large, sharp knife, cut the pasta into the desired width by pressing down evenly with the knife. Unravel the noodles and place them in loose bundles on a wood surface or tablecloth, uncovered. The noodles can be cooked immediately, or allowed to dry and cooked later. They can be kept, at room temperature, for several days.

Pasta Made by Machine

There is no doubt that the best homemade pasta is made by hand. This pasta has a porous surface that sauces cling to perfectly. The smoother surface of machine-rolled pasta does not hold sauces as well. Ever since I began teaching Italian cooking almost twenty years ago, my aim has always been to get you in the kitchen and encourage you to make fresh pasta using a method acceptable to you. The two methods below give you ample choice. However, I say no, no to the extruders—pasta machines that mix the flour and eggs and push them out in the finished shape—because they produce a pasta that has a gummy, limp texture.

The ingredients are the same as for hand-rolled pasta: unbleached all-purpose flour and eggs. See individual recipes for the proportions. For equipment, you'll need the following:

- A food processor or electric mixer to make the dough.
- A small hand-cranked pasta machine to roll out the dough.
- A scalloped pastry wheel to cut the pasta into the desired shapes.

MAKING THE DOUGH IN A FOOD PROCESSOR

Break the eggs into the food processor fitted with the metal blade, and process briefly to mix the eggs. Add the flour, holding back 3 or 4 tablespoons. Pulse the machine on and off until the dough is all gathered *loosely* around the blade. At this point the dough should be moist and slightly sticky. If the dough is a little too wet, add the reserved flour. If it is too dry, beat an extra egg in a small bowl, add half of it to the dough, and pulse the machine once or twice to mix the egg into the dough.

Put the dough on a wooden board or work surface. Dust your hands with flour and knead the dough for a few minutes by hand. Dough kneaded by food processor is not as elastic as dough kneaded by hand, however, it should still be smooth and pliable. The dough is now ready to be rolled out. If you need to hold the dough for a while, keep it wrapped in plastic wrap and leave at room temperature. Give the dough a brief kneading just before rolling it out.

MAKING THE DOUGH WITH AN ELECTRIC MIXER

Break the eggs into the bowl of an electric mixer fitted with the dough hook, and beat briefly at low speed. Add the flour a little at a time, beating well after each addition. When all the flour has been added, increase the speed and let the mixer knead the dough for 5 to 6 minutes. Check the consistency of the dough. If it is too moist, work in a bit more flour. If it is too dry, work in half of a beaten egg. Remove the dough from the bowl and knead it for a few minutes by hand. The dough is now ready to be rolled out. If you need to hold it for a while, keep it wrapped in plastic wrap. Give the dough a brief kneading just before rolling it out.

ROLLING OUT THE DOUGH BY MACHINE

Set the rollers of the pasta machine at their widest opening. Cut off one small piece of dough, about the size of a large egg, and flatten it with the palm of your hand. Keep the rest of the dough wrapped in plastic wrap. Dust the flattened piece of dough lightly with flour, and run it once through the machine. Fold the dough in half, pressing it down with your fingertips. Run it through the machine again. Repeat the step four to five times, rotating the dough and dusting it with flour until it is smooth and not sticky. During these steps the dough will acquire a firmer consistency since the machine is doing additional kneading. (Do not skimp on this step or as you thin the pasta, as it will probably stick to the rollers.) Now that the dough is smooth and firm, it is ready to be stretched into a long, thin sheet of pasta.

Change the rollers to the next setting and run the dough through once *without folding it anymore.* Keep changing to the next setting and working the pasta sheet through the rollers once each time, until it reaches the desired thinness. For stuffed pasta, the sheet of dough should be almost transparent. For string pasta, the sheet of dough should be thin, but not transparent. (I never use the very last setting on my pasta machine because it makes a dough that is too thin.)

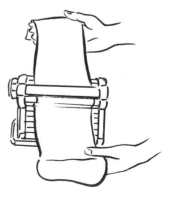

CUTTING THE SHEET OF DOUGH INTO STRING PASTA

If you are planning to make string pasta, like noodles or angel hair, place the sheet of dough on a lightly floured tablecloth and let it dry for 8 to 10 minutes before cutting it. Roll out the remaining dough, one small piece at a time, in the same manner. When the sheets of pasta are no longer sticky, put them through the cutting blades of the pasta machine, according to the desired width of the noodles. Arrange the noodles in soft bundles on a board or a tablecloth. Or they can be allowed to dry and cooked later on. They can be kept at room temperature for a few days.

Here's how to cut some specific string pastas:

- *Tagliatelle*—Roll out the dough into thin sheets and let them dry for 8 to 10 minutes. Put the sheets through the widest cutters of the pasta machine.
- *Fettuccine*—Roll out the dough into thin sheets and let them dry for 8 to 10 minutes. Put the sheets through the widest cutters of the pasta machine.
- *Tagliolini*—Roll out the dough into thin sheets and let them dry for 8 to 10 minutes. Put the sheets through the narrow cutters of the pasta machine.
- *Pappardelle*—Roll out the dough into thin sheets, and with a fluted pastry wheel or a sharp knife, cut the sheets into ¾-inch-wide ribbons.
- *Pizzoccheri*—Roll out the dough into thicker pasta sheets (stop one to two notches before the last). Cut the sheets 6 to 7 inches long, allow to dry for 12 to 15 minutes, and put them through the widest cutter of the pasta machine.
- *Tonnarelli*—The dough for tonnarelli should be thicker than the dough for tagliatelle or fettuccine. In rolling out the dough, stop when you get halfway through the notches of the pasta machine (approximately at number 3 of a hand-cranked machine.) Let the sheets dry for 12 to 15 minutes. Put the sheets through the narrow cutters of the pasta machine. (Because the thick pasta sheets are cut through narrow blades, they will produce thicker, square ribbons.)

STUFFING THE PASTA

The biggest problem in making stuffed pasta is that the sheet of pasta might become too dry to work with. To help avoid that problem, roll out a small piece of dough at a time, cut it into the desired shape, stuff it, and seal it right away. Keep the dough you are not working with wrapped tightly in plastic wrap. Roll out, cut, and stuff the remaining dough in the same manner until the dough is all used up. If your sheet of pasta is still a bit dry and does not seal properly, cut the pasta into the desired shape, stuff it, and lightly moisten the edges with a wet finger or a small brush.

Arrange the stuffed pasta on a large floured platter or cookie sheet. It can be cooked immediately, or it can be prepared a few hours or a day ahead, and refrigerated, uncovered.

Here are methods for some popular stuffed pastas:

- *Ravioli*—Roll out a small, thin sheet of dough at a time and trim it so that it has straight edges and is 5 inches wide. Place 1 tablespoon of the filling every $2\frac{1}{2}$ inches on the sheet of dough, putting the filling closer to the edge near you. Fold the sheet in half over the filling and seal around each mound, pressing out air pockets with your fingertips. Cut between the filling and press the edges to seal.

- For round ravioli, cut the sheet of dough 6 inches wide. Place 1 tablespoon of the filling every 3 inches on the sheet of dough, putting the filling closer to the edge near you. Fold the dough over and seal around each mound, pressing out air pockets with your fingertips. Press a 3-inch round cutter or glass around the filling to cut each raviolo. Repeat with remaining dough.

- *Tortelli*—Roll out and stuff the dough as for ravioli.

- *Tortelloni*—Roll out one small, thin sheet of dough at a time, and cut it into 3-inch squares. Place 1 tablespoon of filling in the center of each square and fold in half to form a triangle. Press the dough around the filling and press the edges firmly together to seal. Bend each tortellone around your finger, pressing one pointed end slightly over the other. Repeat with remaining dough.

- *Cappellacci*—Roll out, stuff, and shape the dough as for tortelloni.
- *Agnolotti*—Roll out, stuff, and shape the dough as for ravioli.
- *Cannelloni*—Roll out one thin sheet of dough at a time and cut it into 4 x 5-inch rectangles. Drop the rectangles in boiling water and cook 30 to 35 *seconds.* Scoop up the pasta with a large strainer and place in a large bowl of cold water. Remove the pasta, spread it out on kitchen towels, and pat dry. Spread a thin layer of filling in the *center* of each rectangle, leaving the borders free. Fold the pasta loosely over the filling to make cannelloni.
- *Lasagne*—Roll out the pasta dough into thin, wide sheets and cut to fit your lasagne baking pan. Parboil the sheets as explained in individual recipes.

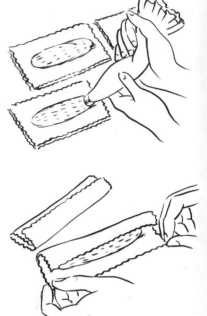

MAKING COLORED PASTA

Traditionally, colored pasta in Italy is generally made only with spinach and tomato paste. To make spinach pasta, add 2 tablespoons of cooked, finely chopped fresh or frozen spinach, thoroughly squeezed of moisture, to the eggs. Mix the spinach with the eggs, then add the flour and proceed to make the dough by hand or by machine. For red pasta, mix 1 tablespoon of tomato paste with the eggs.

For a less traditional but fun approach to colored pasta, add saffron to produce a golden pasta, cooked beets for dark red pasta, and squid ink for black pasta.

SOME TIPS ON PASTA MAKING

If you are a beginner, read the following tips before you start making your first batch of pasta.

1. Unless you are skilled at pasta making, do not attempt to roll out pasta by hand on a hot day because it will dry out very quickly.
2. Besides heat, time is the most important element in rolling out pasta by hand. It should take no longer than 10 minutes to roll out a small batch of dough, or the dough will dry out and it will be impossible to thin out. Start out with a small amount of dough, practice a few times, and be willing to discard it until you know you have it right.
3. If you plan to hand-roll the pasta, wrap the dough with plastic wrap and allow to rest for about 20 minutes, so that the gluten in the dough can relax and the dough will be easier to roll out. If you plan to roll out the pasta dough with a machine, the dough does not need to rest.
4. As you roll out the dough by hand, you might have tears and breakage. Simply patch the holes and go over with a rolling pin.
5. If you roll out pasta with a pasta machine, do not use the very last setting because it produces a sheet of dough that is too thin and breakable. Use the next to the last setting *twice,* and you will have a perfect dough for stuffed pasta.
6. The pasta is ready to be cut into noodles when the sheets that are drying begin to curl up at the edges. If the pasta breaks when you put it through the cutters of the pasta machine, it means it was dried too long. If it sticks together when you put it through the cutters, it was not dried long enough.

Stuffed Pastas

CAPPELLACCI FILLED WITH SQUASH
Capellacci con la Zucca

❧

SERVES 4; MAKES APPROXIMATELY 40 RAVIOLI

Cappellacci are the ravioli of Ferrara, a beautiful city in the northeastern part of the Emilia-Romagna region. These ravioli are filled with sweet squash, crumbled almond cookies, Parmigiano-Reggiano cheese, and nutmeg—a filling that is subtly sweet, complex, and unique at the same time. The traditional sauce for cappellacci is melted sweet butter with fresh sage.

FOR THE FILLING

½ small butternut squash
    (about ½ pound)
2 imported Amaretti di Saronno
    cookies, finely crushed
¼ teaspoon freshly grated
    nutmeg
½ pound ricotta (about 1 cup)
½ cup freshly grated
    Parmigiano-Reggiano cheese
Salt to taste

FOR THE RAVIOLI

2 cups unbleached all-purpose
    flour
3 extra-large eggs

FOR THE SAUCE

3 to 4 tablespoons unsalted
    butter
4 to 5 fresh sage leaves
⅓ to ½ cup freshly grated
    Parmigiano-Reggiano cheese

Prepare the filling: Preheat the oven to 350° F. Cut the squash in half lengthwise and discard the seeds. Wrap the squash in foil, place on a cookie sheet, and bake until tender, about 1 hour. Remove from oven and cool. Scoop out the pulp of the squash and puree it through a food mill. Place the squash in a large, clean kitchen towel and squeeze out about ⅓ cup of the watery juices. Place the puree in a bowl and mix it with the crushed cookies, nutmeg, ricotta, and Parmigiano. Season lightly with salt. Cover the bowl and chill in the refrigerator for a few hours.

Prepare the pasta as instructed on pages 79–87, using the flour and eggs in this recipe. Roll out the dough and prepare the ravioli as instructed on page 85. Cover a large tray or cookie sheet with a kitchen towel. Sprinkle the towel with some flour and place the ravioli in a single layer over it. The ravioli can be used immediately, or they can be refrigerated, uncovered, for a few hours.

Bring a large pot of water to a boil. Add 1 tablespoon of salt and the ravioli. Cook, uncovered, over high heat until the ravioli are tender but still firm to the bite.

Prepare the sauce: While the pasta is cooking, heat the butter in a large skillet over medium heat. Add the sage, stir once or twice, and keep butter warm over low heat.

Scoop up and reserve 1 cup of the pasta cooking water. With a big skimmer or a large slotted spoon, scoop up the ravioli, draining off the excess water against the side of the pot, and place in the skillet. Season lightly with salt and add about half of the Parmigiano. Mix gently over low heat until the ravioli are well coated with the sauce. Stir in a few tablespoons of the reserved pasta water if pasta seems a bit dry. Serve at once with additional Parmigiano.

RAVIOLI WITH WHITE FISH
Ravioli al Pesce Bianco

❧

SERVES 4; MAKES APPROXIMATELY 40 RAVIOLI

Ravioli stuffed with fish have become a standard feature in many upscale restaurants because they are lighter and more delicate than ravioli stuffed with meats. Technically, almost any fish can become a filling for pasta. However, fish with a soft, flaky texture will create a more pleasing, delicate filling than a firmer fleshed fish. This delicious stuffing pairs white fish with shallots, spinach, ricotta, and Parmigiano which taste so good together. Tomatoes, butter, and cream are simmered together into a quick, lovely sauce.

FOR THE FILLING

2 tablespoons unsalted butter
⅓ cup finely minced shallots or yellow onion
1 pound white fish fillets (sea bass, halibut, or sole), cut into 1-inch pieces
½ cup dry white wine
½ pound fresh spinach, stems removed
Salt to taste
1 tablespoon finely minced fresh mint
1 tablespoon chopped fresh parsley
½ cup ricotta
¼ cup freshly grated Parmigiano-Reggiano cheese

FOR THE RAVIOLI

2 cups unbleached all-purpose flour
3 extra-large eggs

FOR THE SAUCE

2 tablespoons unsalted butter
2½ cups canned Italian plum tomatoes with their juice, put through a food mill to remove seeds
¼ cup heavy cream

Prepare the filling: Heat the butter in a medium skillet over medium heat. When the butter foams, add the shallots. Cook, stirring, until they are lightly golden and soft, 6 to 7 minutes. Add the fish and stir until it loses its raw color, 2 to 3 minutes. Raise the heat to high and add the wine. Cook until the wine is all reduced, then turn the heat off under the skillet.

Wash the spinach in several changes of water and place in a small pan only with the water that clings to the leaves. Sprinkle with salt, cover the pan, and place over medium-low heat. Cook until the spinach is tender, 3 to 5 minutes. Drain and squeeze all water out of the spinach.

Mince the fish and spinach very fine by hand or in a food processor. If using a food processor, pulse the machine on and off until everything is chopped fine but not pureed. Put the mixture in a bowl and add the herbs, ricotta, and Parmigiano, then season with salt. Mix until all ingredients are well combined. Taste and adjust the seasoning. (The filling can be prepared several hours ahead. Refrigerate tightly covered.)

Prepare the pasta as instructed on pages 79–87, using the flour and eggs in this recipe. Roll out the pasta dough and prepare the ravioli as instructed on page 85. Cover a large tray or cookie sheet with a kitchen towel. Sprinkle the towel with some flour and place the ravioli in a single layer over it. The ravioli can be used immediately, or they can be refrigerated, uncovered, for a few hours.

Prepare the sauce: Heat the butter in a large skillet over medium heat. Add the tomatoes and cream. Season with salt and simmer, stirring occasionally, for 6 to 8 minutes. Keep the sauce warm over low heat.

Meanwhile, bring a large pot of water to a boil. Add 1 tablespoon of salt and the ravioli. Cook, uncovered, over high heat until the ravioli are tender but still firm to the bite.

With a big skimmer or a large slotted spoon, scoop up the ravioli, draining off the excess water against the side of the pot, and place in the skillet. Mix gently over low heat until the pasta and sauce are well combined. Serve at once.

RAVIOLI WITH SALMON
Ravioli al Salmone

✿

SERVES 4; MAKES APPROXIMATELY 40 RAVIOLI

Stuffed pasta could be considered the signature dish of Biba restaurant. Outstanding stuffed pasta begins, of course, with the pasta itself, which should be thin, almost transparent, light, and delicate. Here the pasta is filled with a delicious mixture of poached and smoked salmon, onions, egg, and just enough Parmigiano to bind everything together. These elegant ravioli are served with sweet butter dotted with small strips of smoked salmon and fresh chives.

FOR THE FILLING

4 cups cold water
1 cup dry white wine
Juice of ½ lemon
Salt to taste
1 pound salmon fillet
1 tablespoon unsalted butter
¼ cup finely minced yellow
   onion
1 ounce smoked salmon, finely
   minced
2 tablespoons chopped fresh
   parsley
¼ cup freshly grated
   Parmigiano-Reggiano cheese
1 medium egg, lightly beaten in
   a small bowl

FOR THE RAVIOLI

2 cups unbleached all-purpose
   flour
3 extra-large eggs

FOR THE SAUCE

3 tablespoons unsalted butter
1½ cups Basic Chicken Broth
   (page 21) or low-sodium
   canned chicken broth
2 ounces smoked salmon, cut
   into ¼-inch strips
1 to 2 tablespoons finely
   minced fresh chives or
   chopped fresh parsley

Prepare the filling: Put the water, wine, and lemon juice in a medium saucepan and bring to a gentle boil. Add the salt and salmon. Reduce the heat to low and simmer, uncovered, for 5 to 6 minutes. Transfer the salmon to a plate and cool. With a large knife, chop the salmon into very small granular pieces and place in a medium bowl.

Heat the butter in a small skillet over medium heat. Add the onion and cook, stirring, until it is lightly golden and soft, 4 to 5 minutes. Add the onion, smoked salmon, parsley, Parmigiano, and egg to the bowl with the salmon, season lightly with salt, and mix everything well. Taste and adjust the seasoning. Tightly cover and refrigerate until ready to use.

Prepare the pasta as instructed on pages 79–87, using the flour and eggs in this recipe. Roll out the pasta dough and prepare the ravioli as instructed on page 85. Cover a large tray or cookie sheet with a kitchen towel. Sprinkle the towel with some flour and place the ravioli in a single layer over it. The ravioli can be used immediately, or they can be refrigerated, uncovered, for a few hours.

Prepare the sauce: Heat the butter in a large skillet over medium heat. When the butter foams, add the broth and boil gently for 2 to 3 minutes. Add the smoked salmon and simmer a couple of minutes longer. Keep the sauce warm over very low heat.

Meanwhile, bring a large pot of water to a boil. Add 1 tablespoon of salt and the ravioli. Cook, uncovered, over high heat until the ravioli are tender but still a bit firm to the bite. Scoop up and reserve about 1 cup of the pasta cooking water.

With a big skimmer or a large slotted spoon, scoop up the ravioli, draining off the excess water against the side of the pot, and place in the skillet. Add the chives or parsley and season lightly with salt. Mix gently over low heat until the pasta is well coated with the sauce. Stir in some of the reserved pasta water if pasta seems a bit dry. Serve at once.

ROASTED RED BEET RAVIOLI WITH LEMON-SAGE BUTTER SAUCE

Ravioli di Barbabietole con Burro, Salvia, e Limone

❧

SERVES 4; MAKES APPROXIMATELY 40 ROUND RAVIOLI

This dish, which is extremely popular at my restaurant in Sacramento, is everything that a great Italian dish should be: fresh tasting and delicate. The light ravioli are tossed in a bubbling butter sauce with fresh sage and Parmigiano. In cooking, the silky thin pasta becomes even more transparent, encircling the ruby red filling like a magnificent flower.

FOR THE FILLING

1½ pounds fresh red beets with their leafy tops
12 ounces whole-milk ricotta
½ cup freshly grated Parmigiano-Reggiano cheese
Grated zest of 1 lemon
Salt to taste

FOR THE SAUCE

3 to 4 tablespoons unsalted butter
6 fresh sage leaves
Salt to taste
⅓ cup freshly grated Parmigiano-Reggiano cheese

FOR THE RAVIOLI

2 cups unbleached all-purpose flour
3 extra-large eggs

Prepare the filling: Preheat the oven to 400° F. Cut off the beet tops and set aside (see Savoring the Beet Greens, page 95). Peel the beets, wrap them in foil, and place on a cookie sheet. Bake until tender when pierced with a thin knife, 40 minutes to 1 hour depending on size. Remove from the oven and cool.

Open the beets, cut into chunks, and put them in a food processor. Pulse the machine on and off until the beets are cut into very small, granular pieces. Do not puree them. Put the beets in a strainer, place the strainer over a bowl, and leave for several hours to drain off the watery juices.

Put the beets in a medium bowl, add the ricotta, Parmigiano, and lemon zest, and season with salt. Mix everything well. Taste and adjust the seasoning. Chill in the refrigerator, uncovered, for 1 or 2 hours.

Prepare the pasta as instructed on pages 79–87, using the flour and eggs in this recipe. Roll out the dough and prepare the ravioli as instructed on page 85. (Because the filling for this pasta is quite wet, do not make the ravioli more than a few hours ahead.)

Bring a large pot of water to a boil. Add 1 tablespoon of salt and the ravioli. Cook, uncovered, over high heat until the ravioli are tender but still firm to the bite. Scoop up and reserve 1 cup of the pasta cooking water.

Prepare the sauce: While the pasta is cooking, heat the butter in a large skillet over medium heat. Add the sage and keep the butter warm over very low heat. (If fresh sage is not available, dress the ravioli with butter and cheese. Do not use dried sage, which is too strong-tasting for this delicate pasta.)

With a big skimmer or a large slotted spoon, scoop up the ravioli, draining off the excess water against the side of the pot, and place in the skillet. Season lightly with salt. Add about half of the Parmigiano and mix well to combine. Stir in some of the pasta cooking water if pasta seems a bit dry. Serve at once with additional Parmigiano if desired.

❧

NOTE

The ravioli can also be tossed into a large heated pasta bowl into which the butter, and then the ravioli and Parmigiano, are added. Toss well.

SAVORING THE BEET GREENS

One of the great bonuses of cooking beets is the leftover greens. To make a crunchy but tender salad of beet greens, remove the leaves from the stems and cook them in plenty of salted water until soft but still bright green. Drain well and toss with extra-virgin olive oil, lemon juice, and salt.

TORTELLI WITH RADICCHIO, RICOTTA, AND GOAT CHEESE

Tortelli al Radicchio, Ricotta, e Caprino

❧

SERVES 4; MAKES APPROXIMATELY 40 TORTELLI

In northern Italy, particularly in the Veneto region where radicchio grows abundantly, pasta stuffed with this wonderfully bitter leaf has become quite popular. The unobtrusive sauce of butter and cheese allows the bracing flavor of the filling to come through brilliantly.

FOR THE FILLING

1 small head radicchio (about 1 pound)
2 tablespoons extra-virgin olive oil
2 ounces pancetta, diced
¼ pound whole-milk ricotta
2 ounces goat cheese
½ cup freshly grated Parmigiano-Reggiano cheese
Salt and freshly ground black pepper to taste

FOR THE TORTELLI

2 cups unbleached all-purpose flour
3 extra-large eggs

FOR THE SAUCE

3 to 4 tablespoons unsalted butter
⅓ cup freshly grated Parmigiano-Reggiano cheese
Salt to taste

Prepare the filling: Discard any bruised or wilted leaves from the radicchio. Detach the leaves and wash them under cold running water. Pat dry with paper towels. Stack the leaves one over the other and cut them into thin strips.

Heat the oil in a large skillet over medium heat. Add the pancetta and sauté until it is lightly golden. Add the radicchio strips and sauté less than 1 minute. Reduce the heat to low, cover the skillet, and cook until the strips are soft and wilted, about 10 minutes. Stir a few times during cooking.

Pour the contents of the skillet into the bowl of a food processor and pulse the machine on and off until the radicchio is finely chopped. Do not puree it. Transfer the radicchio to a medium bowl and add the ricotta, goat cheese, and Parmigiano; mix until everything is well blended. Season lightly with salt and pepper, cover and refrigerate until ready to use.

Prepare the pasta as instructed on pages 79–87, using the flour and eggs in this recipe. Roll out the dough and prepare the tortelli as instructed on page 85. Cover a large tray or cookie sheet with a kitchen towel. Sprinkle the towel with some flour and place the tortelli in a single layer over it. The tortelli can be used immediately, or they can be refrigerated, uncovered, for a few hours.

Bring a large pot of water to a boil. Add 1 tablespoon of salt and the tortelli. Cook, uncovered, over high heat until the tortelli are tender but still firm to the bite. Scoop up and reserve about 1 cup of the pasta cooking water.

Prepare the sauce: While the pasta is cooking, heat the butter in a large skillet over medium heat and keep warm over low heat.

With a big skimmer or a large slotted spoon, scoop up the tortelli, draining off the excess water against the side of the pot, and place in the skillet. Season lightly with salt. Add about half of the Parmigiano and mix gently over low heat until the tortelli are well coated with the sauce. Stir in some of the reserved cooking water if pasta seems a bit dry. Serve at once with additional Parmigiano if desired.

TORTELLI WITH RICOTTA, MASCARPONE, AND SWISS CHARD

Tortelli di Erbette alla Parmigiana

❧

SERVES 4; MAKES APPROXIMATELY 40 TORTELLI

This dish, which comes from Parma, features silky homemade pasta wrapped around a voluptuous filling of ricotta, mascarpone, Swiss chard, and Parmigiano. Traditionally, the tortelli are topped with nothing more than fresh, sweet butter and Parmigiano-Reggiano cheese.

FOR THE FILLING

1 pound Swiss chard
Salt to taste
¼ pound ricotta
¼ pound mascarpone
¼ teaspoon freshly grated
    nutmeg
⅓ cup freshly grated
    Parmigiano-Reggiano cheese
1 large egg, lightly beaten

FOR THE TORTELLI

2 cups unbleached all-purpose
    flour
3 extra-large eggs

FOR THE SAUCE

3 to 4 tablespoons unsalted
    butter
Salt to taste
⅓ to ½ cup freshly grated
    Parmigiano-Reggiano cheese

Prepare the filling: Remove the chard leaves from the stalks. Wash the leaves well in several changes of cold water and put them in a large pot only with the water that clings to the leaves. Add a pinch of salt and turn the heat to medium. Cover the pot and cook until the leaves are tender, about 10 minutes. Stir once or twice during cooking. Drain the chard and squeeze out any remaining moisture. With a large knife, chop the chard very fine.

In a large bowl, combine the chard, ricotta, mascarpone, nutmeg, Parmigiano, and egg. Season with salt. Cover the bowl and refrigerate until ready to use.

Prepare the pasta as instructed on pages 79–87, using the flour and eggs in this recipe. Roll out the pasta dough and prepare the tortelli as instructed on page 85.

Cover a large tray or cookie sheet with a kitchen towel. Sprinkle the towel with some flour and place the tortelli in a single layer over it. The tortelli can be used immediately, or they can be refrigerated, uncovered, for a few hours.

Bring a large pot of water to a boil. Add 1 tablespoon of salt and the tortelli. Cook, uncovered, over high heat until the tortelli are tender but still firm to the bite. Scoop up and reserve about 1 cup of the pasta cooking water.

Prepare the sauce: While the pasta is cooking, heat the butter in a large skillet over medium heat and keep warm over low heat.

With a big skimmer or a large slotted spoon, scoop up the tortelli, draining off the excess water against the side of the pot, and place in the skillet. Season lightly with salt. Add about half of the Parmigiano and mix gently over low heat until the ravioli are well coated with the sauce. Stir in a little of the reserved pasta water if pasta seems too dry. Serve at once with additional Parmigiano.

VERSATILE SWISS CHARD

In Italy, the broad sweet-tasting stalks of Swiss chard are boiled until they are tender, 15 to 20 minutes depending on the size of the stalks, combined with the boiled leaves, and tossed with extra-virgin olive oil, lemon juice, and salt for a refreshing salad. The stalks are so sweet that they are also magnificent simply baked with butter and Parmigiano. In that case, put them in a preheated 400° F. oven and bake for 8 to 10 minutes, or until the cheese has a light golden color.

EGGPLANT–GOAT CHEESE TORTELLI WITH FRESH TOMATOES AND BLACK OLIVES

Tortelli di Melanzane e Caprino con Salsa di Pomodoro e Olive

❦

SERVES 4; MAKES APPROXIMATELY 40 TORTELLI

Eggplant, goat cheese, tomatoes, and black olives—essential ingredients to Mediterranean flavor—form the basis for truly outstanding Italian dishes. In this recipe, the eggplants are roasted for a short time at high temperature, which accomplishes two things: it purges the eggplants of their bitter juices and it cooks them quickly. The sauce for this dish needs to be exceptional. When good fresh tomatoes are not available use canned plum tomatoes such as San Marzano, which are ripe and meaty.

FOR THE FILLING

3 medium eggplants (about 3 pounds), peeled and cut into 2-inch pieces

Salt and freshly ground black pepper to taste

2 tablespoons olive oil

2 tablespoons chopped fresh parsley

3 ounces goat cheese

3 ounces whole-milk ricotta

⅓ to ½ cup freshly grated Parmigiano-Reggiano cheese

FOR THE TORTELLI

2 cups unbleached all-purpose flour

3 extra-large eggs

FOR THE SAUCE

2 tablespoons unsalted butter

2 to 3 tablespoons extra-virgin olive oil

1 large garlic clove, peeled and lightly crushed

1 pound ripe tomatoes, peeled, seeded, and diced (page 9) or 3 cups canned Italian plum tomatoes with their juices

6 to 8 pitted black olives, cut into thin strips

Salt and freshly ground black pepper to taste

Several fresh basil leaves, shredded, or 1 tablespoon chopped fresh parsley

⅓ cup freshly grated Parmigiano-Reggiano cheese

Prepare the filling: Preheat the oven to 500° F. Put the eggplant pieces in a bowl, season with salt and pepper, and toss with the oil. Place eggplant loosely on a large cookie sheet and bake 10 to 15 minutes or until very tender. Remove from oven and cool. Mince the eggplant very fine by hand or with a food processor. Do not puree.

In a medium bowl, combine the eggplant, parsley, goat cheese, and Parmigiano. Season with salt and pepper and mix until the ingredients are well combined. Refrigerate the filling, uncovered, for a few hours.

Prepare the pasta as instructed on pages 79–87, using the flour and eggs in this recipe. Roll out the dough and prepare the tortelli as instructed on page 85. Cover a large tray or cookie sheet with a kitchen towel. Sprinkle the towel with some flour and place the tortelli in a single layer over it. The tortelli can be used immediately, or they can be refrigerated, uncovered, for a few hours.

Prepare the sauce: Heat 1 tablespoon of the butter and the olive oil in a large skillet over medium heat. Add the garlic, brown on all sides, and discard it. Add the tomatoes and the olives, and season with salt and pepper. Cook, stirring a few times, until the tomatoes are soft and their juice has thickened, 4 to 5 minutes. Stir in the remaining tablespoon of butter and turn the heat off under the skillet.

Meanwhile, bring a large pot of water to a boil. Add 1 tablespoon of salt and the tortelli. Cook, uncovered, over high heat until the tortelli are tender but still firm to the bite. Scoop up and reserve 1 cup of the pasta cooking water.

With a big skimmer or a large slotted spoon, scoop up the tortelli, draining off the excess water against the side of the pot, and place in the skillet with the sauce. Add the basil or parsley and season lightly with salt. Toss gently and quickly over low heat until the pasta and sauce are well combined. Add a few tablespoons of the reserved pasta water if the pasta seems too dry. Taste, adjust the seasoning, and serve with a sprinkling of Parmigiano.

MORE ROASTED MELANZANE

I can never consume enough luscious, smoky eggplant. Whenever I roast eggplants I always roast more than I need and prepare little feasts the next day or two. I place the roasted eggplants in a bowl and toss them with just a bit of chopped garlic, some fresh mint when available, extra-virgin olive oil, and strong red wine vinegar. Served next to a slice of good ricotta salata, or fontina cheese, it becomes a light supper of infinite and simple satisfaction.

AGNOLOTTI WITH FOUR CHEESES
Agnolotti ai Quattro Formaggi

✤

SERVES 4; MAKES APPROXIMATELY 40 AGNOLOTTI

Agnolotti are the ravioli of the Piedmont region. They can be filled with a variety of ingredients and topped with many different sauces. (Agnolotti topped with freshly shaved white truffles is an absolute delicacy.) The filling of these agnolotti combines four great Italian cheeses. The sauce is nothing more than unsalted butter, fresh basil, and Parmigiano, but it complements the filling perfectly. This is a rich, delicate dish that will gracefully open an elegant dinner and make cheese lovers swoon.

FOR THE FILLING

2 ounces ricotta salata (firm salted ricotta) or goat cheese
2 ounces fontina cheese
¼ pound ricotta
2 ounces Gorgonzola cheese
2 tablespoons chopped fresh parsley
Salt to taste

FOR THE SAUCE

3 to 4 tablespoons unsalted butter
8 to 10 fresh basil leaves, shredded
Salt to taste
⅓ cup freshly grated Parmigiano-Reggiano cheese

FOR THE AGNOLOTTI

2 cups unbleached all-purpose flour
3 extra-large eggs

Prepare the filling: Grate the ricotta salata and fontina cheeses through the largest holes of a grater. Put all the cheeses and the parsley in a bowl, season lightly with salt (keep in mind that the cheeses are already salty), and mix well to combine. Cover the bowl and refrigerate until ready to use.

Prepare the pasta as instructed on pages 79–87, using the flour and eggs in this recipe. Roll out the dough and prepare the agnolotti as instructed on page 86. Cover a large tray or cookie sheet with a kitchen towel. Sprinkle the towel with some flour and place the agnolotti in a single layer over it. The agnolotti can be used immediately, or they can be refrigerated, uncovered, for a few hours.

Bring a large pot of water to a boil. Add 1 tablespoon of salt and the agnolotti. Cook, uncovered over high heat, until the agnolotti are tender but still a bit firm to the bite. Scoop up and reserve about 1 cup of the pasta cooking water.

While the pasta is cooking, heat the butter in a large skillet over medium-low heat. Add the basil, stir once or twice, then keep warm over low heat.

With a big skimmer or a large slotted spoon, scoop up the agnolotti, draining off the excess water against the side of the pot, and place in the skillet. Season lightly with salt. Add about half of the Parmigiano and mix gently over low heat until the agnolotti are well coated with the sauce. Stir in some of the reserved cooking water if pasta seems a bit dry. Serve at once with additional Parmigiano if desired.

TORTELLONI WITH SWISS CHARD, SPINACH, HAM, AND RICOTTA

Tortelloni con Biete, Spinaci, Prosciutto, e Ricotta

🍂

SERVES 6; MAKES APPROXIMATELY 50 TORTELLONI

In many northern Italian regions, pasta such as tortelloni, tortelli, ravioli, and pansoti are often stuffed with a mixture of greens and a little ricotta, which imparts softness to the filling and holds it together. Of course, other ingredients can go into the filling as well, depending on local traditions or the whims of the cook. This is a typical Italian way of creating recipes that are not only good but also good for you.

In this dish, Swiss chard, spinach, baked ham, ricotta, and Parmigiano are combined in a mouthwatering filling for tortelloni (larger, plumper tortellini), then they are tossed together in a fragrant sauce of ripe tomatoes, pine nuts, and herbs. Omit the ham and you have a sublime vegetarian dish.

FOR THE FILLING

1 pound Swiss chard
½ pound fresh spinach
Salt to taste
¼ pound baked ham, very finely minced
½ to ¾ cup ricotta
1 medium egg
⅓ cup freshly grated Parmigiano-Reggiano cheese

FOR THE TORTELLONI

2 cups unbleached all-purpose flour
3 extra-large eggs

FOR THE SAUCE

⅓ cup extra-virgin olive oil
1 large garlic clove, peeled and lightly crushed
2½ pounds ripe tomatoes, peeled, seeded, and finely minced (page 9)
Salt and freshly ground black pepper to taste
2 tablespoons lightly toasted pine nuts
2 tablespoons chopped fresh oregano leaves, basil, or parsley
1 tablespoon unsalted butter (optional)

Prepare the filling: Remove the Swiss chard leaves from the stalks and the stems from the spinach, and discard any leaves that are bruised or wilted. Reserve the Swiss chard stalks for another use. Wash the leaves well in several changes of cold water and put them in a large pot only with the water that clings to the leaves. Add a pinch of salt and turn the heat on to medium. Cover the pot and cook until the leaves are tender, 10 to 12 minutes. Stir a few times during cooking. Add a little water if needed. Drain the chard and spinach, and squeeze out any remaining moisture. With a large knife, chop the chard and spinach very fine.

In a large bowl, combine the chard, spinach, ham, ricotta, egg, and Parmigiano. Season with salt. Cover the bowl and refrigerate until ready to use.

Prepare the pasta as instructed on pages 79–87, using the flour and eggs in this recipe. Roll out the dough and prepare the tortelloni as instructed on page 85. Cover a large tray or cookie sheet with a kitchen towel. Sprinkle the towel with some flour and place the tortelloni in a single layer over it. The tortelloni can be used immediately, or they can be refrigerated, uncovered, for a few hours.

Prepare the sauce: Heat the oil in a large skillet over medium heat. Add the garlic and brown on all sides. Discard the garlic and add the tomatoes. Season with salt and pepper. Cook, uncovered, stirring occasionally, until the tomatoes are soft and juices have thickened, 5 to 6 minutes. Stir in the pine nuts, oregano, basil, or parsley, and the butter, if using, and turn the heat off under the skillet.

Bring a large pot of water to a boil. Add 1 tablespoon of salt and the tortelloni. Cook, uncovered, over high heat until the tortelloni are tender but still firm to the bite. Drain the tortelloni gently and place in the skillet. Mix well over low heat until the tortelloni are well coated with the sauce. Serve at once.

LASAGNE WITH EGGPLANT, MOZZARELLA, AND TOMATOES

Lasagne con le Melanzane, Mozzarella, e Pomodori

❧

SERVES 6 TO 8

This lasagne is inspired by a traditional southern Italian recipe, in which rigatoni or penne are tossed with a mellow sauce of eggplant, mozzarella, and tomatoes. In this dish, however, it is the homemade pasta that takes center stage. Layered between these harmonious ingredients and baked to a straightforward succulence, this is a dish that will literally melt in your mouth!

Because lasagne is generally rich, serve small portions—and anticipate seconds.

FOR THE FILLING

4 small eggplants (about
   3½ pounds total)
Olive oil for frying
Flour to coat eggplant slices
¼ cup extra-virgin olive oil
2 large garlic cloves, peeled and
   lightly crushed
4 cups canned Italian plum
   tomatoes, put through a food
   mill to remove seeds
Salt and freshly ground black
   pepper to taste
10 to 12 fresh basil leaves,
   shredded, or 1 tablespoon
   chopped fresh parsley

¾ pound mozzarella, diced or
   shredded
1 cup freshly grated
   Parmigiano-Reggiano cheese
1 to 2 tablespoons unsalted
   butter

FOR THE PASTA

2 cups unbleached all-purpose
   flour
3 extra-large eggs

Prepare the filling: Peel the eggplant and cut into ¼-inch round slices. Purge them as instructed on page 10.

Heat ½ inch of the olive oil for frying in a medium skillet over medium heat. Coat the eggplant slices lightly with flour and slip them a few at a time into the hot oil. Cook until they are lightly golden on both sides. Repeat with remaining slices and drain on paper towels, then pat dry thoroughly with additional paper towels.

Heat the olive oil in a medium saucepan over medium heat. Add the garlic and cook until they are golden on all sides. Discard the garlic, add the tomatoes, and season with salt and pepper. As soon as the tomatoes come to a boil, reduce the heat to low and simmer, uncovered, stirring occasionally, until the sauce has a medium-thick consistency, 20 to 25 minutes. Stir the fresh basil into the sauce and turn the heat off under the pan.

Prepare the pasta as instructed on pages 79–87, using the flour and eggs in this recipe. Roll out the dough into lasagne (page 86), and cut to fit your lasagne pan.

Bring a large pot of water to a boil. Add 1 tablespoon of salt and no more than 3 or 4 sheets of pasta at a time. As soon as the water comes back to a boil, cook the sheets no longer than 1 minute. Scoop up the sheets with a large skimmer or slotted spoon, trying not to break them, and place in a bowl of cold water to cool and untangle. Remove the pasta sheets immediately and lay on kitchen towels. Pat dry with another towel. Repeat with remaining pasta sheets.

Butter the bottom and sides of your baking pan. Cover the bottom of the pan with sheets of pasta, trimming the pasta to fit your pan. Spread some sauce over the pasta, top with slices of eggplant, dot with mozzarella, and sprinkle with some Parmigiano. Repeat the process, filling each layer of pasta in this manner for a total of 8 layers. Sprinkle the Parmigiano over the last layer and dot with butter. (The lasagne may be prepared and assembled up to this point 1 day ahead. Refrigerate tightly wrapped. Before baking leave the lasagne at room temperature for 1 to 2 hours.)

Preheat the oven to 400° F. Bake on the middle rack of the oven until the Parmigiano is melted and the top of the lasagne has a nice golden color, 15 to 20 minutes. Remove the dish from the oven and let it set for a few minutes before serving.

CONTINUED

NOTE

Lasagne should have 6 to 8 layers. Never fill the pan to the rim because as it bakes, the pasta will swell up and the sauce and juices will overflow.

COOKING WITH EGGPLANT

❧ *Because eggplant soaks up a great deal of oil, fry it in very hot oil*
so it cooks quickly.

❧ *To reduce the quantity of oil, fry the eggplant in a nonstick skillet or grill it.*
Keep in mind, however, that the slices should be very soft and
cooked all the way through.

❧ *Even though eggplant comes in different shapes and shades, the most common*
is the thick purple type. For this dish, select the thinner kind or
opt for the Japanese variety.

LASAGNE WITH WALNUT PESTO AND RICOTTA
Lasagne al Pesto di Noci e Ricotta

❦

SERVES 6 TO 8

The traditional cooking of Liguria takes wide sheet pasta called lasagne, or *stracci*, "rags," and pairs it with a classic pesto sauce. A more contemporary version combines a walnut and pine nut pesto with a bit of ricotta and cream, which is thinly layered between eight sheets of paper-thin lasagne. The lasagne are then baked just long enough for the top layer to become lightly golden and a bit crisp. The result is an unorthodox but exceptionally smooth and vivacious lasagne.

FOR THE WALNUT PESTO SAUCE

5 cups loosely packed fresh basil leaves

3 tablespoons pine nuts, lightly toasted in the oven

3 tablespoons chopped fresh walnuts

2 garlic cloves

Salt to taste

1 cup extra-virgin olive oil

4 tablespoons ricotta

½ cup freshly grated Parmigiano-Reggiano cheese

⅓ cup heavy cream

FOR THE LASAGNE

2 cups unbleached all-purpose flour

3 extra-large eggs

TO COMPLETE THE DISH

2 tablespoons unsalted butter

⅓ to ½ cup freshly grated Parmigiano-Reggiano cheese

Prepare the pesto: Put the basil, pine nuts, walnuts, garlic, salt, and olive oil in the bowl of a food processor, and process until the mixture has a creamy consistency. (The pesto can be prepared up to this point several days ahead.) Transfer the pesto to a bowl and fold in the ricotta, Parmigiano, and cream. Taste and adjust the seasoning. Cover and set aside until ready to use. (Makes 2¾ cups pesto.)

Prepare the pasta as instructed on pages 79–87, using the flour and eggs in this recipe. Roll out the dough into lasagne (page 86) and cut to fit your pan.

CONTINUED

Bring a large pot of water to a boil. Add 1 tablespoon salt and no more than 3 or 4 sheets of pasta at a time. As soon as the water comes back to a boil, cook the pasta no longer than 1 minute. Scoop up the sheets with a large skimmer or slotted spoon, trying not to break them, and place in a bowl of cold water to cool and untangle. Remove the pasta sheets immediately and lay on kitchen towels. Pat dry with another towel. Repeat with remaining pasta sheets.

Scoop up and reserve about ½ cup of the pasta cooking water. Stir about 3 to 4 tablespoons of the reserved pasta water into the pesto and mix well.

Butter the bottom and sides of your baking pan generously. Cover the bottom of the baking pan with sheets of pasta, trimming the pasta to fit your pan. Spread some pesto lightly over the sheets and sprinkle with a bit of Parmigiano. Repeat the process, filling each layer in the same manner, for a total of 7 layers. Add the last eighth layer of pasta.

Melt the butter in a small skillet over medium heat, and brush it over the last layer of pasta. Sprinkle the Parmigiano generously over the last layer of pasta. (The lasagne may be prepared and assembled up to this point 1 day ahead. Refrigerate tightly wrapped. Before baking, leave the lasagne at room temperature for 1 to 2 hours.)

Preheat the oven to 400° F. Bake on the middle rack of the oven just until the top of lasagne is lightly golden, 10 to 15 minutes. Remove the dish from the oven and let it set for a few minutes before serving.

PESTO PERFECTION

🌿 *Spread the pesto very lightly over each layer of pasta,*
or the dish will be overpowering.

🌿 *In making pesto, do not use too much garlic or its taste will*
obscure that of the other ingredients.

LASAGNE WITH SPECK AND MIXED MUSHROOMS

Lasagne con Speck e Funghi Misti

❧

SERVES 6 TO 8

Lasagne is not a dish for everyday. In fact, in the Italian tradition, lasagne is prepared mostly for special occasions, for holidays, or for Sunday meals with family and friends. The dish can be by turns sumptuous, voluptuous, delicate, rustic and quite hearty. But no matter what the filling is, fresh, homemade pasta is the only suitable one for lasagne.

In this recipe seven layers of delicate homemade pasta are layered with sautéed mixed mushrooms, speck (smoked Italian ham), béchamel sauce, and Parmigiano-Reggiano cheese. The result is a remarkably delicious dish, elegant enough to serve on the most special occasions.

FOR THE MUSHROOM FILLING

⅓ to ½ cup olive oil

1½ pounds mixed mushrooms (white cultivated, shiitake, cremini, chanterelles), wiped clean and thinly sliced

Salt and freshly ground black pepper to taste

2 tablespoons chopped fresh parsley

FOR THE LASAGNE

2 cups unbleached all-purpose flour

3 extra-large eggs

FOR THE BÉCHAMEL SAUCE

3 cups milk

4 tablespoons unsalted butter

4½ tablespoons all-purpose flour

Pinch of salt

TO COMPLETE THE DISH

¼ pound sliced speck or prosciutto, cut into ¼-inch-wide strips

1 cup freshly grated Parmigiano-Reggiano cheese

1 tablespoon cold unsalted butter, cut into small cubes

CONTINUED

Prepare the filling: Heat the oil in a large skillet over medium heat. Add the mushrooms without crowding the pan and cook, stirring, until they are lightly golden. Scoop up the mushrooms with a slotted spoon and place in a strainer. Put the strainer over a bowl to allow excess oil to drip off. Cook remaining mushrooms in the same manner. When all the mushrooms are done, put them in a bowl, season with salt and pepper, and stir in the parsley.

Prepare the pasta as instructed on pages 79–87, using the flour and eggs in this recipe. Roll out the dough into lasagne (page 86) and cut to fit your pan.

Bring a large pot of water to a boil. Add 1 tablespoon of salt and no more than 3 to 4 sheets of pasta at a time. As soon as the water comes back to a boil, cook the pasta no longer than 1 minute. Scoop up the sheets with a large skimmer or slotted spoon, trying not to break them, and place in a bowl of cold water to cool and untangle. Remove the pasta sheets immediately and lay on kitchen towels. Pat dry with another towel. Repeat with remaining pasta sheets.

Prepare the béchamel sauce: Heat the milk in a small saucepan over low heat. Melt the butter in a medium saucepan over medium heat. When the butter foams, add the flour, lower the heat to medium-low, and stir the mixture with a wooden spoon or a small whisk. Cook and stir for about 2 minutes, making sure not to let the flour turn brown. Remove the saucepan from the heat and add the hot milk all at once. Mix energetically to prevent lumps. Put the saucepan back over low heat, season with salt, and cook gently, stirring constantly, until the sauce has a medium-thick consistency, 3 to 4 minutes. If the béchamel is too thick, stir in a bit more milk. If it is too thin, cook a bit longer. (Makes approximately 3 cups sauce.) (For preparing béchamel ahead, see below.)

Preheat the oven to 400° F. Butter the bottom and sides of a lasagne pan generously. Cover the bottom of the pan with sheets of pasta, trimming the pasta to fit the pan. Spread a light layer of béchamel over the pasta, scatter the mushrooms over the béchamel, top with strips of speck, and sprinkle with Parmigiano. Repeat the process for a total of 6 layers. Add the seventh layer of pasta and spread the remaining béchamel over it. Sprinkle with the Parmigiano and dot with butter. (The lasagne may be prepared and assembled up to this point 1 day ahead. Refrigerate tightly wrapped. Before baking, leave the lasagne at room temperature for 1 to 2 hours.)

Bake on the middle rack of the oven until the top of the lasagne is lightly golden, 15 to 20 minutes. Remove the dish from the oven and let it settle a few minutes before serving.

❦

PREPARING BÉCHAMEL AHEAD

If béchamel is made to wait, butter a sheet of plastic wrap and press it over the béchamel to avoid forming a thin crust. When béchamel cools too long, it thickens and firms up. Reheat it gently, adding a little bit of milk and whisking constantly until it again has a smooth consistency.

SPINACH LASAGNE WITH ENRICHED BOLOGNESE MEAT RAGÙ

Lasagne Verdi al Ragù Arricchito

❦

SERVES 6 TO 8

Trattoria Boni in Bologna is a family-run establishment where food is prepared according to what is available in the market that day. During one of my visits to Boni I had a spinach lasagne that was positively incredible. Eight layers of thin spinach pasta, laced with a filling of succulent pork, veal, prosciutto, and fresh porcini mushroom ragù enriched with a creamy béchamel sauce.

This is Boni lasagne. The only change I made was to use dried porcini instead of fresh, which are seldom available. This dish is a labor of love, for it requires a bit of time and patience, but the result is well worth it. To make it a little easier on yourself, you can prepare this lasagne in two stages: The ragù can be refrigerated for two days or frozen for a month.

CONTINUED

FOR THE MEAT RAGÙ

2 ounces dried porcini
　　mushrooms, soaked in
　　2 cups lukewarm water for
　　20 minutes
2 tablespoons unsalted butter
2 tablespoons extra-virgin
　　olive oil
½ cup finely minced yellow
　　onion
½ cup finely minced carrot
½ cup finely minced celery
½ pound chopped veal,
　　preferably from the shoulder
½ pound ground pork,
　　preferably from
　　Boston butt
¼ pound prosciutto, finely
　　chopped
¼ pound chicken livers
Salt and freshly ground black
　　pepper to taste
½ cup dry Marsala wine
3 cups canned Italian plum
　　tomatoes with their juice, put
　　through a food mill to
　　remove seeds

1 cup Basic Chicken Broth
　　(page 21) or low-sodium
　　canned chicken broth
¼ cup milk

FOR THE LASAGNE

2 cups unbleached all-purpose
　　flour
3 extra-large eggs
2 tablespoons finely chopped
　　cooked fresh or frozen
　　spinach

FOR THE BÉCHAMEL SAUCE

1¼ cups milk
2 tablespoons unsalted butter
2 tablespoons all-purpose flour
Pinch of salt

TO COMPLETE THE DISH

1 cup freshly grated
　　Parmigiano-Reggiano cheese
1 tablespoon cold unsalted
　　butter, cut into small cubes

Prepare the ragù: Drain the porcini mushrooms and reserve their soaking water. Rinse the mushrooms well under cold running water and chop them fine. Line a strainer with paper towels and strain the mushroom water into a bowl to get rid of the sandy deposits. Set aside.

Heat the butter and oil in a wide-bottomed, heavy saucepan over medium heat. When the butter begins to foam, add the vegetables and cook, stirring, until they are lightly golden and soft, 6 to 7 minutes. Raise the heat to high, and add the veal, pork, prosciutto, and chicken livers. Season with salt and pepper. Cook, stirring, to break up the meat with a large spoon until light golden in color, 5 to

6 minutes. Add the porcini mushrooms and the wine. Cook until the wine is almost all reduced, then add the tomatoes, broth, and 1 cup of the reserved mushroom water. As soon as the liquid comes to a boil, reduce the heat to low and partially cover the pan. Cook the ragù at the slowest of simmer for about 2 hours, stirring from time to time. When done the sauce should have a medium-thick consistency and a light brown color. If too dry, add a little additional broth or water. Add the milk and cook a few minutes longer. Taste, adjust the seasoning, and turn the heat off. (Makes approximately 4½ cups sauce.) (The sauce can be refrigerated, tightly covered, for 2 days or kept in the freezer up to a month.)

Prepare the pasta as instructed on pages 79–87, using the flour, eggs, and spinach in this recipe. Roll out the dough into lasagne (page 86) and cut to fit your baking pan.

Bring a large pot of water to a boil. Add 1 tablespoon of salt and no more than 3 or 4 sheets of pasta at a time. As soon as the water comes to a boil, cook the sheets no longer than 1 minute. Scoop up the sheets with a large skimmer or slotted spoon, trying not to break them, and place in a bowl of cold water to cool and untangle. Remove the pasta sheets immediately and lay on kitchen towels. Pat dry with another kitchen towel. Repeat with remaining pasta sheets.

Prepare the béchamel sauce as instructed on page 112, using the proportions in this recipe. When done, remove from the heat and cool slightly. (Makes approximately 1½ cups sauce.) (For preparing the béchamel ahead, see page 113.)

Preheat the oven to 400° F. Butter the bottom and sides of your lasagne pan generously. Add the béchamel to the meat sauce and mix well to combine. Cover the bottom of the pan with sheets of pasta, trimming the pasta to fit the pan. Spread a thin layer of sauce over the pasta and sprinkle with Parmigiano. Repeat the process, layering pasta, meat-béchamel sauce, and Parmigiano for an additional 7 layers. Dot the last layer of pasta with butter. (The lasagne may be prepared and assembled up to this point 1 day ahead. Refrigerate tightly wrapped. Before baking, leave the lasagne at room temperature for 1 to 2 hours.)

Bake on the middle rack of the oven until the top of the lasagne is lightly golden, 15 to 20 minutes. Remove the dish from the oven and let it set a few minutes before serving.

CANNELLONI WITH
SHRIMP STUFFING
Cannelloni con Ripieno di Gamberi

❦

SERVES 8; MAKES APPROXIMATELY 16 CANNELLONI

A delicate homemade pasta wrapped around a sumptuous filling: the result is nothing less than splendid.

Don't let the many steps of this dish scare you, because most of the work here can be done a day ahead. Actually, cannelloni is perhaps one of the best dishes to do for company, since all you have to do at the last moment is to bake them.

FOR THE FILLING

1 to 2 tablespoons unsalted
  butter
½ cup finely minced yellow
  onion
1½ pounds medium shrimp,
  peeled and deveined
1 garlic clove, minced
½ cup dry red vermouth
⅓ cup heavy cream
1 large egg, lightly beaten in a
  small bowl
2 tablespoons chopped fresh
  parsley
⅓ to ½ cup freshly grated
  Parmigiano-Reggiano cheese
Salt to taste

FOR THE CANNELLONI

1½ cups unbleached
  all-purpose flour
3 medium eggs

FOR THE BÉCHAMEL SAUCE

3 cups milk
Pinch of saffron
3 tablespoons unsalted butter
3 tablespoons all-purpose flour
Salt to taste

TO COMPLETE THE DISH

1 to 2 tablespoons cold butter,
  cut into small pieces to top
  the cannelloni

Prepare the filling: Heat the butter in a large skillet over medium heat. Add the onion and cook, stirring, until the onion is lightly golden and soft, about 5 minutes. Raise the heat to high and add the shrimp. Cook until shrimp are lightly golden on all sides, 2 to 3 minutes. Add the garlic, stir once or twice, then add the vermouth. Stir until the vermouth is almost all reduced, about 2 minutes. Stir in the cream and cook until only a few tablespoons of thick sauce is left in the skillet.

Transfer the shrimp to the bowl of a food processor and pulse the machine on and off until shrimp are finely minced but not pureed. Transfer the mixture to a bowl. Add the egg, parsley, and Parmigiano and season with salt. Cover the bowl and set aside or refrigerate until ready to use.

Prepare the pasta as instructed on pages 79–87, using the flour and eggs in this recipe. Roll out the pasta dough and prepare the cannelloni as instructed on page 86.

Bring a large pot of water to a boil. Add 1 tablespoon of salt and no more than 4 or 5 pieces of pasta to the water. As soon as the water comes back to the boil, cook the pasta no longer than 1 minute. Scoop up the pasta squares with a large skimmer or slotted spoon, trying not to break them, and place in a bowl of cold water to cool and untangle. Remove the pasta squares from the cold water immediately and lay on kitchen towels. Pat dry with another towel. Repeat with remaining pasta squares.

Lay the dried pasta on a work surface and place approximately 2 tablespoons of the filling down the center of each square. Fold the two opposite edges of the pasta over the filling to make a tube. Butter a large baking dish generously and lay the cannelloni, seams facing up, next to each other, leaving a little space between them.

Prepare the béchamel sauce as instructed on page 112, using the proportions in this recipe. When the béchamel is done, remove from the heat and cool slightly. (Makes approximately 3 cups sauce.) Spoon béchamel sauce over the cannelloni, coating them completely. Cover the dish tightly with plastic wrap and refrigerate until ready to use.

Preheat the oven to 400° F. When the oven is hot, dot the cannelloni with butter and place on the middle rack of the oven. Bake until the cannelloni are lightly golden, about 10 minutes. Remove the cannelloni from the oven and allow to set for a minute or two before serving.

SPINACH CANNELLONI WITH DUCK AND WILD MUSHROOM STUFFING

Cannelloni Verdi con Anatra e Funghi

❧

SERVES 8; MAKES APPROXIMATELY 16 CANNELLONI

Cannelloni are large, freshly made pasta squares that can be filled with a variety of ingredients. A cannelloni dish is perhaps one of the most elegant ways to use homemade pasta. Cannelloni, like lasagne, can be prepared a day or two ahead and baked at the last moment. The homemade pasta in this recipe is imperative. No crepes, no wonton wrappers, or any other substitute will do.

FOR THE FILLING

1 ounce dried porcini mushrooms, soaked in 1 cup lukewarm water for 20 minutes
2 tablespoons unsalted butter
⅓ cup finely minced shallots or yellow onion
1 pound duck breasts, skin removed and meat cut into ½-inch pieces
¼ pound sliced prosciutto, cut into strips
½ cup dry imported Marsala wine, such as Florio or Pellegrino
Salt and freshly ground black pepper to taste
1 large egg

2 tablespoons chopped fresh parsley
½ to ¾ cup freshly grated Parmigiano-Reggiano cheese

FOR THE CANNELLONI

1½ cups unbleached all-purpose flour
3 medium eggs
1 heaping tablespoon finely chopped cooked fresh or frozen spinach

FOR THE BÉCHAMEL SAUCE

3 cups milk
3 tablespoons unsalted butter
3 tablespoons flour
Salt to taste

1 to 2 tablespoons unsalted
butter, cut into small
pieces
½ cup freshly grated
Parmigiano-Reggiano
cheese

1 to 2 tablespoons unsalted
butter
2½ cups canned Italian plum
tomatoes with their juice,
put through a food mill to
remove seeds
Salt and freshly ground black
pepper to taste

Prepare the filling: Drain the porcini mushrooms and reserve their soaking water for other use. Rinse the mushrooms well under cold running water and chop them fine.

Heat the butter in a medium skillet over medium heat. When the butter begins to foam, add the shallots or onion and cook, stirring, until shallots are lightly golden, 4 to 5 minutes. Add the duck. Cook until duck has a nice golden color, 4 to 5 minutes. Add the mushrooms and prosciutto, and stir once or twice. Raise the heat to high and add the wine. Cook, stirring and scraping up the bits and pieces attached to the bottom of the skillet, until the wine is almost all reduced, 2 to 3 minutes. Season lightly with salt and pepper.

Transfer the contents of the skillet to the bowl of a food processor and pulse the machine on and off until the mixture is finely minced but not pureed. Transfer to a bowl. Add the egg, parsley, and Parmigiano and mix well. Taste and adjust the seasoning. Cover the bowl and set aside or refrigerate until ready to use.

Prepare the pasta as instructed on pages 79–87, using the flour and eggs in this recipe. Roll out the pasta dough and prepare the cannelloni as instructed on page 86.

Bring a large pot of water to a boil. Add 1 tablespoon of salt and no more than 5 or 6 pieces of pasta to the water. As soon as the water comes back to the boil, cook the pasta no longer than 1 minute. Scoop up the pasta squares with a large skimmer or slotted spoon, trying not to break them, and place in a bowl of cold water to cool and untangle. Remove the pasta from the cold water immediately and lay on kitchen towels to dry. Pat dry with another towel. Repeat with remaining pasta squares.

Lay the dried pasta on a work surface and place approximately 2 tablespoons of the filling down the center of each square. Fold the two opposite edges of the pasta over the filling to make a tube. Butter a large baking dish generously and lay the cannelloni next to each other, leaving a little space between them.

CONTINUED

Prepare the béchamel sauce as instructed on page 112, using the proportions in this recipe. When béchamel is done, cool slightly. (Makes approximately 3 cups sauce.) Scoop up ½ cup of béchamel and reserve. Spoon the remaining sauce over the cannelloni, coating them completely. Cover the dish tightly with plastic wrap and refrigerate until ready to use.

Preheat the oven to 400° F. When the oven is hot, dot the cannelloni with butter, sprinkle with the Parmigiano, and place on the middle rack of the oven. Bake until the cannelloni are lightly golden, about 10 minutes.

Meanwhile, prepare the tomato sauce: Heat the butter in a medium skillet over medium heat. When the butter begins to foam, add the tomatoes and season with salt and pepper. Simmer for 2 to 3 minutes, then stir in the reserved béchamel sauce and simmer a few minutes longer.

Remove the cannelloni from oven and allow to set for a few minutes. Spread a few tablespoons of sauce on flat serving dishes, place two cannelloni on each dish, and serve at once.

String Pastas

TONNARELLI WITH SPICY SCALLOP SAUCE

Tonnarelli con Sugo di Cape Sante

❧

SERVES 4

At my restaurant in Sacramento, we serve a variety of bruschette topped with vegetables, cheeses, or seafood. One of my favorite toppings is a concoction of spicy scallops, garlic, and sun-dried tomatoes, which can also become a quick, appetizing pasta sauce.

When cooking fresh pasta, keep in mind that it will be done in no time at all. Drain it while it is still al dente, since it will finish cooking while it is tossed with the sauce.

FOR THE TONNARELLI

2 cups unbleached all-purpose
  flour
3 extra-large eggs

FOR THE SAUCE

⅓ cup extra-virgin olive oil
¾ pound sea scallops, cut into
  ½-inch cubes
1 garlic clove, finely minced
1 tablespoons finely minced
  sun-dried tomatoes

Chopped fresh red chili pepper
  or hot red pepper flakes to
  taste
Salt to taste
½ cup dry white wine
1 cup canned Italian plum
  tomatoes with their juice, put
  through a food mill to
  remove seeds
2 tablespoons chopped fresh
  parsley
1 tablespoon unsalted butter

Prepare the pasta as instructed on pages 79–87, using the flour and eggs in this recipe. Roll out the dough and cut into tonnarelli as instructed on page 84. (The pasta can be prepared ahead and left, uncovered, at room temperature for 2 days. Do not refrigerate.)

CONTINUED

Prepare the sauce: Heat the oil in a large skillet over high heat. Add the scallops and cook, stirring, until scallops lose their raw appearance, 1 to 2 minutes. Add the garlic, sun-dried tomatoes, and chili pepper. Season with salt and stir a few times. Add the wine. Cook until the wine and juices from the scallops are reduced approximately by half, 1 to 2 minutes. Add the tomatoes and cook until the sauce begins to thicken, about 4 minutes. Stir in the parsley and the butter and turn the heat off under the skillet.

Meanwhile, bring a large pot of water to a boil. Add 1 tablespoon of salt and the pasta. Cook, uncovered, over high heat until the pasta is tender but still firm to the bite. Scoop up and reserve about 1 cup of the pasta cooking water.

Drain the pasta and place in the skillet with the sauce. Toss everything quickly over low heat until pasta and sauce are well incorporated. Add some of the reserved pasta water if pasta seems a bit dry. Taste, adjust the seasoning, and serve at once.

YELLOW AND GREEN NOODLES
WITH MORTADELLA,
PEAS, AND MUSHROOMS
Paglia e Fieno con Mortadella, Piselli, e Funghi

※

SERVES 4

Paglia e fieno, or "straw and hay," is the name of spinach and yellow noodles that are traditionally served with an exquisite sauce of ham, fresh peas, and cream. In this version, mortadella takes the place of ham and the mushrooms provide a contrast to the sweetness of the peas. The noodles here are tonnarelli, which resemble a thicker version of tagliolini. Fettuccine or tagliatelle can also be used. The dish is at its best when paired with homemade pasta. If time is short, use a good brand of imported fettuccine or tagliatelle.

FOR THE YELLOW TONNARELLI

1 cup unbleached all-purpose
    flour
2 medium eggs

FOR THE GREEN TONNARELLI

1 cup unbleached all-purpose
    flour
2 medium eggs
1 tablespoon finely chopped
    cooked fresh or frozen
    spinach

FOR THE SAUCE

1 cup cooked fresh peas or
    thawed frozen green peas

¼ cup extra-virgin olive oil
½ pound white cultivated
    mushrooms, wiped clean and
    thinly sliced
6 ounces mortadella, thickly
    sliced and cut into
    ¼-inch-wide strips
1 cup heavy cream
Salt and freshly ground black
    pepper to taste
1 tablespoon unsalted butter
½ cup freshly grated
    Parmigiano-Reggiano cheese

Prepare the pastas as instructed on pages 79–87, using the flour and eggs in these recipes. Roll out the doughs and cut into tonnarelli as instructed on page 84. (For preparing the pasta ahead, see page 121.)

Prepare the sauce: Drain the peas. Heat the oil in a large skillet over high heat. Add the mushrooms and cook, stirring, until mushrooms are golden, 2 to 3 minutes. Reduce the heat to medium, add the mortadella and peas, and stir a few times. Pour in the cream and season with salt and pepper. Cook, stirring from time to time, until the cream is reduced approximately by half, 3 to 4 minutes. Stir the butter into the sauce and turn the heat off under the skillet.

Meanwhile, bring a large pot of water to a boil. Add 1 tablespoon of salt and the tonnarelli. Cook, uncovered, over high heat, stirring occasionally, until the pasta is tender but still firm to the bite. Scoop up and reserve about 1 cup of the pasta cooking water.

Drain the pasta and add it to the sauce. Add half of the Parmigiano and toss well over low heat until the creamy sauce clings to the pasta. Add some of the reserved pasta water if pasta seems a bit dry. Taste, adjust the seasoning, and serve with additional Parmigiano if desired.

CONTINUED

RED TAGLIATELLE WITH BRESAOLA AND PORCINI MUSHROOMS

Tagliatelle Rosse con Bresaola e Porcini

SERVES 4

Years ago, there was an excellent restaurant in Bologna called A1 Cantunzein ("The Little Corner"), which used to make the best and most varied pasta in the whole city. One of their signature dishes was a tasting of three different colored tagliatelle: yellow with saffron, green with spinach, and red with tomato paste or beets. It was a delicious and colorful dish—one which I delight in whenever I have the opportunity.

This dish is a variation that pairs delicately red tagliatelle with an appetizing sauce of bresaola, porcini mushrooms, and cream.

FOR THE TAGLIATELLE

2 cups unbleached all-purpose
flour
3 extra-large eggs
1 tablespoon tomato paste

FOR THE SAUCE

1 ounce dried porcini
mushrooms, soaked in
2 cups lukewarm water
for 20 minutes
¼ cup extra-virgin olive oil
½ cup finely minced carrot

3 ounces thickly sliced bresaola,
cut into ¼-inch-wide strips
½ cup dry white wine
Salt and freshly ground black
pepper to taste
½ cup heavy cream
1 tablespoon unsalted butter
2 tablespoons chopped fresh
parsley
½ cup freshly grated
Parmigiano-Reggiano
cheese

Prepare the pasta as instructed on pages 79–87, using the flour, eggs, and tomato paste in this recipe. Roll out the dough and cut into tagliatelle as instructed on page 84. (For preparing the pasta ahead, see page 121.)

Prepare the sauce: Drain the porcini mushrooms and reserve the soaking water. Rinse the mushrooms well under cold running water and chop them roughly. Line a strainer with paper towels and strain the mushroom water into a bowl to get rid of the sandy deposits. Set aside.

Heat the oil in a large skillet over medium heat. Add the carrot and cook, stirring occasionally, until lightly golden and soft, 5 to 6 minutes. Add the porcini mushrooms and the bresaola, and stir for about 1 minute. Add the wine and 1 cup of the reserved mushroom water, and season lightly with salt and pepper. Cook, stirring occasionally, until the liquid is reduced approximately by half. Add the cream and butter. As soon as the cream begins to thicken, after 1 or 2 minutes, stir in the parsley. Taste, adjust the seasoning, and turn the heat off under the skillet.

Meanwhile, bring a large pot of water to a boil. Add 1 tablespoon of salt and the tagliatelle. Cook, uncovered, over high heat until the pasta is tender but still firm to the bite. Scoop up and reserve about 1 cup of the pasta cooking water.

Drain the pasta, place in the skillet with the sauce, and add about half of the Parmigiano. Add a bit of pasta water if needed. Toss everything quickly over low heat until pasta and sauce are well incorporated. Taste, adjust the seasoning, and serve with additional Parmigiano.

CHESTNUT FLOUR TAGLIATELLE WITH CABBAGE AND FONTINA CHEESE

Tagliatelle con Farina di Castagne con Cavoloe Fontina

❧

SERVES 4

Pasta made with chestnut flour is not an everyday Italian staple. So when I came across a recipe in an old cookbook belonging to my sister-in-law's mother, I was thrilled. The recipe simply stated "to mix the chestnut flour with the white flour and make broad tagliatelle." That much I understood. So, after a few attempts I found the formula and made my first batch of delicious chestnut tagliatelle. The sauce combines garlic-scented butter and fontina cheese with cabbage. If you could see and smell this dish, you would get in the kitchen to make it at once because, yes, it is that good.

FOR THE CHEXTNUT TAGLIATELLE

1⅓ cups unbleached all-purpose flour

1 cup finely milled chestnut flour

3 extra-large eggs

1 to 2 tablespoons milk

FOR THE SAUCE

½ pound Savoy cabbage, cored and leaves cut into thin strips

3 to 4 tablespoons unsalted butter

2 garlic cloves, peeled and lightly crushed

¼ pound fontina cheese, cut into small pieces

Salt and freshly ground black pepper to taste

½ cup freshly grated Parmigiano-Reggiano cheese

Prepare the pasta as instructed on pages 79–87, using the flours, eggs, and milk in this recipe. Roll out the dough and cut into tagliatelle, as instructed on page 84. (For preparing the pasta ahead, see page 121.)

Prepare the sauce: Bring a large pot of water to a boil. Add 1 tablespoon salt and the cabbage. Cook, uncovered, until the cabbage begins to soften, 2 to 3 minutes. Add the tagliatelle to the cabbage, and cook until the pasta is tender but still firm to the bite. Scoop up and reserve about 1 cup of the pasta cooking water.

While the pasta and cabbage cook, heat the butter in a large skillet over medium heat. When the butter foams, add the garlic and brown on all sides. Discard the garlic and add the fontina cheese and ½ cup of the reserved pasta water; stir.

Drain the pasta and the cabbage and place in the skillet. Season with salt and generously with pepper. Add half of the Parmigiano and the remaining pasta water. Toss the pasta well over low heat until the cheese melts and the sauce thickens and thoroughly coats the pasta. Add more water if pasta seems a bit dry. Taste, adjust the seasoning, and serve with additional Parmigiano.

SPINACH TAGLIATELLE WITH CLAMS AND SCALLOPS

Tagliatelle Verdi con Frutti di Mare

🐚

SERVES 4

In many parts of Italy the traditional pasta for this type of seafood sauce is spaghetti or linguine. In Emilia-Romagna, however, where delicate homemade pasta is almost sacred, tagliatelle, tagliolini, and pappardelle are often paired with sauces containing seafood. The result is a rich, luxurious dish.

FOR THE SPINACH TAGLIATELLE

2 cups unbleached all-purpose flour

3 extra-large eggs

2 tablespoons finely chopped cooked fresh or frozen spinach

FOR THE SAUCE

½ cup water

3 pounds manilla clams (or the smallest you can get), cleaned (page 11)

⅓ cup extra-virgin olive oil

½ pound scallops, cut into ½-inch cubes

2 garlic cloves, minced

½ cup dry white wine

1 pound ripe tomatoes, peeled, seeded, and diced (page 9)

Salt to taste

Chopped fresh red chili pepper or hot red pepper flakes to taste

1 tablespoon unsalted butter

CONTINUED

Prepare the pasta as instructed on pages 79–87, using the flour, eggs, and spinach in this recipe. Roll out the dough and cut into tagliatelle, as instructed on page 84. (For preparing the pasta ahead, see page 121.)

Prepare the sauce: Put the water in a large skillet and place over medium heat. Add the clams and cover the skillet. As soon as the clams open, transfer them to a bowl. Line a strainer with paper towels, strain the liquid into a bowl, and set aside. Detach the clams from the shells and, if they are large, cut them into two or three pieces. Place the clams in a bowl and set aside.

Heat the oil in a large skillet over high heat. Add the scallops and cook, stirring, for a minute or two. Add the garlic, stir for less than a minute, then add the wine and the reserved clam liquid. Cook, stirring occasionally, until the liquid is reduced approximately by half. Lower the heat to medium and add the tomatoes. Simmer until the tomato sauce begins to thicken, 3 to 4 minutes. Add the clams and season with salt and chili pepper. Stir the butter into the sauce and turn the heat off under the skillet.

Meanwhile, bring a large pot of water to a boil. Add 1 tablespoon of salt and the pasta. Cook, uncovered, over high heat, stirring occasionally, until the pasta is tender but still firm to the bite.

Drain the pasta and add it to the sauce. Toss everything quickly over low heat until the pasta and sauce are well combined. Taste, adjust the seasoning, and serve.

TAGLIATELLE WITH FRESH
PORCINI MUSHROOMS
Tagliatelle con Porcini

SERVES 4

If you can get your hands on fresh porcini mushrooms—which in this country is not an easy feat—you must try this dish. Here, the fresh porcini with their meaty texture and woodsy fragrance are combined with tomatoes, cream, and fresh mint. Delicate homemade tagliatelle or fettuccine are the perfect vehicle for this appetizing sauce.

To use Parmigiano in this dish boils down to personal choice. I prefer this pasta without it because the clear flavor of the mushrooms comes through better. If using, go at it with a light hand.

FOR THE TAGLIATELLE

2 cups unbleached all-purpose
  flour
3 extra-large eggs

FOR THE SAUCE

¼ to ⅓ cup extra-virgin olive oil
¾ pound fresh porcini
  mushrooms, portobello,
  shiitake, or cremini
  mushrooms, wiped clean and
  thinly sliced
1 to 2 tablespoons unsalted
  butter
⅓ cup finely minced yellow
  onion

1 garlic clove, finely minced
3 cups canned Italian plum
  tomatoes with their juice, put
  through a food mill to
  remove seeds
Salt and freshly ground black
  pepper to taste
2 to 3 tablespoons heavy cream
8 to 10 fresh mint leaves,
  minced, or 1 to 2 tablespoons
  chopped fresh parsley
⅓ cup freshly grated
  Parmigiano-Reggiano cheese
  (optional)

Prepare the pasta as instructed on pages 79–87, using the flour and eggs in this recipe. Roll out the pasta dough and cut into tagliatelle as instructed on page 84. (For preparing the pasta ahead, see 121.)

CONTINUED

Prepare the sauce: Heat the oil in a large skillet over high heat. When the oil is hot, add the mushrooms without crowding the skillet. (Sauté in a couple of batches if necessary.) Cook, stirring, until the mushrooms are lightly golden, 2 to 3 minutes. With a slotted spoon, transfer the mushrooms to a plate.

Put the skillet back over medium heat and add the butter. Add the onion and cook, stirring, until the onion is lightly golden, 4 to 5 minutes. Add the garlic and stir quickly once or twice. Add the sautéed mushrooms, stir a few times, then add the tomatoes. Season with salt and several grinds of pepper. As soon as the sauce comes to a boil, reduce the heat to low and simmer, stirring occasionally, until the sauce has a medium thick consistency, about 10 minutes. Add the cream and simmer 2 to 3 minutes longer. Stir in the mint or the parsley, taste, and adjust the seasoning.

Meanwhile, bring a large pot of water to a boil. Add 1 tablespoon of salt and the tagliatelle. Cook, uncovered, over high heat until the pasta is tender but still firm to the bite.

Drain the pasta and place in the skillet with the sauce. Add ¼ cup of the Parmigiano, if using, and mix everything quickly over low heat until the pasta and sauce are well combined. Taste, adjust the seasoning, and serve at once with additional Parmigiano if desired.

BUCKWHEAT NOODLES WITH BRUSSELS SPROUTS AND SPECK

Pizzoccheri con Cavolini di Brusselle e Speck

🍂

SERVES 4

Pizzoccheri are broad, short noodles made with a combination of soft buckwheat flour and white flour. They are a specialty of the Valtellina, a beautiful valley between Milan and the Swiss border.

The traditional way of serving pizzoccheri is with a sturdy sauce of butter, garlic, cabbage, potatoes, and soft cheese. This version, which I developed on a cold, wintry day in Sacramento, uses Brussels sprouts, leeks, speck (smoked Italian ham), butter, and Parmigiano. It's a hearty dish with wholesome appeal.

FOR THE PIZZOCCHERI

1 cup buckwheat flour
1 cup unbleached all-purpose
   flour
3 extra-large eggs
2 tablespoons milk

FOR THE SAUCE

1 pound Brussels sprouts (see
   Selecting and Storing
   Brussels Sprouts, page 132)

1 medium leek (about ¾ pound)
4 tablespoons unsalted butter
2 garlic cloves, finely minced
¼ pound thickly sliced speck
   or prosciutto, cut into
   ½-inch-wide strips
Salt and freshly ground black
   pepper to taste
½ cup freshly grated
   Parmigiano-Reggiano
   cheese

Prepare the pasta as instructed on pages 79–87, using the flours, eggs, and milk in this recipe. Roll out the dough and cut into pizzoccheri, as instructed on page 84. (For preparing the pasta ahead, see 121.)

Prepare the sauce: Trim the stem ends of the Brussels sprouts and remove any loose or discolored leaves. Bring a medium saucepan of water to a boil, then add a pinch of salt and the sprouts. Cook, uncovered, over medium heat until the sprouts are tender but still a bit firm to the bite, about 10 minutes. Drain and immediately plunge them in a large bowl of ice water to stop the cooking and set their green color. Drain the sprouts, cut them into thin slices, and place in a bowl until ready to use.

Cut off the root of the leek and remove the green stalk. Cut leek in half lengthwise and slice it thinly. Place in a colander and wash well under cold running water, making sure to remove all dirt. Drain well and pat dry with paper towels.

Heat 3 tablespoons of the butter in a large skillet over medium heat. Add the leek and cook, stirring occasionally, until pale yellow and soft, 8 to 10 minutes. Add the garlic and stir for about 1 minute. Add the speck or prosciutto and the sprouts, and season with salt and pepper. Stir for 2 to 3 minutes, until sprouts are heated all the way through.

Meanwhile, bring a large pot of water to a boil. Add 1 tablespoon of salt and the pizzoccheri. Cook, uncovered, over high heat until pizzoccheri are tender but still firm to the bite. Scoop out and reserve about 1 cup of the pasta cooking water.

Drain the pasta and place in the skillet. Season with salt and pepper. Add the remaining 1 tablespoon butter, about half of the Parmigiano, and ½ cup of the reserved pasta water. Toss the pasta well over low heat until it is well incorporated with the sauce. Add more water if pasta seems a bit dry. Taste, adjust the seasoning, and serve with additional Parmigiano.

SELECTING AND STORING BRUSSELS SPROUTS

Brussels sprouts are like miniature cabbages with a milder taste.
Even though sprouts are available most of the year, their peak season is
from October through December. Select them just as you would a large cabbage.
Make sure they have a bright green color and a firm compact body, and
store in airtight bags in the refrigerator.

PAPPARDELLE WITH
RABBIT RAGÙ
Pappardelle alla Lucchese

❧

SERVES 4

Ristorante la Mora, in the outskirts of the city of Lucca, is a destination point. This rustic, elegant restaurant serves great local fare. Years ago, when I was doing research for a book on the food of the Italian *trattorie,* I was totally captivated by its delicious food. One of the dishes I particularly liked was the *tacconi alla Lucchese,* or pasta with rabbit sauce. Once back in Sacramento I wrote them, praising the dish and asking for the recipe. A year and half later, after the book on the *trattorie* was published, the recipe arrived. Italians are never in a hurry!

In Italy, a lot of pasta dishes are topped with sauces from the juices and meats of roasts or braised meats, game, and fowls. The meat is served one night topped by a bit of its sauce or pan juices, and the next day what sauce is left is turned into a delicious pasta sauce.

FOR THE PAPPARDELLE

2 cups unbleached all-purpose
   flour
3 extra-large eggs

FOR THE RABBIT SAUCE

⅓ cup extra-virgin olive oil
1 rabbit (about 2½ pounds),
   thoroughly washed and cut
   into serving pieces
½ cup minced yellow onion
⅓ cup minced carrot
⅓ cup minced celery

1 cup medium-body red wine
1 pound ripe tomatoes, peeled,
   seeded, and minced (page 9)
2 tablespoons Italian tomato
   paste, mixed with 2 cups
   Basic Chicken Broth (page
   21) or low-sodium canned
   chicken broth
Salt and freshly ground black
   pepper to taste
1 tablespoon unsalted butter
½ cup freshly grated
   Parmigiano-Reggiano cheese

Prepare the pasta as instructed on pages 79–87, using the flour and eggs in this recipe. Roll out the dough and prepare the pappardelle as instructed on page 84. (For preparing the pasta ahead, see page 121.)

CONTINUED

Prepare the sauce: Heat the oil in a large skillet over medium heat. Add the rabbit pieces and cook until lightly golden on all sides, 4 to 5 minutes. Transfer the rabbit to a plate. Add the vegetables to the skillet and stir until they are lightly golden, about 5 minutes. Return the rabbit to the skillet, stir it briefly with the vegetables, and add the wine. Cook until wine is reduced by half, 3 to 4 minutes. Add the tomatoes and broth mixture and season with salt and pepper. Bring the liquid to a gentle simmer, reduce the heat to low, and cover the skillet, leaving the cover slightly askew. Cook, basting occasionally, until the meat is tender and begins to fall away from the bones, 1 to 1½ hours.

Place the rabbit on a cutting board and cool. Puree the sauce through a food mill or in a food processor. Return the sauce to the skillet. Remove the meat from the bones and mince it very fine with a large knife. Add the meat and the butter to the sauce, and stir it over low heat just long enough for the butter to melt and blend with the sauce. (If the sauce is too thick, stir in a little more broth.) Taste, adjust the seasoning, cover and set aside or refrigerate until ready to use, up to a day ahead. (Makes approximately 5½ cups sauce.)

Bring a large pot of water to a boil. Add 1 tablespoon of salt and the pappardelle. Cook, uncovered, over high heat until the pasta is tender but still a bit firm to the bite.

Drain the pasta and place it in a large heated pasta bowl. Add about half of the sauce and half of the Parmigiano. Mix everything well, until pasta and sauce are well combined. Add more sauce if needed. Serve at once with additional Parmigiano if desired.

RABBIT AL FORNO

This dish is braised on top of the stove, as it is typically done in Italy. It can however, also be cooked in the oven. In that case, preheat the oven to 350° F. Brown the rabbit and vegetables in an ovenproof skillet or sauté pan, add the wine, broth, and tomatoes, and bring to a gentle boil. Cover the skillet or sauté pan, place in the oven, and cook 1 to 1½ hours, basting the rabbit a few times during cooking.

PAPPARDELLE WITH PIETRO'S MEAT RAGÙ

Pappardelle di Pietro alla Petroniana

❧

SERVES 4

The most famous and celebrated meat ragù of Italy is *ragù alla Bolognese,* a rich blending of slowly simmered meat and vegetables. There are, however, several renditions of this dish, all of which proclaim their authenticity. This version comes from Pietro Bondi, long-time friend and chef for many years of the venerable Diana restaurant in Bologna. This ragù, lightly hinting of nutmeg, comes very close to one my mother used to make, which she used to toss with homemade tagliatelle, the noodles of Bologna. This ragù is best when made only a few hours ahead.

FOR THE PAPPARDELLE

2 cups unbleached all-purpose flour
3 extra-large eggs

FOR THE MEAT RAGÙ

3 tablespoons unsalted butter
½ cup finely minced yellow onion
½ cup finely minced carrot
½ cup finely minced celery
½ pound ground beef chuck
2 ounces chicken livers, finely minced
2 ounces chicken giblets, finely minced

⅛ teaspoon freshly grated nutmeg
Salt and freshly ground black pepper to taste
½ cup dry white wine
3 tablespoons tomato paste, diluted in 2½ cups Basic Chicken Broth (page 21) or low-sodium canned chicken broth
½ cup milk
⅓ to ½ cup freshly grated Parmigiano-Reggiano cheese

Prepare the pasta as instructed on pages 79–87, using the flour and eggs in this recipe. Roll out the dough and cut into pappardelle, as instructed on page 84. (For preparing the pasta ahead, see page 121.)

CONTINUED

Prepare the ragù: Heat 2 tablespoons of the butter in a wide-bottomed, heavy saucepan over medium heat. When the butter begins to foam, add the vegetables and cook, stirring, until they are lightly golden and soft, 6 to 7 minutes. Raise the heat to high and add the meat, chicken livers, and giblets. Cook, stirring, until the meat has a light golden color, 5 to 6 minutes. Add the nutmeg and season with salt and pepper. Stir in the wine and cook until it is almost all reduced. Add the broth mixture. As soon as the liquid comes to a boil, reduce the heat to low and partially cover the pan. Cook the ragù at the slowest of simmers for 1½ hours. Add the milk and cook ½ hour longer. Stir the ragù from time to time and check its consistency. At the end of cooking, the ragù should be moist and slightly liquidy. If too dry, stir in a little more broth. Taste, adjust the seasoning, and turn the heat off. (Makes approximately 3 cups of sauce.) (When prepared a few hours ahead, keep at room temperature and reheat gently just before using.)

Bring a large pot of water to a boil. Add 1 tablespoon of salt and the pappardelle. Cook, uncovered, over high heat, until the pasta is tender but still a bit firm to the bite.

Drain the pasta and place in a large heated pasta bowl. Add about half of the ragù, half of the Parmigiano, and the remaining tablespoon butter. Toss everything quickly and thoroughly, until pasta and ragù are well combined. Add more ragù if needed. Serve at once with freshly grated Parmigiano.

TASTY OPTIONS FOR RAGÙ

This classic ragù has a nice compact texture and a light brown color. Its flavor is full and rich without being heavy. Use it with moderation because a little goes a long way. Any leftover ragù can be used over penne or rigatoni.

TAGLIOLINI WITH ZUCCHINI, SHRIMP, AND SAFFRON

Tagliolini con Zucchine, Gamberetti, e Zafferano

❧

SERVES 4

In this dish, zucchini are sautéed to a bright golden color, then tossed with sautéed shrimp, diced tomatoes, saffron, and basil and mixed with homemade tagliolini. This great sauce can be done in less than 10 minutes. If you don't have time to make your own pasta, buy a good brand of imported factory-made tagliolini, tagliatelle, or fettuccine.

FOR THE TAGLIOLINI

2 cups unbleached all-purpose flour
3 extra-large eggs

FOR THE SAUCE

⅓ cup extra-virgin olive oil
3 medium zucchini (about ¾ pound), cut into thin rounds
1 pound medium shrimp, peeled, deveined, and cut into ½-inch pieces
2 ripe tomatoes, peeled, seeded, and diced (page 9)

1 garlic clove, minced
⅛ teaspoon saffron diluted in ½ cup Basic Chicken Broth (page 21) or low-sodium canned chicken broth
8 to 10 fresh basil leaves, finely shredded, or 2 tablespoons chopped fresh parsley
Salt and freshly ground black pepper to taste
1 tablespoon unsalted butter

Prepare the pasta as instructed on pages 79–87, using the flour and eggs in this recipe. Roll out the dough and cut into tagliolini, as instructed on page 84. (For preparing the pasta ahead, see page 121.)

Prepare the sauce: Heat the oil in a large skillet over high heat. Add the zucchini and cook until they are lightly golden, 2 to 3 minutes. Scoop up the zucchini with a slotted spoon and drain on paper towels.

CONTINUED

Put the skillet back over high heat. Add a bit more oil if needed. Add the shrimp and cook, stirring, until they are lightly golden, 1 to 2 minutes. Add the tomatoes and garlic, and stir for 2 to 3 minutes. Add the broth mixture and the basil or parsley. Season with salt and pepper and stir for about a minute. Stir the butter into the sauce and turn the heat off under the skillet.

Meanwhile, bring a large pot of water to a boil. Add 1 tablespoon of salt and the tagliolini. Cook, uncovered over high heat until the tagliolini are tender but still a bit firm to the bite. Scoop up and reserve about 1 cup of the pasta water.

Drain the pasta and place in the skillet with the sauce. Mix quickly over low heat until pasta and sauce are well combined. Add a few tablespoons of the pasta water if sauce seems a bit dry. Taste, adjust the seasoning, and serve.

COOKING HOMEMADE PASTA

Fresh homemade pasta in general, and tagliolini in particular, will cook in no time at all. Drop the tagliolini into boiling water. As soon as the water returns to a boil, taste for doneness. Remove when the pasta is still firm, as it will finish cooking in the skillet with the sauce.

TAGLIOLINI WITH LOBSTER AND FRESH TOMATOES

Taglioline con l'Aragosta e Pomodori Freschi

❧

The time to prepare this beautiful pasta dish is summer, when tomatoes are sweet and fragrant. If you want to splurge, use a fresh whole lobster (see Cooking Live Lobsters, page 140).

FOR THE TAGLIOLINI

2 cups unbleached all-purpose flour
3 extra-large eggs

FOR THE LOBSTER SAUCE

2 fresh or frozen lobster tails (about 9 ounces each)
⅓ cup extra-virgin olive oil
2 garlic cloves, minced
Chopped fresh red chili pepper or hot red pepper flakes to taste

1 tablespoon minced sun-dried tomatoes
1 to 2 tablespoons capers
1½ pounds ripe tomatoes, peeled, seeded, and diced (page 9)
Salt to taste
2 tablespoons chopped fresh parsley
1 tablespoon unsalted butter

Prepare the pasta as instructed on pages 79–87, using the flour and eggs in this recipe. Roll out the dough and cut the tagliolini as instructed on page 84. (For preparing the pasta ahead, see page 121.)

Prepare the sauce: With a large knife or poultry scissors, cut the flat part of the lobster shells down the middle. Hold the cut shells with a kitchen towel and pry it open. Remove the meat, and cut it into ½-inch pieces.

Heat the oil in a large skillet over medium heat. Add the lobster pieces and cook, stirring for a minute or two. Add the garlic, chili pepper, sun-dried tomatoes, and capers and stir once or twice. Add the diced tomatoes, season with salt, and cook for 3 to 4 minutes. Stir in the parsley and turn the heat off under the skillet.

Meanwhile, bring a large pot of water to a boil. Add 1 tablespoon of salt and the pasta. Cook, uncovered, over high heat stirring occasionally, until the pasta is tender but still firm to the bite. Scoop up and reserve 1 cup of the pasta cooking water.

Drain the pasta and add it to the sauce. Add the butter and mix everything quickly over low heat until the pasta and the sauce are well combined. Add some of the reserved pasta water if sauce seems a bit dry. Taste, adjust the seasoning, and serve.

COOKING LIVE LOBSTERS

If you are using a live lobster, drop it in boiling water and cook until done; then remove the meat, dice it, and use as instructed.

TAGLIOLINI WITH BUTTER AND CREAM

Tagliolini in Bianco

🎋

SERVES 4

This is the type of quick, delicious preparation that many regions call their own. Even though the ingredients can be counted on one hand, they produce one of the purest of all Italian dishes.

FOR THE TAGLIOLINI

2 cups unbleached all-purpose flour
3 extra-large eggs

FOR THE SAUCE

3 to 4 tablespoons unsalted butter

1 cup heavy cream
⅛ teaspoon freshly grated nutmeg
Salt to taste
½ cup freshly grated Parmigiano-Reggiano cheese

Prepare the pasta as instructed on pages 79–87, using the flour and eggs in this recipe. Roll out the dough and prepare the tagliolini as instructed on page 84. (For preparing the pasta ahead, see page 121.)

Prepare the sauce: Heat the butter in a large skillet over medium heat. As soon as the butter begins to foam, add the cream and nutmeg, and season with salt. Simmer until the cream begins to thicken, 2 to 3 minutes. Turn the heat off under the skillet.

Meanwhile, bring a large pot of water to a boil. Add 1 tablespoon of salt and the tagliolini. Cook, uncovered, over high heat until the pasta is tender but still firm to the bite. Scoop up and reserve about 1 cup of the pasta cooking water.

Drain the pasta and add it to the skillet. Season the pasta lightly with salt. Add ¼ cup of the Parmigiano and toss quickly over low heat until the sauce thoroughly coats the pasta. Add some of the reserved water if pasta seems a bit dry. Taste, adjust the seasoning, and serve with additional Parmigiano.

FETTUCCINE WITH LAMB RAGÙ
Fettuccine con Ragù
di Agnello

❧

SERVES 4

Lamb is the essential meat of the Romans. It is the centerpiece of the Easter meal, and throughout the year, it is consumed in myriad ways. This delicious dish comes from a tucked-away *trattoria* in the outskirts of Rome, Trattoria Paola. This is a dish with a history and a continuity. It is basic, comforting fare prepared with ease and served with love. And the sauce is equally good served over factory-made pasta. Rigatoni and penne would complement the sauce quite well.

FOR THE FETTUCCINE

2 cups unbleached all-purpose
    flour
3 extra-large eggs

FOR THE SAUCE

⅓ cup extra-virgin olive oil
⅓ cup finely minced yellow
    onion
⅓ cup finely minced carrot
⅓ cup finely minced celery
1 pound chopped lamb,
    preferably from the shoulder
1 cup dry white wine
3 cups canned Italian plum
    tomatoes with their juice, put
    through a food mill to
    remove seeds

1½ cups Basic Chicken Broth
    (page 21) or low-sodium
    canned chicken broth
Salt and freshly ground black
    pepper to taste
1 cup shelled fresh peas or
    thawed frozen peas
2 to 3 tablespoons heavy cream
1 cup freshly grated
    Parmigiano-Reggiano cheese

Prepare the pasta as instructed on pages 79–87, using the flour and eggs in this recipe. Roll out the dough and prepare fettuccine as instructed on page 84. (For preparing the pasta ahead, see page 121.)

Prepare the sauce: Heat the oil in a large skillet or wide-bottomed saucepan over medium heat. Add the onion, carrot, and celery and cook, stirring, until the vegetables are lightly golden and soft, 7 to 8 minutes. Raise the heat to high and add the lamb. Stir until it loses its raw color. Add the wine and cook until almost all reduced, 2 to 3 minutes. Add the tomatoes and broth, and season with salt and pepper. Bring the sauce to a boil, then reduce the heat to low and cover the skillet partially. Simmer 30 to 35 minutes, stirring occasionally, until sauce has a medium-thick consistency. Add fresh peas, if using, and simmer 7 to 8 minutes longer. Add the cream and stir for about a minute. Taste and adjust the seasoning. If using thawed peas, add them when you add the cream. (Makes approximately 3⅓ cups sauce.)

Bring a large pot of water to a boil. Add 1 tablespoon salt and the fettuccine. Cook, uncovered, over high heat until the pasta is tender but still firm to the bite.

Drain the pasta and place it in a large heated pasta bowl. Add about half of the sauce and ⅓ cup of Parmigiano. Mix everything well until pasta and sauce are well combined. Add more sauce if needed. Serve at once with additional Parmigiano if desired.

FETTUCCINE WITH CHANTERELLES, PROSCIUTTO, TOMATOES, AND CREAM

Fettuccine con Gallinacci, Prosciutto, Pomodori, e Panna

❧

SERVES 4

If you have the time and the know-how, make this dish with homemade fettuccine. If you don't, look for a good brand of imported pasta, such as Fini, Barilla, or Agnesi. And if you can't find any of the mushrooms listed in the recipe, then you can always use that old standby, white cultivated mushrooms. As they say in this country, "If you only have lemons, make lemonade."

FOR THE FETTUCCINE

2 cups unbleached all-purpose
    flour
3 extra-large eggs

FOR THE SAUCE

⅓ cup extra-virgin olive oil
½ pound fresh chanterelles,
    shiitake, or cremini
    mushrooms, cleaned
¼ pound prosciutto, cut in
    1 thick slice and diced

1 garlic clove, minced
4 to 5 fresh sage leaves,
    shredded, or 1 tablespoon
    chopped fresh parsley
4 cups canned Italian plum
    tomatoes with their juice, put
    through a food mill to
    remove seeds
Salt and freshly ground black
    pepper to taste
¼ cup heavy cream

Prepare the pasta as instructed on pages 79–87, using the flour and eggs in this recipe. Roll out the dough and prepare the fettuccine as instructed on page 84. (For preparing the pasta ahead, see page 121.)

Prepare the sauce: Heat the oil in a large skillet over high heat. Add the mushrooms and cook, stirring, until they are golden, 2 to 3 minutes (see Golden Mushrooms, page 145). Add the prosciutto, garlic, and fresh sage or parsley, then stir for about 1 minute. Add the tomatoes and season with salt and pepper. As soon as the tomatoes begin to boil, reduce the heat to low and simmer uncovered, stirring occasionally, until sauce has a medium-thick consistency, 8 to 10 minutes. Add the cream and simmer a few minutes longer. Taste, adjust the seasoning, and turn the heat off.

Meanwhile, bring a large pot of water to a boil. Add 1 tablespoon of salt and the pasta. Cook, uncovered, over high heat, stirring a few times, until the pasta is tender but still a bit firm to the bite.

Drain the pasta and add it to the skillet with the sauce. Toss well over low heat until pasta and sauce are well combined. Taste, adjust the seasoning, and serve.

GOLDEN MUSHROOMS

Mushrooms should always be cooked in a large skillet over high heat. They should never be crowded in a pan or they won't brown properly and their juices will not evaporate quickly. Add the mushrooms to the skillet when the oil begins to smoke, and in no time at all, you will have perfectly golden mushrooms.

FETTUCCINE WITH PANCETTA, PLUM TOMATOES, AND PEAS

Fettuccine con Pancetta, Perini, e Piselli

SERVES 4

Onion, pancetta, and tomatoes cooked for a short time, produce a sauce that is savory, sweet, and satisfying within minutes.

It is a good idea to always have at hand a few boxes of good, imported factory-made pasta for those days when there is no time to make our own. Barilla, Fini, De Cecco are all excellent brands. Penne rigate, garganelli, rigatoni, and bow ties will also be quite good with this sauce.

CONTINUED

FOR THE FETTUCCINE

2 cups unbleached all-purpose
  flour
3 extra-large eggs

FOR THE SAUCE

1 cup shelled fresh or thawed
  frozen peas
Salt and freshly ground black
  pepper to taste
⅓ cup extra-virgin olive oil
1 cup finely minced yellow
  onion

¼ pound pancetta, finely
  chopped
1 pound ripe, juicy plum
  tomatoes, seeded, and diced
2 tablespoons tomato paste,
  diluted in 1 cup Basic
  Chicken Broth (page 21)
  or low-sodium canned
  chicken broth
1 tablespoon unsalted butter
⅓ cup freshly grated
  Parmigiano-Reggiano
  cheese

Prepare the pasta as instructed on pages 79–87, using the flour and eggs in this recipe. Roll out the dough and prepare the fettuccine as instructed on page 84. (For preparing the pasta ahead, see page 121.)

Prepare the sauce: If using fresh peas, bring a small saucepan of water to a boil. Add a pinch of salt and the peas. Boil the peas over medium heat until they are tender, 5 to 10 minutes depending on size. Drain and set aside until ready to use.

Heat the oil in a large skillet over medium heat. Add the onion and pancetta and cook, stirring, until they are lightly golden, 4 to 5 minutes. Add the diced tomatoes and stir for a few minutes. Add the diluted tomato paste and season lightly with salt and pepper. Reduce the heat to low and simmer uncovered, stirring occasionally, for 10 to 12 minutes. Add the butter and peas, stir a few times, and turn the heat off under the skillet.

Meanwhile, bring a large pot of water to a boil. Add 1 tablespoon of salt and the pasta. Cook, uncovered, over high heat until the pasta is tender but still firm to the bite. Drain the pasta and place in the skillet with the sauce. Mix everything quickly over low heat until pasta and sauce are well combined. Taste, adjust the seasoning, and serve with Parmigiano.

Barley and Porcini Mushroom Soup

OPPOSITE PAGE:
Chick-pea and Clam Soup

ABOVE:
Peeling the roasted beets for the ravioli filling

RIGHT:
Placing the beet filling on the pasta sheet

Roasted Red Beet Ravioli with Lemon-Sage Butter Sauce

RIGHT:
Pappardelle

BELOW:
Pappardelle with Rabbit Ragù

Ingredients for Cavatelli with Fava Beans and Fresh Tomatoes

Orecchiette with Arugula

ABOVE:
Spaghetti with Oven-Roasted Tomatoes and Garlic

LEFT:
Oven-roasted tomatoes

LEFT:
Saffron

BELOW:
Spaghetti with Mussels and Saffron

OPPOSITE PAGE:
Risotto with Blueberries

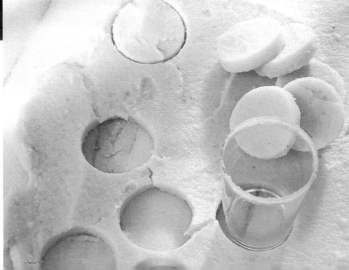

ABOVE:
Potato Gnocchi with Osso Buco Sauce

RIGHT:
Cutting the dough to make Baked Semolina Gnocchi with Smoked Mozzarella

Polenta cornmeal

Molded Polenta with Pork Skewers

Factory-Made Pasta

Garganelli with Speck, Asparagus Tips, Peas, and Cream
Garganelli with Lobster and Broccoli Rabe
Cavatelli with Mussels and Beans
Cavatelli with Arugula and Tomato Sauce
Cavatelli with Fava Beans and Fresh Tomatoes
Orecchiette with Arugula
Perciatelli with Fava Beans, Pancetta, and Oven-Roasted Tomatoes
Bucatini with Fava Beans and Pancetta Roman Style
Bucatini with Monkfish
Bucatini with Shellfish and Porcini Sauce
Rigatoni with Squash
Rigatoni with Artichoke Sauce
Pennette with Eggplant
Pennette with Swordfish, Eggplant, and Sun-dried Tomatoes
Spinach Penne with Endive, Pancetta, and Cream
Linguine with Broccoli Rabe, Squid, and Hot Pepper
Spaghetti with Mussels and Saffron
Spaghetti with Spicy Eggplant-Tomato Sauce

Spaghettini with Leeks
Pasta with Roasted Onions and Pancetta
Spaghettini with Tomatoes, Capers, Olives, and Anchovies
Spaghetti with Oven-Roasted Tomatoes and Garlic
Summer Spaghetti with Uncooked Tomatoes and Herbs
Bigoli with Tuna, Anchovies, and Onions
Pasta with Vodka, Bresaola, and Cream
Bow Ties with Onion, Zucchini, and Cherry Tomatoes
Bow Ties with Roasted Almonds and Cream
Paternostri with Tuna, Tomatoes, and Chili Pepper
Paternostri with Peas, Leeks, and Pancetta
Baked Fusilli with Smoked Mozzarella and Tomatoes
Pasta with Stewed Vegetables
Pasta with Cotechino Sausage, Broccoli Rabe, and Tomatoes
Pasta with Cauliflower and Pancetta
Pasta with Spicy Broccoli
Pasta with Sausage, Red Bell Peppers, and Tomato Ragù
Pasta with Veal-Prosciutto Ragù with Marsala
Pasta with Sicilian Pesto
Ziti with Peppers and Crisp Bread Crumbs
Ziti with Neapolitan Pork Ragù
Shells with Porcini Mushrooms, Sausage, and Cream

*G*ood factory-made pasta, spaghetti, penne, linguine, and fusilli is made with durum wheat flour (100 percent semolina) and water. Nothing else. This pasta, which has the golden color of wheat, is sturdier and more compact than homemade pasta. It cannot be made successfully at home because it requires large commercial machines to knead the hard dough and temperature-controlled chambers to dry the pasta. Good-quality factory pasta, when properly cooked, swells considerably in size while maintaining its toothsomeness. What I love most about factory-made pasta is its wholesomeness and immediacy. Just reach for a box of imported pasta, and in no time at all you have a great golden pasta dish on your table.

Unfortunately, some people have the notion that factory-made pasta is inferior to the homemade version. That, of course, is not true. Personally, I would rather eat good-quality factory pasta than the so-called fresh pasta found in supermarket and specialty stores.

In choosing factory-made pasta, look for an imported Italian brand. Some of my favorites are Del Verde, De Cecco, Barilla, Voiello, La Molisana, and Fini.

SOME GOLDEN RULES FOR COOKING AND SAUCING PASTA

Italians take the tasks of cooking and saucing pasta very seriously. With quick, precise, fluid motions, they drop the pasta into the water, stir it religiously, taste it, drain it, toss it with the sauce, and just like the crescendo of a grand opera, rush it to the table, where the whole family waits. Pasta! There is no food more Italian than pasta!

Whether you are planning to cook homemade or factory-made pasta, you need a large pot of water. For one pound of pasta, you need approximately 5 quarts of water. Cover the pot so the water will come to a boil faster.

When the water boils, add the salt and pasta. Cover the pot again. As soon as the water comes back to a boil, remove the lid and stir the pasta with a long fork or tongs. The salt will season the pasta, highlighting its wholesome flavor. If you have plenty of water in the pot and you give it an occasional stir, the pasta will not stick together. Never add oil to the water.

The cooking time of the pasta will depend on the size, type, and shape. Rigatoni, for example, might take as long as 14 minutes to cook. Taste the pasta often to determine its doneness. Remove the pasta from the heat when it is tender but still decisively firm to the bite—al dente—because it will keep cooking as it is tossed with the hot sauce.

Before draining the pasta, scoop up and reserve some of the cooking water. The pasta cooking water is the secret ingredient of Italian cooks. If a sauce is too thin, they add some pasta water; the starch in the water thickens the sauce.

Once pasta is cooked, drain it and toss it immediately with the sauce. *Never* rinse the pasta unless you are making lasagne or cannelloni. Also, *never* precook your pasta unless you are making lasagne or cannelloni. These are the only instances when pasta is quickly precooked, rinsed to stop the cooking, and dried before it is stuffed and baked.

And finally, remember that pasta does not wait for anyone! (My mother's favorite motto.) Pasta is at its best immediately after it has been tossed with the sauce. If pasta is made to wait, it will become overcooked and limp, and the sauce will dry out.

GARGANELLI WITH SPECK, ASPARAGUS TIPS, PEAS, AND CREAM

Garganelli con Speck, Asparagi, Piselli, e Panna

※

SERVES 4 TO 6

In my region of Emilia-Romagna, this dish is made with prosciutto and either peas or asparagus tips. It is a sauce to die for. In this version, I use both asparagus tips and fresh peas, and have substituted speck for the prosciutto because I love the flavor of smoked ham with cream. I have also reduced the amount of cream and, to stretch the amount of sauce, I have added some chicken broth. Luscious and lower in fat.

3 pounds fresh asparagus (the thinnest you can get)

Salt and freshly ground black pepper to taste

1 cup shelled fresh green peas or thawed frozen peas

¼ pound speck, cut in 1 thick slice

3 tablespoons unsalted butter

1 cup heavy cream

¾ cup Basic Chicken Broth (page 21) or low-sodium canned chicken broth

1 pound garganelli or pennette rigate (small grooved penne)

½ cup freshly grated Parmigiano-Reggiano cheese

Detach the asparagus tips from the stalks and reserve stalks for another use. Wash the asparagus tips under cold running water. Bring a small saucepan with salted water to a boil and add the tips. Cook until tender but still a bit firm to the bite, 2 to 5 minutes, depending on size. Drain and set aside.

If using fresh peas, fill up the same saucepan with water and bring to a boil. Add a pinch of salt and the peas, and cook until peas are tender but still a bit firm. Drain and set aside.

CONTINUED

Cut the speck into thin strips. Heat 2 tablespoons of the butter in a large skillet over medium heat. Add the speck and stir for a minute or two. Add the asparagus and the fresh or frozen peas and stir briefly to coat with the butter. Add the cream and broth, and season with salt and pepper. Reduce the heat to medium-low and cook, stirring constantly, until the cream has a medium-thick consistency, 2 to 3 minutes. Turn the heat off under the skillet.

Meanwhile, bring a large pot of water to a boil. Add 1 tablespoon of salt and the pasta. Cook, uncovered, over high heat, stirring occasionally, until the pasta is tender but still a bit firm to the bite.

Drain the pasta and add it to the sauce. Add the remaining tablespoon butter and ⅓ cup of Parmigiano. Mix everything quickly over low heat until the creamy sauce clings to the pasta. Add a bit more cream or chicken broth if sauce looks a little dry. Taste, adjust the seasoning, and serve with more Parmigiano if desired.

GARGANELLI WITH LOBSTER AND BROCCOLI RABE

Garganelli con Aragosta e Broccoli Rape

SERVES 4 TO 6

One thing I noticed during my last trip to Italy is that while traditional regional food can still be found, especially in tucked-away *trattorie,* there's less rigidity to the rules. Home cooks and chefs are more willing to experiment. This delicious dish proves it. Broccoli rabe, a slightly bitter vegetable much used in many southern Italian olive-oil-based preparations, is paired with a cream-lobster sauce and tossed with garganelli, a typical pasta of Emilia-Romagna in northern Italy. The delightful element of this dish is that, as the sauce simmers and reduces, the broccoli rabe literally melts into the sauce, imparting a unique flavor.

3 bunches (2 pounds) broccoli
   rabe
2 fresh or frozen lobster tails
   (about 9 ounces each)
¼ cup extra-virgin olive oil
2 garlic cloves, peeled and
   lightly crushed
1 cup heavy cream

Salt to taste
Chopped fresh red chili pepper
   or hot red pepper flakes to
   taste
1 tablespoon unsalted butter
1 pound garganelli, mezze
   penne, or penne rigate

Trim and discard any large woody stalks and wilted leaves from the broccoli rabe. Separate the florets from the leaves and wash them well under cold running water. Bring a large pot of water to a boil. Add a generous pinch of salt and the broccoli rabe. Cook, uncovered, over high heat until rabe is tender, 3 to 5 minutes. Scoop up and reserve 1 cup of the cooking water. Drain the broccoli rabe and set aside.

With a large knife or poultry scissors, cut the shells of the lobster tails down the middle of the belly (the flat part of the tail). Hold the cut shells with a kitchen towel and pry it open. Remove the meat and cut into ½-inch pieces.

Heat the oil in a large skillet over medium heat. Add the garlic, cook until it is golden on all sides, then discard it. Add the lobster pieces and cook until they are lightly colored, 2 to 3 minutes. With a slotted spoon, transfer the lobster to a plate. Add the broccoli rabe, ½ cup of the reserved cooking water, and the cream. As soon as the cream comes to a boil, reduce the heat to low and simmer, stirring and mashing the rabe down with a wooden spoon, until the sauce has a medium-thick consistency, 4 to 5 minutes. Return the lobster to the skillet, season with salt and chili pepper, and swirl in the butter. Simmer the sauce for a minute or two, then turn off the heat.

Meanwhile, bring a large pot of water to a boil. Add 1 tablespoon of salt and the pasta. Cook, uncovered, over high heat, stirring occasionally, until the pasta is tender but still a bit firm to the bite. Drain the pasta and add it to the sauce. Mix everything quickly over low heat until the sauce is well reduced and clings to the pasta. Taste, adjust the seasoning, and serve.

CAVATELLI WITH MUSSELS
AND BEANS
Cavatelli con Cozze e Fagioli

❧

SERVES 4 TO 6

The region of Puglia is the heel of Italy's boot. This beautiful, sunny area is inexhaustible in its creativity with pasta. Every vegetable, every type of fish or shellfish, every legume is combined with pasta, and everything is tied together by the superlative olive oil of the region. The cooking of Puglia is simple, rustic, and unaffected. This is one of my very favorite dishes. You simply must try it.

½ cup dried cannellini or
    kidney beans, picked over
    and soaked overnight
    (page 11)
3 pounds mussels, cleaned
    (page 11)
⅓ cup extra-virgin olive oil
1 garlic clove, minced
3 anchovy fillets, minced
1½ cups canned Italian plum
    tomatoes with their juice, put
    through a food mill to
    remove seeds

Salt to taste
Chopped fresh red chili pepper
    or hot red pepper flakes to
    taste
1 pound cavatelli, orecchiette,
    or shells
1 tablespoon chopped fresh
    parsley

Drain the beans and cook as instructed on page 11. Set aside until ready to use. (The beans can be cooked 2 days ahead. Cool them in their cooking liquid, cover, and refrigerate.)

Put ½ cup of water in a large skillet and place over medium heat. Add the mussels, cover the skillet, and cook just until the mussels open. Transfer them to a bowl as they open. Line a strainer with paper towels and strain the liquid into a bowl. Detach the mussels from the shells and, if they are very large, cut them into 2 pieces and place in a separate bowl. If you wish, reserve 6 of the nicest mussels in their shells for decoration. (The mussels can be prepared 2 hours ahead. Refrigerate tightly covered.)

Wipe the skillet in which the mussels have opened with paper towels. Heat the oil in the skillet over medium heat. Add the garlic and the anchovies, and stir until garlic begins to color, about 1 minute. Add the reserved liquid from the mussels and the tomatoes, and season with salt and chili pepper. Bring the sauce to a gentle boil and add the beans. Reduce the heat to low and simmer, uncovered, stirring occasionally, until sauce begins to thicken, 6 to 8 minutes. Stir the mussels into the sauce during the last few minutes of cooking. Turn the heat off under the skillet.

Meanwhile, bring a large pot of water to a boil. Add 1 tablespoon of salt and the cavatelli. Cook, uncovered, over high heat, stirring occasionally, until the pasta is tender but still a bit firm to the bite.

Drain the pasta and add it to the sauce. Stir in the parsley and mix everything well over low heat until the pasta and sauce are well combined. Taste, adjust the seasoning, and serve.

CAVATELLI WITH ARUGULA AND TOMATO SAUCE

Cavatelli con la Rugola e Pomodoro

✤

SERVES 4 TO 6

Once again Puglia provides great, simple food perfected by cooks over the centuries: Tomatoes simmered just long enough to reduce and thicken a bit; pasta cooked with peppery arugula and tossed with the tomato sauce and pecorino cheese into a large heated bowl which can be taken directly to the table. This is comfort food Italian style.

⅓ cup extra-virgin olive oil

3 garlic cloves, peeled and lightly crushed

3 cups canned Italian plum tomatoes with their juice, put through a food mill to remove seeds

Salt and freshly ground black pepper to taste

1 pound fresh arugula, thoroughly washed and stems removed

1 pound cavatelli, orecchiette, or shells

¼ cup freshly grated pecorino Romano cheese or ⅓ cup freshly grated Parmigiano-Reggiano cheese

Heat the oil in a medium saucepan over medium heat. Add the garlic and cook until it is golden on all sides. Discard the garlic and add the tomatoes. When the tomatoes come to a boil, reduce the heat to low, season with salt and pepper, and cook, uncovered, at the gentlest of simmers. Simmer, 13 to 15 minutes, or until the sauce has a medium-thick consistency. Turn the heat off under the pan.

Meanwhile, bring a large pot of water to a boil. Add 1 tablespoon of salt, the arugula, and the cavatelli. Cook, uncovered, over high heat, stirring occasionally, until the pasta is tender but still a bit firm to the bite.

Drain the pasta and arugula and place it in a large, heated serving bowl. Add about half of the sauce and half of the pecorino cheese or ¼ cup of the Parmigiano. Mix well until pasta and sauce are well combined. Add more sauce as needed. Taste, adjust the seasoning, and serve with a sprinkle of additional cheese.

CAVATELLI WITH FAVA BEANS
AND FRESH TOMATOES
Cavatelli con le Fave e Pomodori

❦

SERVES 4 TO 6

When I first tested this dish in the middle of spring, I was able to buy one of the first crops of the season. The fava beans were small and very tender—so tender, in fact, that after I shelled and blanched them briefly in boiling water, their outer skins slipped off instantly and the beans did not need any additional cooking. They were tender and marvelous.

⅓ cup extra-virgin olive oil
1 large garlic clove, peeled and
    lightly crushed
1 tablespoon capers, rinsed and
    chopped
2 anchovy fillets, chopped
1½ pounds ripe plum tomatoes,
    seeded and diced

3 pounds fresh unshelled fava
    beans, shelled and peeled
    (page 11)
Salt and freshly ground black
    pepper to taste
1 pound cavatelli, orecchiette,
    or shells

Heat the oil in a large skillet over medium heat. Add the garlic and cook until it is golden on all sides, then discard it. Add the capers, anchovies, and tomatoes. Cook and stir until the tomatoes begin to soften, 4 to 5 minutes. Add the fava beans and season with salt and generously with pepper. Stir for a minute or two, then turn the heat off under the skillet.

Meanwhile, bring a large pot of water to a boil. Add 1 tablespoon of salt and the pasta. Cook, uncovered, over high heat, stirring occasionally, until the pasta is tender but still a bit firm to the bite.

Drain the pasta and add it to the skillet with the sauce. Toss well until pasta and sauce are well combined. Taste, adjust the seasoning, and serve.

ORECCHIETTE WITH ARUGULA
Orecchiette con la Rugola

※

SERVES 4 TO 6

Wheat, olive oil, vegetables and fish are the basic staples of Puglia's gastronomy, which is strongly rooted in the land. This is a simple dish that relies entirely on the quality of its ingredients. Look for imported orecchiette, extra-virgin olive oil from Puglia, and fresh young arugula.

½ cups peeled and diced
  potatoes (about the size of
  small green olives)
⅓ cup extra-virgin olive oil
4 anchovy fillets, chopped
3 garlic cloves, minced
Salt and freshly ground black
  pepper to taste
1 pound fresh arugula,
  thoroughly washed and
  stems removed

1 pound orecchiette, cavatelli,
  or shells
¼ cup freshly grated pecorino
  Romano cheese or ⅓ cup
  freshly grated Parmigiano-
  Reggiano cheese

Bring a saucepan of water to a boil over medium heat. Add the potatoes and cook until they are tender but still a bit firm to the bite, 5 to 6 minutes. Drain the potatoes, place in a bowl, and set aside until ready to use.

Heat the oil in a large skillet over medium heat. Add the anchovies and garlic, and cook, stirring, until the garlic begins to color, about 1 minute. Add the potatoes, season them with salt and generously with pepper, and mix them well with the savory base. Turn the heat off under the skillet.

Meanwhile, bring a large pot of water to a boil. Add 1 tablespoon of salt, the arugula, and the pasta. Cook, uncovered, over high heat, stirring occasionally, until the pasta is tender but still a bit firm to the bite. Scoop up ½ cup of the cooking pasta water.

Drain the pasta and add it to the skillet. Add the pecorino or Parmigiano cheese and mix everything well over low heat. Add a bit of the pasta water if pasta looks too dry. Taste, adjust the seasoning, and serve.

PERCIATELLI WITH FAVA BEANS, PANCETTA, AND OVEN-ROASTED TOMATOES

Perciatelli con Fave, Pancetta, e Pomodori al Forno

❧

SERVES 4 TO 6

This is an immensely appetizing pasta, provided you prepare it with fresh fava beans, which are only available in spring, from April to June. Choose the smaller pods, which offer younger, tenderer beans. I have made this dish also with dried fava beans, and the result was still quite good. Canned fava beans should not even be considered.

1½ pounds ripe plum tomatoes, cut into ⅓-inch round slices
Salt and freshly ground black pepper to taste
⅓ to ½ cup extra-virgin olive oil
⅓ cup finely minced yellow onion
1 garlic clove, minced
¼ pound pancetta, sliced ⅛ inch thick, cut into medium strips

2 pounds fresh unshelled fava beans, or ½ pound dried beans, prepared as instructed on page 11
1 pound perciatelli, bucatini (see Note, below), spaghetti, or vermicelli

Preheat the oven to 250°.

Line a baking sheet with parchment paper or aluminum foil and brush the parchment or foil lightly with olive oil. Place the tomato slices on the baking sheet and season with salt. Roast the tomatoes for 3 to 3½ hours, or until they have lost all their liquid and look dried and shriveled. Remove tomatoes from oven, cool them, and peel off their skins. Roughly dice the tomatoes and set aside until ready to use. (The tomatoes can be prepared 2 days ahead. Place them in a small bowl, cover with olive oil, and refrigerate until ready to use.)

CONTINUED

Heat the oil in a large skillet over medium heat. Add the onion and cook, stirring, until lightly golden, 4 to 5 minutes. Add the garlic, stir less than 1 minute, then add the pancetta. Cook until golden, 2 to 3 minutes. Add the fava beans and tomatoes, then season with salt and pepper. Cook and stir for a minute or two, then turn the heat off under the skillet.

Meanwhile, bring a large pot of water to a boil. Add 1 tablespoon of salt and the pasta. Cook, uncovered, over high heat, stirring occasionally, until the pasta is tender but still a bit firm to the bite. Scoop up and reserve about 1 cup of the pasta cooking water.

Drain the pasta and add it to the skillet. Season the pasta lightly with salt and add about ½ cup of the reserved pasta water. Toss well over low heat until the pasta and sauce are thoroughly combined. Add more water if the pasta looks a bit dry. Taste, adjust the seasoning, and serve.

$$\text{❧}$$

NOTE

Perciatelli is a thick spaghetti with a very thin hole through its length. Perciatelli and bucatini are interchangeable.

BUCATINI WITH FAVA BEANS AND PANCETTA ROMAN STYLE

Bucatini con Fave e Pancetta alla Romana

%

SERVES 4 TO 6

Fava beans with *guanciale,* or "pork jowl," is a traditional Roman vegetable dish found in Roman *trattorie* during the spring. Because I consider pasta and vegetables one of the best things under the sun, one day I combined this vegetable dish with bucatini, tossed it with lots of black pepper, and sat back to enjoy what has become one of my favorite pasta dishes. The only liberty I took with this classic preparation was to substitute pancetta for the pork jowl.

⅓ to ½ cup extra-virgin olive oil
⅓ cup finely minced yellow
   onion
5 ounces pancetta, sliced ⅛ inch
   thick, cut into small strips
2 pounds fresh unshelled fava
   beans (page 11), or ½ pound
   dried fava beans, prepared as
   instructed on page 11

Salt and freshly ground black
   pepper to taste
1 pound bucatini, spaghetti, or
   rigatoni

Heat the oil in a large skillet over medium heat. Add the onion and cook, stirring, until lightly golden, 4 to 5 minutes. Add the pancetta and cook for 2 to 3 minutes, until also lightly golden. Add the fava beans, then season with salt and generously with pepper. Cook and stir for a minute or two, then turn the heat off under the skillet.

Meanwhile, bring a large pot of water to a boil. Add 1 tablespoon of salt and the pasta. Cook, uncovered, over high heat, stirring occasionally, until the pasta is tender but still a bit firm to the bite. Scoop up ½ cup or so of the pasta water.

Drain the pasta and add it to the skillet. Season the pasta with salt and pepper, and stir in some of the pasta water. Toss well over low heat until the pasta and sauce are well combined. Taste, adjust the seasoning, and serve.

BUCATINI WITH MONKFISH

Bucatini con Sugo di Pescatrice

❧

SERVES 4 TO 6

This is the type of food I like to cook on my day off. Fresh and fast and simple. The firm white meat of the monkfish, gently cooked with a savory tomato sauce, retains its tender succulence, while the fresh mint adds a refreshing taste. This is typical food of several Italian coastal regions. If monkfish is not available, prawns would make a good substitute.

⅓ cup extra-virgin olive oil
1 pound monkfish fillet, cut into small cubes, or 1 pound prawns
½ cup finely minced yellow onion
1 garlic clove, finely minced
3 anchovy fillets, minced
4 cups canned Italian plum tomatoes with their juice, put through a food mill to remove seeds

Salt to taste
Chopped fresh red chili pepper or hot red pepper flakes to taste
10 to 12 fresh mint leaves, roughly shredded, or 1 to 2 tablespoons chopped fresh parsley
1 pound bucatini, perciatelli, or spaghetti

Heat the oil in a large skillet over medium heat. Add the monkfish pieces and cook until they begin to color, 2 to 3 minutes. With a slotted spoon, transfer the fish to a plate. Add the onion to the skillet and cook, stirring, until lightly golden, 4 to 5 minutes. Add the garlic and anchovies, and stir until garlic begins to color, about 1 minute. Add the tomatoes, then season with salt and chili pepper. As soon as the sauce begins to simmer, reduce the heat to medium-low and cook, stirring occasionally, until sauce has a medium-thick consistency, 10 to 12 minutes. Return the monkfish to the skillet, add the mint or parsley, and simmer the sauce for 3 to 4 minutes longer. Turn the heat off under the skillet.

Meanwhile, bring a large pot of water to a boil. Add 1 tablespoon of salt and the pasta. Cook, uncovered, over high heat, stirring occasionally, until the pasta is tender but still a bit firm to the bite. Drain the pasta and add it to the sauce. Mix everything quickly over low heat until the pasta and sauce are well combined. Taste, adjust the seasoning, and serve.

PASTA BAKED IN PARCHMENT

This sauce also works beautifully in pasta baked in parchment, which brings out the fragrance and aroma of the ingredients within its wrapping, especially seafood. It is also a beautiful, impressive dish to prepare for company.

Prepare the sauce as instructed above. Preheat the oven to 400° F. Cook the pasta in plenty of boiling water only halfway through; *it should have a pronounced al dente consistency. Then drain pasta and toss with the sauce in the skillet. (The dish can be prepared up to this point one hour or so ahead.)*

Just before baking, place 2 large sheets of parchment paper or foil on a large baking sheet. Divide the pasta between the 2 parchment sheets. Fold the parchments over the pasta and fold the edges tightly to seal. Bake about 8 minutes or until the bundles puff up and turn lightly brown. Unwrap the bundles and place the pasta on warm serving dishes. (Individual smaller bundles can also be prepared.)

BUCATINI WITH SHELLFISH
AND PORCINI SAUCE

Bucatini con Intingolo di Frutti
di Mare e Porcini

SERVES 4 TO 6

This dish, which comes from Puglia, pairs traditional shellfish with fresh porcini mushrooms and a local thick homemade pasta called troccoli, a type of thick spaghetti. Since fresh porcini are hard to come by, I have substituted reconstituted dried porcini, which are loaded with flavor. And when ripe tomatoes are available, use them instead of the canned.

1 ounce dried porcini
   mushrooms, soaked in
   1 cup lukewarm water
   for 20 minutes
1 pound mussels, cleaned
   (page 11)
1 pound clams, cleaned
   (page 11)
⅓ cup extra-virgin olive oil
5 ounces medium shrimp,
   peeled, deveined, and finely
   diced
5 ounces sea scallops, finely
   diced

1 garlic clove, finely minced
½ cup dry white wine
3 cups canned Italian plum
   tomatoes with their juice, put
   through a food mill to
   remove seeds
Salt and freshly ground black
   pepper to taste
1 to 2 tablespoons chopped
   fresh parsley
1 pound bucatini or spaghetti

Drain the mushrooms and rinse them well under cold running water. Chop roughly and set aside.

Put ½ cup water in a large skillet and place over medium heat. Add the mussels and clams, cover the skillet, and cook just long enough for the shellfish to open. Transfer them to a bowl as they open. Line a strainer with paper towels and strain the liquid into a bowl. Dice the mussels and clams into small pieces and set aside.

Wipe the skillet clean with paper towels. Heat the oil in the skillet over high heat. Add the shrimp and scallops, and stir until they begin to color, 1 to 2 minutes. With a slotted spoon, transfer them to a plate. Add the garlic and porcini, and stir for a few minutes. Add the wine and cook until it is almost all reduced, 2 to 3 minutes. Add the tomatoes and the reserved shellfish liquid, and bring to a gentle boil. Reduce the heat to medium, and season with salt and pepper. Let the sauce bubble gently until it has a medium-thick consistency, 7 to 8 minutes. Add the shellfish and simmer a few minutes longer. Stir in the parsley, adjust the seasoning, and turn the heat off under the skillet.

Meanwhile, bring a large pot of water to a boil. Add 1 tablespoon of salt and the pasta. Cook, uncovered, over high heat, stirring occasionally, until the pasta is tender but still firm to the bite. Drain the pasta and add it to the sauce. Mix everything well over low heat until pasta and sauce are well combined. Taste, adjust the seasoning, and serve.

RIGATONI WITH SQUASH
Rigatoni con la Zucca

❦

SERVES 4 TO 6

Every time I am in Mantova, I have dinner at Trattoria dei Martini. It is everything that a sophisticated, well-run, family-owned *trattoria* should be: the service is excellent and the food is terrific. This is one of their dishes, which I have adapted slightly because of the unavailability of a few ingredients. The great golden color and lightly sweet taste of this pasta, given by the squash and the amaretti cookies, has roots in the Renaissance, when many dishes had sweet and savory flavors. An appealing, great fall dish, this fits well into a semi-traditional Thanksgiving dinner. It should be served in small quantities as a first course.

1 small butternut squash (about 1 pound)

3 imported Amaretti di Saronno cookies, finely crushed (see Note, below)

¼ teaspoon freshly grated nutmeg

4 tablespoons unsalted butter

⅓ cup finely minced scallions

1 cup heavy cream

½ cup Basic Chicken Broth (page 21) or low-sodium canned chicken broth

Salt to taste

1 pound rigatoni or penne rigate

1 to 2 tablespoons chopped fresh parsley

1 cup freshly grated Parmigiano-Reggiano cheese

Preheat the oven to 350° F.

Cut the squash in half lengthwise, remove and discard the seeds, and wrap the squash in foil. Place the squash on a cookie sheet and bake until tender, about 1 hour. Remove from oven and cool. Scoop out the pulp and puree it through a food mill or a ricer. Place the puree in a bowl and mix it with the crushed cookies and the nutmeg. (Makes approximately 1½ cups pureed squash.)

Heat 3 tablespoons of the butter in a large skillet over medium-low heat. When the butter begins to foam, add the scallions and cook, stirring, until very soft and lightly golden, 5 to 6 minutes. Raise the heat to medium and add the cream and broth. When the cream begins to simmer, add the pureed squash. Season with salt and simmer for 2 to 3 minutes. If the sauce becomes too thick, stir in a little more broth.

Meanwhile, bring a large pot of water to a boil. Add 1 tablespoon of salt and the rigatoni. Cook, uncovered, over high heat until the pasta is tender but still a bit firm to the bite.

Drain the pasta and place it in the skillet with the sauce. Add the parsley and ⅓ cup of the Parmigiano, and mix well. Stir over low heat until the pasta and sauce are well combined. Serve with a bit of additional Parmigiano if desired.

NOTE

Amaretti di Saronno are almond cookies imported from Italy. They can be found in Italian markets and specialty food stores.

RIGATONI WITH
ARTICHOKE SAUCE
Rigatoni con Sugo di Carciofi

❧

SERVES 4 TO 6

This delicious *sugo di carciofi* comes from Liguria, where it is used not only over pasta but also over meat preparations. In Liguria, meaty fresh porcini are added to the sauce. Here, dried porcini replace the fresh ones, and as always their flavorful soaking water is added to the sauce, enriching it considerably.

1½ pounds small baby
    artichokes, cleaned and
    cooked (page 9)
1 ounce dried porcini
    mushrooms, soaked in 1 cup
    lukewarm water for
    20 minutes
⅓ cup extra-virgin olive oil
½ cup finely minced yellow
    onion
1 garlic clove, minced
½ cup dry white wine

4 cups canned Italian plum
    tomatoes with their juice, put
    through a food mill to
    remove seeds
Salt and freshly ground black
    pepper to taste
1 tablespoon unsalted butter
1 tablespoon chopped fresh
    parsley
1 pound rigatoni, penne rigate,
    or mezze maniche

Cut the artichokes into thin slices. Set aside until ready to use.

Drain the porcini mushrooms and reserve the soaking water. Rinse the mushrooms well under cold running water and chop them roughly. Line a strainer with paper towels and strain the mushroom water into a bowl to get rid of the sandy deposits. Set aside.

Heat the oil in a medium saucepan over medium heat. Add the onion and cook until lightly golden, 4 to 5 minutes. Add the garlic and the porcini mushrooms, and stir for a minute or two. Add the artichokes and mix well with the savory base. Raise the heat to high and add the wine. Cook and stir until the wine is almost all reduced. Add the tomatoes and the reserved porcini soaking water. Season with salt and pepper. Bring the liquid to a boil, then reduce the heat to low.

Cover the saucepan, leaving the lid slightly askew, and simmer for 30 to 40 minutes or until the sauce has a medium-thick consistency. Check and stir the sauce a few times during cooking. Swirl in the butter and the parsley, and stir once or twice. Turn the heat off under the saucepan. (This sauce can be prepared a few hours ahead.)

Meanwhile, bring a large pot of water to a boil. Add 1 tablespoon of salt and the rigatoni. Cook, uncovered, over high heat until the pasta is tender but still a bit firm to the bite. Drain the pasta and place it in a large heated serving bowl. Add about half of the sauce and mix everything well until the pasta and sauce are well combined. Add a bit more sauce if needed. Bring the bowl to the table and serve at once.

ONE SAUCE, MANY MEALS

This sauce freezes so well and tastes so great over potato gnocchi or trenette, or as a topping for crostini bruschetta, I have deliberately given measurements that provide leftovers. Though you'll need only 2 to 2½ cups of sauce for this dish, this recipe produces 4½ to 5 cups.

PENNETTE WITH EGGPLANT
Pennette con Melanzane
al Funghetto

❧

SERVES 4 TO 6

*A*l *funghetto* is a traditional Italian combination of sautéed eggplant, mushrooms, or zucchini in olive oil, garlic, and parsley. Vegetables cooked *al funghetto* can be served as appetizers, side dishes, or, as we finally have discovered, as a topping for pasta. As the diced eggplant is cooking, it will soak up most of the oil in the skillet. Resist the temptation to add more oil and keep cooking until they have a nice golden color.

Pennette rigate are short, grooved, narrow tubes of pasta that give just the right texture to this dish.

1 medium eggplant (about 1½ pounds), purged (page 10)	Salt and freshly ground black pepper to taste
½ cup extra-virgin olive oil	1 pound pennette rigate, penne, spaghetti, or linguine
2 garlic cloves, minced	
2 anchovy fillets, chopped	
2 tablespoons chopped fresh parsley	

Cut the eggplant into ½-inch cubes. Heat the oil in a large skillet over high heat. Add the eggplant and cook, stirring, until the cubes have a bright golden color. Add the garlic, anchovies, and parsley and stir quickly until garlic begins to color, less than 1 minute. Season with salt and generously with pepper, and turn the heat off under the skillet.

Meanwhile, bring a large pot of water to a boil. Add 1 tablespoon of salt and the pasta. Cook, uncovered, over high heat, stirring occasionally, until the pasta is tender but still a bit firm to the bite. Scoop up and reserve 1 cup of the pasta cooking water.

Drain the pasta and add it to the sauce. Add ½ cup of the reserved pasta water and mix everything quickly over low heat until the pasta and sauce are well combined. Stir in a bit more water if the pasta looks too dry. Taste, adjust the seasoning, and serve.

MAKE IT SPICY, MAKE IT SAUCY

By adding or removing an ingredient or two, this sauce acquires a new identity. By adding sun-dried tomatoes, capers and chili pepper, or a few cups of tomato sauce and cooking it for 5 to 6 minutes, you have entirely different dishes.

COOKING EGGPLANT LIGHT

If you want to cut down on the amount of oil, cut the eggplant into ¼-inch-thick slices, purge them as instructed on page 10, and grill them. Cut the slices into ½-inch cubes, place them in a hot skillet with just a little oil, and toss quickly with some garlic and parsley.

PENNETTE WITH SWORDFISH, EGGPLANT, AND SUN-DRIED TOMATOES

Pennette con Pesce Spada, Melanzane, e Pomodori Secchi

⁂

SERVES 4 TO 6

How many recipes like this are there in Italian cooking? A thousand! And yet while many dishes seem similar to the untrained eye, they all have their own unique character, individuality, and taste. The basic thread that unites these dishes is one single, vital ingredient: olive oil! Flavorful and voluptuous, with a pale yellow, deep green, or golden color, olive oil is without doubt the most important ingredient in Italian cooking.

Select the freshest swordfish, the best eggplant, and the most aromatic sun-dried tomatoes, but please do pay attention to the oil you buy, for it could make or break your dish. (See page 5 for a short discussion on olive oil.)

1 medium eggplant (about 1¼ pounds), purged (page 10)
⅓ to ½ cup extra-virgin olive oil
⅓ cup finely minced yellow onion
2 garlic cloves, minced
½ pound swordfish steak, cut into ½-inch cubes
2 tablespoons capers, rinsed
1 tablespoon finely minced sun-dried tomatoes

Salt and freshly ground black pepper to taste
1 pound pennette, penne, spaghetti, or linguine
6 to 8 leaves fresh basil, shredded, or 1 to 2 tablespoons chopped fresh parsley

Cut the eggplant into ½-inch cubes. Heat ⅓ cup oil in a large skillet over high heat. Add the eggplant and cook until eggplant has a bright golden color. With a slotted spoon, scoop up the eggplant and transfer to paper towels to drain.

Put the skillet back over medium heat and add a little additional oil if needed. Add the onion and garlic, and cook, stirring, until the onion is lightly golden, 4 to

5 minutes. Add the swordfish and stir until it begins to color, 2 to 3 minutes. Add the capers and sun-dried tomatoes, stir once or twice, then add the eggplant. Season with salt and generously with pepper, and turn the heat off under the skillet.

Meanwhile, bring a large pot of water to a boil. Add 1 tablespoon of salt and the pasta. Cook, uncovered, over high heat, stirring occasionally, until the pasta is tender but still a bit firm to the bite. Scoop up and reserve 1 cup of the pasta cooking water.

Drain the pasta and add it to the sauce. Add the basil or parsley and ½ cup of the reserved pasta water, and mix everything quickly over low heat until the pasta and sauce are well combined. Stir in a bit more pasta water if sauce looks too dry. Taste, adjust the seasoning, and serve.

AS A TOMATO SAUCE

For Pennette with Swordfish, Eggplant, and Tomatoes, add 3 cups of canned strained tomatoes to the sauce instead of the sun-dried tomatoes and simmer the sauce for 10 to 12 minutes. Then add the eggplant, stir for a few minutes, and turn off the heat.

SPINACH PENNE WITH ENDIVE, PANCETTA, AND CREAM

Penne Verde con Indivia Belga, Pancetta, e Panna

❦

SERVES 4 TO 6

A year or so ago, a friend of mine returning from a trip to Italy told me about a pasta dish he had eaten in Milan, at a restaurant called Boeucc. He explained the dish and asked me to prepare it for him. The only thing he was sure of was that the sauce had cream and, he could have sworn, also Worcestershire sauce! Well, now I was intrigued. So after a couple of attempts to duplicate this phantom dish, I came up with this version, which my friend thought was very good and close enough to the real thing. But use the Worcestershire sauce with restraint: too much of it will overpower and obliterate the taste of the other ingredients.

3 medium Belgian endive
   (about ¾ pound total)
¼ cup extra-virgin olive oil
¼ pound pancetta, in 1 thick
   slice, cut into medium strips
1 to 2 tablespoons
   Worcestershire sauce
½ cup dry white wine
1 cup Basic Chicken Broth
   (page 21) or low-sodium
   canned chicken broth

⅓ cup heavy cream
Salt and freshly ground white
   pepper to taste
1 pound spinach penne, shells,
   or fusilli
1 tablespoon unsalted butter
⅓ cup freshly grated
   Parmigiano-Reggiano cheese

Remove the bruised outer leaves of the endive and slice them into thin strips.

Heat the oil in a large skillet over medium heat. Add the endive and cook, stirring, until soft, almost wilted, 6 to 7 minutes. Add the pancetta and cook until lightly golden. Add the Worcestershire sauce and stir quickly once or twice, then stir in the wine. Cook until the wine is reduced by half, 2 to 3 minutes. Add the broth and cream. Season with salt and pepper. As the sauce begins to bubble, reduce the heat to low and simmer a few minutes, until sauce has a medium-thick consistency. Turn the heat off under the skillet.

Meanwhile, bring a large pot of water to a boil. Add 1 tablespoon of salt and the pasta. Cook, uncovered, over high heat, stirring occasionally, until the pasta is tender but still a bit firm to the bite. Scoop up and reserve 1 cup of the pasta cooking water.

Drain the pasta and add it to the sauce. Add the butter, ¼ cup Parmigiano, and a bit of the cooking water if needed. Mix everything quickly over low heat until the pasta and sauce are well combined. Taste, adjust the seasoning, and serve with a bit of additional Parmigiano.

LINGUINE WITH BROCCOLI RABE, SQUID, AND HOT PEPPER

Linguine con Rapini, Calamari, e Peperoncino

❧

SERVES 4 TO 6

*A*glio e olio, that great classic southern Italian invention, is the foundation of many other pasta dishes and lends itself to innumerable variations. This dish begins with oil, garlic, and chili pepper, to which are added calamari, bread crumbs, and broccoli rabe.

Broccoli rabe, a delicious green leafy vegetable with a slightly bitter nutty taste, is available year-round, with its peak season from late fall to early spring.

2 pounds broccoli rabe
⅓ cup extra-virgin olive oil
2 garlic cloves, minced
Chopped fresh red chili pepper or hot red pepper flakes to taste
12 ounces whole squid, cleaned (page 12), cut into ½-inch circles

2 tablespoons plain bread crumbs
Salt to taste
1 pound linguine or spaghetti

Trim and discard any large woody stalks and wilted leaves from the broccoli rabe. Wash the rabe well under cold running water and set aside.

Heat the oil in a large skillet over medium heat. Add the garlic, chili pepper, and squid, and cook, stirring, only until the squid becomes chalky white, 1 to 2 minutes. Raise the heat to high and add the bread crumbs. Stir quickly until bread crumbs turn lightly golden, 10 to 15 seconds. Season with salt and turn the heat off under the skillet.

Meanwhile, bring a large pot of water to a boil. Add 1 tablespoon of salt, the broccoli rabe, and the pasta. Cook, uncovered, over high heat, stirring occasionally, until the pasta is tender but still a bit firm to the bite. Scoop up and reserve ½ cup of the pasta cooking water.

Drain the pasta and add it to the skillet. Season the pasta lightly with salt and add the reserved water. Mix everything well over low heat until the pasta and sauce are well combined. Taste, adjust the seasoning, and serve.

SPAGHETTI WITH MUSSELS AND SAFFRON
Spaghetti con Cozze e Zafferano

❦

SERVES 4 TO 6

The combination of shellfish with saffron and pasta has become quite popular in Italy. The saffron adds a rich color and a definite taste to the dish, while the chili pepper lifts the mood. Clams can be used instead of or in addition to the mussels. Rigatoni, penne, or linguine can take the place of spaghetti.

½ cup water

3 pounds mussels, cleaned (page 11)

¼ teaspoon powdered saffron (page 12)

⅓ cup extra-virgin olive oil

½ cup finely minced leek, thoroughly washed

2 garlic cloves, minced

½ cup dry white wine

Salt to taste

Chopped fresh red chili pepper or hot red pepper flakes to taste

1 tablespoon unsalted butter

1 tablespoon chopped fresh parsley

1 pound spaghetti, spaghettini, or linguine

Put the water in a large skillet and place over medium heat. Add the mussels and cover the skillet. Cook just until the mussels open. Transfer them to a bowl as they open. Line a strainer with paper towels, strain the liquid into a bowl, and stir in the saffron. Set aside. Detach the mussels from the shells, cut the mussels into 2 to 3 pieces, and place in a separate bowl.

CONTINUED

Heat the oil in a large skillet over medium heat. Add the leek and cook, stirring, until lightly golden and soft, 6 to 7 minutes. Add the garlic and stir a few times. Add the reserved liquid with the saffron and the wine. Raise the heat to high and cook, stirring, until the liquid is reduced a little more than half. Season with salt and chili pepper. Add the butter and parsley, and stir until the sauce has a medium-thick consistency. Add the mussels and stir them for a minute or so with the sauce. Taste and adjust the seasoning. Turn the heat off.

Meanwhile, bring a large pot of water to a boil. Add 1 tablespoon of salt and the pasta. Cook, uncovered, over high heat, stirring occasionally, until the pasta is tender but still a bit firm to the bite.

Drain the pasta and place in a large heated serving bowl. Add the mussels and all the sauce, and toss until everything is well combined. Taste, adjust the seasoning, and serve.

SPAGHETTI WITH SPICY EGGPLANT-TOMATO SAUCE
Spaghetti con Intingolo di Melanzane, Pomodori, e Peperoncino

SERVES 4 TO 6

Perhaps the best-known pasta dish of Sicily is *pasta con la Norma,* "pasta with eggplant."

This version is enhanced by the vegetables of Sicily. Here the tomato sauce has garlic, anchovies, and olives. It is cooked only briefly to retain its freshness and bright red color, then it is pureed. The eggplant is diced into cubes, fried, and added to the sauce during the last minutes of cooking. This is the kind of food that makes you want to sing!

1 medium eggplant (about
    1¼ pounds), purged
    (page 10)
½ cup extra-virgin olive oil
2 garlic cloves, minced
4 anchovy fillets, chopped
10 black pitted olives, cut into
    quarters
Chopped fresh red chili pepper
    or hot red pepper flakes to
    taste
3 cups canned Italian plum
    tomatoes with their juice, put
    through a food mill to
    remove seeds

Salt to taste
¼ cup loosely packed fresh
    oregano leaves, or
    2 tablespoons chopped
    fresh parsley
1 pound spaghetti, bucatini, or
    fusilli

Cut the eggplant into ½-inch cubes. Heat ⅓ cup of the oil in a large skillet over high heat. Add the eggplant and cook until the cubes have a bright golden color. With a large slotted spoon, scoop up the fried eggplant and transfer to paper towels to drain.

Put the skillet back over medium heat and add a little additional oil if needed. Add the garlic, anchovies, olives, and chili pepper and stir for a minute or two. Add the tomatoes and season with salt. As soon as the sauce comes to a boil, reduce the heat to low and simmer, uncovered, 8 to 10 minutes. Puree the sauce through a food mill or in a food processor and return to the skillet. Add the fried eggplant to the sauce and simmer 2 to 3 minutes longer. Stir in the fresh oregano or parsley, and turn the heat off under the skillet.

Meanwhile, bring a large pot of water to a boil. Add 1 tablespoon of salt and the pasta. Cook, uncovered, over high heat, stirring occasionally, until the pasta is tender but still a bit firm to the bite.

Drain the pasta and add it to the sauce, and mix everything quickly over low heat until pasta and sauce are well combined. Taste, adjust the seasoning, and serve.

SPAGHETTINI WITH LEEKS
Spaghettini con Porri

❦

SERVES 4 TO 6

When leeks are stewed slowly for a long time, they lose their pungency and their flavor becomes mild and almost sweet. Here, the sweetness of the onion blends remarkably well with the spiciness of the chili pepper.

4 large leeks (about
   1¾ pounds total)
3 tablespoons unsalted butter
2 tablespoons olive oil
2 to 3 garlic cloves, minced
1 cup water
2 tablespoons chopped fresh
   parsley

Salt to taste
Chopped fresh red chili pepper
   or hot red pepper flakes to
   taste
1 pound spaghettini or
   spaghetti

Cut off the roots of the leeks and remove half of the green stalks. Cut the leeks in half lengthwise and slice them into small strips. Place them in a large colander and wash well under cold running water, making sure to remove all the dirt. Drain leeks thoroughly, place on paper towels, and pat them dry.

Heat 2 tablespoons of the butter and the oil in a large skillet over medium heat. When the butter foams, add the leeks and garlic, and stir just long enough to coat with the butter. Add the water, reduce the heat to low, and cover the skillet partially. Simmer for 25 to 30 minutes, stirring occasionally, until the leeks are meltingly soft and moist. Add a little more water if the juices in the skillet should reduce too much. Stir in the parsley, then season with salt and generously with chili pepper.

Meanwhile, bring a large pot of water to a boil. Add 1 tablespoon of salt and the pasta. Cook, uncovered, over high heat, stirring occasionally, until the pasta is tender but still a bit firm to the bite. Scoop up and reserve 1 cup of the pasta cooking water.

Drain the pasta and add it to the sauce. Season the spaghettini with salt, add the remaining tablespoon butter and ½ cup of the pasta cooking water, and mix quickly over low heat until the pasta and the sauce are well combined. Taste, adjust the seasoning, and serve.

PLAY WITH YOUR FOOD

*Since this basic preparation lends itself to so many variations,
do what Italian cooks do—improvise.*

Brown some strips of pancetta and toss it with the leeks.

Toss some boiled bitter greens into the sauce.

Add some canned tuna, chopped very fine.

Add some cubes of fried eggplant.

PASTA WITH ROASTED ONIONS
AND PANCETTA

Pasta con Cipolle al Forno e Pancetta

❧

SERVES 4 TO 6

When onions roast in the oven in their own skins, they become as sweet as honey. Here, the onions are roasted, skins removed, and put back in the oven to brown further. Cut into pieces, the onions are quickly sautéed with pancetta and thyme and turned into a luscious sauce for pasta. This is a dish that will cost you almost nothing in terms of money and time. Double the amount of onions you are roasting and use them as a salad, drizzled with extra-virgin olive oil and just a bit of good balsamic vinegar.

3 medium yellow onions (about 1½ pounds total), with tips and roots trimmed

¼ cup extra-virgin olive oil

2 to 3 ounces thickly sliced pancetta, cut into ½-inch pieces

1 tablespoon minced fresh thyme or fresh chopped parsley

Salt and finely ground black pepper to taste

1 pound garganelli, penne, or rigatoni

1 tablespoon unsalted butter

½ cup freshly grated Parmigiano-Reggiano cheese

Preheat the oven to 400° F. Place the onions on a lightly oiled baking sheet and roast until they are easily pierced with a knife, about 1 hour. When the onions are cool enough to handle, remove their skins and put them back in the oven to roast until they have a nice golden color, 10 to 15 minutes. Slice into thin wedges and cut the wedges into small pieces. Gather the onions and as much of their juices as you can and place in a bowl. Set aside until ready to use.

Heat the oil in a large skillet over medium heat. Add the pancetta and cook, stirring, until lightly golden, about 2 minutes. Add the roasted onions and the thyme or parsley, season with salt and generously with pepper, and stir just long enough to heat the onions through.

Meanwhile, bring a large pot of water to a boil. Add 1 tablespoon of salt and the pasta. Cook, uncovered, over high heat until the pasta is tender but still firm to the bite. Scoop up and reserve about ⅓ cup of the pasta cooking water.

Drain the pasta and place it in the skillet with the sauce. Add the reserved cooking water, the butter, and a small handful of the Parmigiano. Season lightly with salt. Mix well over low heat until pasta and sauce are well combined. Taste, adjust the seasoning, and serve with additional Parmigiano.

SPAGHETTINI WITH TOMATOES, CAPERS, OLIVES, AND ANCHOVIES
Spaghettini alla Puttanesca

❦

SERVES 4 TO 6

Spaghetti alla puttanesca means spaghetti "harlot style." It is said that the ladies of the night would prepare this dish for their customers to seduce them. And I maintain that this is a dish that would seduce *anyone* because it is so utterly direct and appealing.

The traditional recipe calls for coursely chopped canned tomatoes. In Rome, however, I had this dish with canned tomatoes that had been put through a food mill, as I do in this version. You can also substitute tomato sauce.

⅓ cup extra-virgin olive oil
4 anchovy fillets, chopped
1 garlic clove, minced
1 tablespoon chopped fresh parsley
2 tablespoons capers, rinsed
10 black pitted olives, thinly sliced

4 cups canned Italian plum tomatoes with their juice, put through a food mill to remove seeds
Salt and freshly ground black pepper to taste
1 pound spaghettini or spaghetti

CONTINUED

Heat the oil in a large skillet over medium heat. Add the anchovies and garlic, and stir for about 1 minute. Add the parsley, capers, and olives and stir for a minute or two. Add the tomatoes and season with salt and pepper. When the sauce begins to bubble, reduce the heat to low and simmer, uncovered, about 15 minutes.

Meanwhile, bring a large pot of water to a boil. Add 1 tablespoon of salt and the spaghetti. Cook, uncovered, over high heat, stirring occasionally, until the pasta is tender but still firm to the bite.

Drain the pasta and add it to the sauce. Mix everything quickly over low heat until the pasta and sauce are well combined. Taste, adjust the seasoning, and serve.

SPAGHETTI WITH OVEN-ROASTED TOMATOES AND GARLIC

Spaghetti con Pomodori al Forno e Aglio

SERVES 4 TO 6

The popularity of sun-dried tomatoes has inspired chefs with simpler alternatives to the lengthy process of drying tomatoes in the sun.

The first time I tried this effective technique, I put the tomatoes and garlic in the preheated 250° F. oven and went to a movie. When I returned the tomatoes had shriveled to half their original size, but their sweet aroma had filled the entire house.

3 pounds ripe plum tomatoes, cut into ½-inch-thick rounds

4 to 5 garlic cloves, peeled

Salt to taste

⅓ cup extra-virgin olive oil

2 tablespoons capers, rinsed

⅓ cup fresh oregano leaves, or 1 to 2 tablespoons chopped fresh parsley

Chopped fresh red chili pepper or hot red pepper flakes to taste

1 pound spaghetti

Preheat the oven to 250° F.

Line 2 baking sheets with parchment paper or aluminum foil and brush the parchment or foil very lightly with olive oil. Place tomato slices on the baking sheet and scatter the garlic in the empty spaces between the slices. Season with salt. Roast the tomatoes for 3 to 3½ hours, or until they have lost all their liquid and look shriveled. Remove the tomatoes from oven, cool them, and remove their skins. Roughly dice the tomatoes and the garlic.

Heat the oil in a large skillet over medium heat. Add the tomatoes, garlic, capers, fresh oregano or parsley, and hot pepper. Stir just long enough to heat everything through, 1 to 2 minutes. Turn the heat off under the skillet.

Bring a large pot of water to a boil, add 1 tablespoon of salt, and add the spaghetti. Cook, uncovered, stirring the pasta occasionally, until the spaghetti are tender but still firm to the bite. (Thin spaghetti generally cook between 6 to 8 minutes, depending on the brand.)

Drain the pasta and add it the skillet. Season with salt. Toss the spaghetti and tomatoes well over medium heat for about 1 minute. Taste, adjust the seasoning, and serve.

STORING HOMEMADE DRIED TOMATOES

If you have leftover dried tomatoes, place them in a jar, cover them with olive oil, and use within a few days. Or place the tomatoes in small resealable plastic bags, seal them thoroughly, and freeze them.

SUMMER SPAGHETTI WITH UNCOOKED TOMATOES AND HERBS

Spaghetti Estivi al Sugo Crudo

❧

SERVES 4 TO 6

During the long, hot days of summer, Italians love to prepare uncooked tomato sauces because they are quick, healthy, and wonderfully fresh-tasting. This sauce calls for very ripe tomatoes and aromatic fresh herbs. Even though it can be made only with one or two types of herbs, it really bursts with flavor when prepared with all the herbs listed. Do not chop your herbs too far ahead, for they tend to blacken.

2 pounds ripe plum tomatoes, peeled, seeded, and finely minced (page 9)

2 garlic cloves, minced

½ cup mixed chopped fresh herbs (marjoram, oregano, mint, basil, and parsley)

½ cup extra-virgin olive oil

Salt and freshly ground black pepper to taste

1 pound spaghetti or linguine

Place the tomatoes in a large pasta bowl with all their juices. Add the garlic, herbs, and oil. Season with salt and generously with pepper. Mix everything well, taste, and adjust the seasoning. Cover the bowl with plastic wrap and chill in the refrigerator for about 15 minutes.

Meanwhile, bring a large pot of water to a boil. Add 1 tablespoon of salt and the spaghetti. Cook, uncovered, over high heat until the pasta is tender but still firm to the bite.

Remove the sauce from the refrigerator. Drain the pasta, add it to the bowl with the sauce, and mix well. Taste, adjust the seasoning, and serve.

BIGOLI WITH TUNA, ANCHOVIES, AND ONIONS

Bigoli alla Veneziana

SERVES 4 TO 6

This is a traditional Venetian dish in which thick, whole wheat spaghetti strands are tossed with a sauce of meltingly soft onion and fresh anchovies. In this variation, the onions are simmered slowly until the water evaporates and the onions become *very* soft. Then tuna and anchovies are added for a sweet and savory repast.

⅓ cup extra-virgin olive oil
3 cups thinly sliced yellow
   onion
½ cup water
8 anchovy fillets
1 (3½-ounce) can white tuna
   packed in oil, drained and
   broken into small pieces

Salt and freshly ground black
   pepper to taste
1 pound bigoli or whole wheat
   spaghetti or linguine
2 tablespoons chopped fresh
   parsley

CONTINUED

Heat the oil in a large skillet over medium-low heat. Add the onion and water. Cover the skillet partially and cook, stirring occasionally, until the onion is very soft and the water is completely evaporated, about 15 minutes. Raise the heat to high and cook, stirring constantly, until the onion turns lightly golden, 2 to 3 minutes. Add the anchovies and tuna, and stir for a minute or two, then turn the heat off under the skillet.

Bring a large pot of water to a boil. Add 1 tablespoon of salt and the pasta. Cook, uncovered, over high heat until the pasta is tender but still firm to the bite. Scoop out and reserve about ½ cup of the cooking water.

Drain the pasta and place it in the skillet with the onions. Stir in the parsley and season with salt and pepper. Mix everything quickly over low heat until the pasta and sauce are well combined. If the sauce is a bit dry, stir in a little of the reserved pasta water. Taste, adjust the seasoning, and serve.

A SAUCY VERSION

If you want to transform this into a tomato-based sauce, for Spaghetti with Onion, Tuna, Anchovies, and Tomatoes, put 2 cups canned Italian plum tomatoes with their juice through a food mill to remove the seeds, then add to the sauce. Season with a bit of hot pepper flakes and simmer for about 10 minutes.

PASTA WITH VODKA, BRESAOLA, AND CREAM

Pasta con Vodka, Bresaola, e Panna

⁂

SERVES 4 TO 6

Bresaola—cured dried beef—and vodka do wonderful things to the basics of Italian cooking. Vodka, like wine, leaves behind a certain depth of flavor; the bresaola makes the sauce assertive and savory.

1 medium leek
¼ cup extra-virgin olive oil
¼ pound thickly sliced bresaola or prosciutto, cut into thin strips
⅓ cup vodka (see Note, below)
1 cup heavy cream
Salt and freshly ground white pepper to taste

1 pound garganelli, bow ties, or pennette
1 tablespoon unsalted butter
1 to 2 tablespoons chopped fresh parsley
½ cup freshly grated Parmigiano-Reggiano cheese

Cut off the root of the leek and remove half of the green stalk. Cut the leek in half lengthwise and slice it into small strips. Place in a colander and wash well under cold running water, making sure to remove all the dirt. Drain well, pat dry with paper towels, and set aside.

Heat the oil in a large skillet over medium heat. Add the leek and cook, stirring, until it is golden and soft, 10 to 12 minutes. Add the bresaola or prosciutto, and stir a few times. Remove the skillet from the heat and add the vodka (see Note). Put the skillet back on the heat and stir gently until the vodka is almost all evaporated, about 2 minutes. Add the cream, season lightly with salt and pepper, and let it bubble gently for 2 to 3 minutes.

Meanwhile, bring a large pot of water to a boil. Add 1 tablespoon of salt and the pasta. Cook, uncovered, over high heat until the pasta is tender but still a bit firm to the bite. Scoop up and reserve about 1 cup of the pasta cooking water.

CONTINUED

Drain the pasta and place in the skillet with the sauce. Season pasta lightly with salt. Add ½ cup of the reserved cooking water, the butter, parsley, and ¼ cup of the Parmigiano. Stir well over low heat until the pasta and sauce are well combined. Add some more water if sauce seems a bit dry. Taste, adjust the seasoning, and serve with additional Parmigiano if desired.

NOTE

If you are not used to cooking with alcohol, be careful. Remove the skillet from the heat and add the vodka. Put the skillet back on the heat carefully and stir gently until the vodka is almost all evaporated. Chances are that, because of the high alcohol content of the vodka, it will flame up no matter how careful you are. It is okay; allow the alcohol to burn off and the flame will subside. Or remove the pan from the heat and blow on the flame. Or put a lid or another skillet on the flame to subdue it.

Know that accidents can occur in the kitchen. If a fire should start while you are cooking, never throw water on it. Throw salt or baking soda, or use a fire extinguisher if you have one at hand.

BOW TIES WITH ONION, ZUCCHINI, AND CHERRY TOMATOES
Farfalle Vegetariane

SERVES 4 TO 6

For me, one of the joys of summer is the abundance of fresh produce and herbs. I make this light, fresh-tasting pasta with the first crop of organic cherry tomatoes, sweet onions, tender young zucchini, and fresh basil and oregano from my garden. If you don't have access to organic tomatoes and fresh herbs, make it with ripe, juicy tomatoes and fresh parsley. Use good extra-virgin olive oil. Do not add any garlic; just let the flavors of these fresh ingredients speak for themselves.

½ cup extra-virgin olive oil

2 cups thinly sliced yellow
onion

4 small zucchini, cut into small
cubes

1 pound red and yellow cherry
tomatoes, halved, or 1 pound
ripe plum tomatoes, peeled,
seeded, and diced (page 9)

Salt and freshly ground pepper
to taste

1 tablespoon unsalted butter

1 pound bow ties or penne

⅓ cup loosely packed fresh basil
and oregano leaves, torn into
small pieces

Heat the oil in a large skillet over medium heat. Add the onion and cook, stirring, until lightly golden and soft, about 8 minutes. Raise the heat to high and
add the zucchini. Cook and stir until the zucchini begin to color, about 5 minutes.
Add the tomatoes, stir well, and season with salt and pepper. Reduce the heat to
low and simmer, stirring occasionally, until the tomatoes are soft and the juices in
the skillet have thickened, about 10 minutes. Add the butter, stir well, and turn
the heat off under the skillet.

Meanwhile, bring a large pot of water to a boil. Add 1 tablespoon of salt and
the pasta. Cook, uncovered, over high heat until the pasta is tender but still firm
to the bite. Scoop out and reserve about 1 cup of the pasta cooking water.

Drain the pasta and add it to the skillet. Add the basil and oregano, and mix
well. If the sauce looks a bit dry, stir in a little of the reserved pasta water. Taste,
adjust the seasoning, and serve.

BOW TIES WITH ROASTED ALMONDS AND CREAM
Farfalle con Mandorle e Panna

🦋

SERVES 4 TO 6

There comes a time, when an uncompromisingly rich dish is needed for one's emotional well-being! And if we want to sin, we should do it in style. Almonds, cream, and Parmigiano are the ingredients that cling to this pasta in perfect harmony.

3 ounces blanched whole
    almonds
3 tablespoons unsalted butter
2 garlic cloves, finely minced
1 cup Basic Chicken Broth
    (page 21) or low-sodium
    canned chicken broth
1½ cups heavy cream
Salt and freshly ground white
    pepper to taste

1 pound bow ties, garganelli, or
    pennette
8 to 10 fresh basil leaves,
    shredded, or 2 tablespoons
    chopped fresh parsley
½ cup freshly grated
    Parmigiano-Reggiano cheese

Preheat the oven to 350° F.

Put the almonds on a cookie sheet and place in the oven until they are lightly golden, 2 to 3 minutes. Remove from the oven and cool. Chop the almonds roughly.

Heat the butter in a large skillet over medium heat. When the butter begins to foam, add the garlic and almonds, and stir for less than 1 minute. Add the broth and cream. Season with salt and pepper. When the cream begins to simmer, reduce the heat to low and cook, stirring occasionally, until the sauce has a medium-thick consistency, 6 to 7 minutes. Turn the heat off under the skillet.

Meanwhile, bring a large pot of water to a boil. Add 1 tablespoon of salt and the pasta. Cook, uncovered, over high heat until the pasta is tender but still firm to the bite.

Drain the pasta and place it in the skillet with the sauce. Add the basil or parsley and about ¼ cup of the Parmigiano. Mix well over low heat until the pasta and sauce are well combined and the sauce clings to the pasta. Taste and adjust the seasoning. Serve with a bit of additional Parmigiano if desired.

PATERNOSTRI WITH TUNA, TOMATOES, AND CHILI PEPPER

Paternostri con Tonno, Pomodori, e Peperoncino

SERVES 6

Paternostri is a short tubular pasta often used in soups. In several southern Italian regions, however, small pasta such as paternostri, ditalini, or chioccioline (remember, any pasta that finishes with *ini* means small) are also served as a *pasta asciutta*—a pasta with sauce—and quite often the sauce has some type of seafood.

This pastina seems to swell considerably after it is cooked and tends to soak up the sauce quickly. One pound of paternostri or ditalini will feed 6 people generously.

1 (7-ounce) can white tuna
    packed in oil
⅓ to ½ cup extra-virgin olive oil
½ cup finely minced yellow
    onion
2 garlic cloves, minced
Chopped fresh red chili pepper
    or hot red pepper flakes to
    taste
1½ cups Basic Fish Broth
    (page 23)

3 cups canned Italian plum
    tomatoes with their juice, put
    through a food mill to
    remove seeds
Salt to taste
1 pound paternostri, ditalini,
    farfalline, or chioccioline
2 tablespoons chopped fresh
    parsley

CONTINUED

Drain the tuna from its oil, place on a cutting board, and chop it very fine. Set aside.

Heat the oil in a large skillet over medium heat. Add the onion and cook, stirring, until it is lightly golden, 4 to 5 minutes. Add the garlic and chili pepper, and stir for about 1 minute. Stir the tuna into the savory base, add the broth and the tomatoes, and season with salt. Simmer, uncovered, stirring occasionally, until sauce has a medium-thick consistency, 8 to 10 minutes. Turn the heat off under the skillet.

Meanwhile, bring a large pot of water to a boil. Add 1 tablespoon of salt and the pasta. Cook, uncovered, over high heat, stirring once or twice, until the pasta is tender but still a bit firm to the bite. Scoop up and reserve 1 cup of the pasta cooking water.

Drain the pasta and add it to the sauce. Add the parsley and mix well over low heat until the pasta and sauce are well combined. Add a bit of the reserved pasta cooking water if sauce looks too dry. Taste, adjust the seasoning, and serve.

PATERNOSTRI WITH PEAS, LEEKS, AND PANCETTA

Paternostri con Piselli, Porri, e Pancetta

SERVES 6

In the traditional Sicilian preparation, the small, tubular paternostri—also known as tubi, tubetti, or ditalini—are paired with leeks and sweet spring peas. Here, it is enriched by golden crisp pancetta.

2 cups shelled fresh or thawed
   frozen peas
Salt and freshly ground black
   pepper to taste
1 medium leek
⅓ to ½ cup extra-virgin olive oil
¼ pound thickly sliced
   pancetta, diced

1 pound paternostri, farfalline,
   or chioccioline
¼ cup freshly grated pecorino
   Romano cheese or ½ cup
   freshly grated Parmigiano-
   Reggiano cheese

If using fresh peas, bring a small saucepan of water to a boil. Add the peas to the water with a pinch of salt. Cook, uncovered, until tender, 5 to 10 minutes depending on size. Drain peas and set aside until ready to use.

Cut off the root of the leek and remove the dark green stalk. Cut the leek in half lengthwise and slice it into thin strips. Place the leek in a colander and wash well under cold running water, making sure to remove all the dirt. Shake the colander well to remove as much water as possible.

Heat the oil in a large skillet over medium heat. Add the leek and cook, stirring, until lightly golden and soft, 10 to 12 minutes. Add the pancetta and cook until golden, 1 to 2 minutes. Add the cooked or thawed peas and stir for a minute or two. Season with salt and several grinds of pepper.

Bring a large pot of water to a boil. Add 1 tablespoon of salt and the pasta. Cook, uncovered, over high heat until the pasta is tender but still a bit firm to the bite. Scoop up and reserve 1 cup of the pasta cooking water.

Drain the pasta and place it in the skillet with the sauce. Add about half of the cheese and mix everything quickly over low heat until the pasta and sauce are well combined. Add a bit of the reserved pasta cooking water if the sauce looks too dry. Serve at once with additional cheese.

BAKED FUSILLI WITH SMOKED
MOZZARELLA AND TOMATOES
Fusilli al Forno

🌿

SERVES 4 TO 6

Tomatoes, mozzarella, and pasta are synonymous with the cooking of Naples and the Campania region. Here pasta is tossed with a light tomato sauce and laced with smoked mozzarella, then baked until the cheese melts. It is simply delicious.

⅓ cup extra-virgin olive oil

2 garlic cloves, peeled and
   lightly crushed

5 cups canned Italian plum
   tomatoes with their juice, put
   through a food mill to
   remove seeds

Salt and freshly ground black
   pepper to taste

1 pound fusilli or penne

¼ pound smoked mozzarella,
   cut into small pieces or
   shredded

1 to 2 tablespoons unsalted
   butter, cut into small pieces

Heat the oil in a large skillet over medium heat. Add the garlic and cook until golden on all sides. Discard the garlic and add the tomatoes. When the tomatoes come to a boil, reduce the heat to low, season with salt and pepper, and simmer, uncovered, 8 to 10 minutes. Turn the heat off under the skillet.

Meanwhile, bring a large pot of water to a boil. Add 1 tablespoon of salt and the pasta. Cook, uncovered, over high heat, stirring occasionally, until the pasta is tender but a bit firmer than usual. It should have a decisive al dente texture.

While the pasta is cooking, preheat the oven to 400° F., and butter a large baking dish.

Drain the pasta and add it to the sauce. Mix well until the pasta and sauce are well combined. Taste and adjust the seasoning. Put the pasta in the baking dish and sprinkle with the diced mozzarella and the butter. Bake on the middle rack of the oven for 6 to 8 minutes, or until the cheese is melted. Serve hot.

PASTA WITH STEWED
VEGETABLES
Pasta con Verdure Stufate

☙

SERVES 4 TO 6

Stewed vegetables are staples of many Italian kitchens. There is the *peperonata* of Emilia-Romagna, which uses peppers, tomatoes, and onions. The *peperonata* of Sicily adds green olives to the peppers and tomatoes. The *cianfotta* of the Campania region stews peppers, eggplant, zucchini, and potatoes. While the vegetables might be different, the basic philosophy is the same: stew the vegetables gently in a base of good olive oil until they are soft but not completely mushy, then serve them warm or at room temperature. Traditionally these rustic dishes are always served as a vegetable. However, they are also absolutely wonderful sauce for pasta.

⅓ cup extra-virgin olive oil

2 large red bell peppers (about ½ pound), seeded and diced

1 small eggplant (about ¾ pound), cut into 1-inch cubes and purged (page 10)

2 garlic cloves, minced

2 medium tomatoes (about ½ pound), seeded and diced

1 tablespoon tomato paste diluted in 1½ cups cold water

Salt to taste

Chopped fresh red chili pepper or hot red pepper flakes to taste

1 teaspoon good balsamic vinegar (optional)

1 pound ziti, fusilli, rigatoni, or penne

Heat the oil in a large skillet over medium heat. Add the peppers and cook, stirring, until they begin to color, 5 to 6 minutes. Add the eggplant and cook for 3 to 4 minutes. Add the garlic, tomatoes, and diluted tomato paste. Season with salt and chili pepper. Reduce the heat to low, cover the skillet partially, and cook, stirring occasionally, until the vegetables are soft but not mushy, 20 to 25 minutes. Add the balsamic vinegar if using (see Balsamic as Highlight, page 198), and stir briefly into the sauce. Turn the heat off under the skillet. (The sauce can be prepared to this point a day ahead. Refrigerate tightly covered.)

CONTINUED

Meanwhile, bring a large pot of water to a boil. Add 1 tablespoon of salt and the pasta. Cook, uncovered, over high heat, stirring occasionally, until the pasta is tender but still a bit firm to the bite.

Drain the pasta and place it in a large heated serving bowl. Add the vegetables and mix everything until the pasta and vegetables are well combined. Taste, adjust the seasoning, and serve.

BALSAMIC AS HIGHLIGHT

If you are using balsamic vinegar, make sure not to go overboard with it.
A teaspoon or so will highlight the taste of the vegetables,
too much will be overpowering.

PASTA WITH COTECHINO SAUSAGE, BROCCOLI RABE, AND TOMATOES

Pasta con Cotechino, Rapini, e Pomodori

❧

SERVES 4 TO 6

This dish combines a typical northern Italian ingredient—cotechino sausage—with broccoli rabe, a vegetable that is much loved by southern Italians. The result is a delicious and hearty dish.

1 small cotechino sausage, about 1 pound (see Lucky Cotechino, page 200)

2 pounds broccoli rabe

⅓ cup extra-virgin olive oil

½ cup finely minced yellow onion

4 cups canned Italian plum tomatoes with their juice, put through a food mill to remove seeds

Salt and freshly ground black pepper to taste

1 pound shells, fusilli, or orecchiette

Soak the sausage in a large bowl of cold water for several hours or overnight. Drain, pierce in several places with a fork, and place in a large saucepan. Cover with water and bring the water to a gentle boil. Reduce the heat to low and simmer, uncovered, for 1 hour. Leave the cotechino in its own water until ready to use.

Trim and discard any large woody stalks and wilted leaves from the broccoli rabe. Wash the rabe well under cold running water and set aside.

Heat the oil in a large skillet over medium heat. Add the onion and cook, stirring, until lightly golden, 4 to 5 minutes. Add the tomatoes. When the tomatoes come to a boil, reduce the heat to low, season with salt and pepper, and simmer gently for 8 to 10 minutes. Remove the skin from the sausage and chop the meat into small, rough pieces. Add to the tomato sauce and simmer 3 to 4 minutes longer.

CONTINUED

Meanwhile, bring a large pot of water to a boil. Add 1 tablespoon of salt, the broccoli rabe, and the pasta. Cook, uncovered, over high heat, stirring occasionally, until the pasta is tender but still a bit firm to the bite.

Drain the pasta and the broccoli rabe and add it to the sauce. Mix everything well over low heat until the pasta and sauce are thoroughly combined. Taste, adjust the seasoning, and serve.

LUCKY COTECHINO

Cotechino is a large, tender, fresh sweet pork sausage from the Emilia-Romagna region. It is traditionally served next to bollito misto, or mixed boiled meats. Cotechino with lentils is a time-honored combination and a favorite dish to serve on New Year's Day, for it is believed to bring good luck.

Cotechino is available in Italian markets and specialty food shops.

Substitute sweet Italian sausage if cotechino is not available.

PASTA WITH CAULIFLOWER
AND PANCETTA
Pasta con Cavolfiore e Pancetta

❧

SERVES 4 TO 6

When I made this dish for the first time for my husband, he took a look at the golden pancetta and crisp bread crumbs and said, "Where is the sauce?" And when I told him that what he saw *was* the sauce, he seemed puzzled and a bit worried. I told him to trust me and just sit down at the table. Then I cooked the pasta with the cauliflower, drained it, and added it to the "sauce." I tossed it all together, seasoned it with salt and generously with pepper, and brought the skillet to the table. After his first bite, my husband, obviously pleased, ate that simple peasant dish with great gusto and deep satisfaction.

1 medium head cauliflower (about 2½ pounds)	Salt and freshly ground black pepper to taste
⅓ cup extra-virgin olive oil	1 pound penne
¼ pound pancetta, cut in 1 thick slice and diced	2 tablespoons chopped fresh parsley
2 tablespoons plain bread crumbs	

Separate the florets from the cauliflower and cut them into even, small pieces. Wash the florets well under cold running water. Set aside.

Heat the oil in a large skillet over medium heat. Add the pancetta and cook until lightly golden, 1 to 2 minutes. Raise the heat to high and add the bread crumbs. Stir quickly until bread crumbs turn lightly golden, about 10 seconds. Season with salt and generously with pepper. Turn the heat off under the skillet.

Meanwhile, bring a large pot of water to a boil. Add 1 tablespoon of salt, the pasta, and the cauliflower florets. Cook, uncovered, over high heat, stirring occasionally, until the pasta is tender but still a bit firm to the bite. Scoop up and reserve ½ cup of the pasta cooking water.

CONTINUED

Drain the pasta and cauliflower and add it to the skillet. Add the parsley and season the pasta lightly with salt. Add some of the reserved pasta water. Mix everything over low heat until the pasta and sauce are well combined. Taste, adjust the seasoning, and serve.

MEATLESS SAUCE

For a vegetarian version, omit the pancetta and instead sauté the garlic with some thinly sliced green or black olives, chili pepper, and sun-dried tomatoes in oil. Cook the pasta and cauliflower together, drain, and toss with this appetizing sauce.

PASTA WITH SPICY BROCCOLI
Pasta con Broccoli e Peperoncino

SERVES 4 TO 6

During the last five years I seem to have developed a maddening fondness for pasta with vegetables, especially if made with extra-virgin olive oil and hot red pepper. In some regions of Italy, such as Abruzzi, Puglia, Campania, and Lazio, these dishes are tremendously popular. They are also healthy, quick to prepare, and economical.

This dish is a bit unusual because the broccoli is boiled until literally mushy, then cooked again with the tomato sauce until it totally disintegrates into the sauce. I found this dish to be immensely appetizing.

1½ pounds broccoli
Salt to taste
⅓ cup extra-virgin olive oil
2 garlic cloves, minced
Chopped fresh red chili pepper
    or hot red pepper flakes to
    taste
3 cups canned Italian plum
    tomatoes with their juice, put
    through a food mill to
    remove seeds

¼ cup heavy cream
1 pound mezzemaniche,
    rigatoni, or penne
¼ cup freshly grated
    Parmigiano-Reggiano cheese

Separate the florets from the broccoli stalks. Wash the florets well under cold running water. Bring a medium pot of water to a boil. Add a generous pinch of salt and the florets and cook until florets are very tender, almost mushy. Drain the florets, place in a bowl, and set aside until ready to use.

Heat the oil in a large skillet over medium heat. Add the garlic and chili pepper, and cook, stirring, until garlic begins to color, about 1 minute. Add the tomatoes and broccoli, and season with salt. Simmer, stirring and mashing the broccoli down with a wooden spoon, for 5 to 6 minutes. Add the cream, simmer for a minute or two, then turn off the heat.

Meanwhile, bring a large pot of water to a boil. Add 1 tablespoon of salt and the pasta. Cook, uncovered, over high heat, stirring occasionally, until the pasta is tender but still a bit firm to the bite. Scoop up and reserve ½ cup of the pasta cooking water.

Drain the pasta and add it to the sauce. Add the Parmigiano and mix well over low heat until the pasta and sauce are well combined. Add a bit of the reserved pasta water if the sauce looks too dry. Taste, adjust the seasoning, and serve.

PASTA WITH SAUSAGE, RED BELL PEPPERS, AND TOMATO RAGÙ

Pasta con Ragù di Salsiccia, Peperoni, e Pomodori

❧

SERVES 4 TO 6

I n the outskirts of Bologna, the lovely Trattoria dei Cacciatori prepares some delightful pasta. This is one of their dishes. For this dish, use sweet sausage without the addition of fennel or hot pepper.

2 large red bell peppers, roasted
(page 10)

½ pound ripe plum tomatoes,
peeled, seeded, and diced
(page 9)

¼ cup extra-virgin olive oil

⅓ cup finely minced yellow
onion

2 tablespoons finely minced
carrot

2 tablespoons finely minced
celery

¼ pound mild Italian sausage,
casing removed, chopped

½ cup full-bodied red wine

1½ cups canned Italian plum
tomatoes with their juice, put
through a food mill to
remove seeds

1½ cups Basic Chicken Broth
(page 21) or low-sodium
canned chicken broth

Salt and freshly ground black
pepper to taste

1 tablespoon unsalted butter

1 pound penne or shells

⅓ to ½ cup freshly grated
Parmigiano-Reggiano cheese

Cut the peppers into ½-inch pieces. Place in a bowl and set aside. Place the tomatoes in the bowl and set aside.

Heat the oil in a large skillet over medium heat. Add the onion, carrot, and celery and cook, stirring, until the vegetables are lightly golden and soft, 6 to 7 minutes. Raise the heat to high and add the sausage. Stir with a large wooden spoon to break up the sausage, cooking until it looses its raw color, 2 to 3 minutes. Add the wine and cook until it is almost all reduced. Add the diced peppers and tomatoes. Cook, stirring, for a few minutes, then add the canned tomatoes and broth. Season with salt and pepper. Bring the sauce to a boil, then reduce the heat to low and simmer, uncovered, 15 to 20 minutes. Stir the butter into the sauce and turn the heat off under the skillet. Add a bit more broth if the sauce becomes too thick.

Meanwhile, bring a large pot of water to a boil. Add 1 tablespoon of salt and the pasta. Cook, uncovered, over high heat until the pasta is tender but still firm to the bite.

Drain the pasta and place in a large, heated serving bowl. Reheat the sauce if needed, and add half to the pasta with a small handful of Parmigiano. Mix well and add more sauce as needed. Taste, adjust the seasoning, and serve.

PASTA WITH VEAL-PROSCIUTTO RAGÙ WITH MARSALA

Pasta con Ragù alla Romagnola

❧

SERVES 4 TO 6

While I was growing up in Bologna it was possible to guess who was preparing a ragù in the building where I lived by the rhythmical sound of the mezzaluna (half-moon knife) on the chopping board, and by the appetizing aroma that would spread throughout the building. Of the many meat ragùs of Emilia-Romagna, perhaps the most celebrated is *ragù alla Bolognese.* This flavorful, long-simmered ragù is typically paired with tagliatelle, the homemade noodles of Bologna. Another ragù that is positively delicious is *ragù alla Romagnola.* This begins with the essential savory base of sautéed onion, carrot, and celery but gets its particular flavor from veal, prosciutto, and Marsala. The béchamel sauce, added during the last few minutes of cooking, enriches the ragù with its voluptuous, creamy texture.

FOR THE BÉCHAMEL

1 cup milk
2 tablespoons unsalted butter
2 tablespoons all-purpose flour
Pinch of salt
¼ teaspoon freshly grated
  nutmeg

FOR THE RAGÙ

2 tablespoons unsalted butter
2 tablespoons olive oil
½ cup finely minced yellow
  onion
⅓ cup finely minced carrot
⅓ cup finely minced celery
2 tablespoons chopped fresh
  parsley

1 pound ground veal
¼ pound chicken livers
¼ pound finely chopped
  prosciutto
1 cup dry Marsala wine
3 tablespoons tomato paste
  diluted with 3 cups Basic
  Chicken Broth (page 21) or
  low-sodium canned broth
Salt and freshly ground black
  pepper to taste

TO COMPLETE THE DISH

1 pound rigatoni, garganelli,
  penne rigate, or tagliatelle
½ cup freshly grated
  Parmigiano-Reggiano cheese

Prepare the béchamel: Make the sauce as instructed on page 112, using the proportions in this recipe. When the béchamel is done, stir in the nutmeg. Set aside.

Prepare the ragù: Heat the butter and oil in a large skillet over medium heat. Add the onion, carrot, celery, and parsley and cook, stirring, until the vegetables are lightly golden, 4 to 5 minutes. Raise the heat to high and add the veal, chicken livers, and prosciutto. Cook, stirring, until the veal begins to color, 3 to 4 minutes. Add the wine and stir until it is reduced approximately by half. Add the broth mixture and season with salt and pepper. Bring the broth to a boil, then reduce the heat to low and cover the skillet partially. Simmer 1 to 1½ hours, stirring occasionally, until the sauce has a medium-thick consistency. If the sauce reduces too much during cooking, add a little more broth. Stir the béchamel into the sauce, and cook 4 to 5 minutes longer. Taste, adjust the seasoning, and set aside until ready to use. (Makes about 3½ cups sauce.)

Bring a large pot of water to a boil. Add 1 tablespoon of salt and the pasta. Cook, uncovered, over high heat, stirring occasionally, until the pasta is tender but still a bit firm to the bite.

Reheat the sauce if needed. Drain the pasta and add it to a large, heated serving bowl. Add about half of the sauce and half of the Parmigiano, and toss until the pasta is well coated with the ragù. Add a little more sauce if needed. Taste and adjust the seasoning. Take the bowl to the table and serve at once with the additional Parmigiano if desired.

SECRETS OF THE RAGÙ

*The real tricks to this ragù are a perfect browning of the vegetables
and the meat, and a long, slow cooking.*

PASTA WITH SICILIAN PESTO
Pasta con Pesto alla Siciliana

✤

SERVES 4 TO 6

This great summer dish comes from Trapani, a beautiful city on the west coast of Sicily. In Sicily, almonds—an important Sicilian crop—are used instead of pine nuts to make a light pesto. To make this dish outstanding, you need, ripe, juicy tomatoes, green extra-virgin olive oil (preferably from Sicily), and a very light hand with the garlic.

1½ pounds ripe tomatoes, peeled, seeded, and diced (page 9)
¼ cup blanched whole almonds
1½ cups loosely packed fresh basil leaves
1 garlic clove
½ cup extra-virgin olive oil

2 to 3 tablespoons freshly grated pecorino Romano cheese or ⅓ cup freshly grated Parmigiano-Reggiano cheese
Salt to taste
1 pound bucatini, spaghetti, or linguine

Put the diced tomatoes in a strainer and put the strainer over a bowl. Leave for about 1 hour or until the tomatoes lose their watery juices.

Preheat the oven to 350° F. Put the almonds on a cookie sheet and place in the oven until they are lightly golden, 2 to 3 minutes. Remove from oven and cool.

Put the almonds, basil, and garlic in the bowl of a food processor. Add ⅓ cup of the oil and process until smooth. Transfer the pesto to a bowl and stir in the cheese. Taste, adjust the seasoning, and set aside. (Makes approximately ¾ cup pesto.)

Put the tomatoes in a large bowl, add the pesto, and mix well. Add the remaining oil if the mixture looks a bit dry. Taste, adjust the seasoning, and leave at room temperature for about half an hour.

Meanwhile, bring a large pot of water to a boil. Add 1 tablespoon of salt and the pasta. Cook, uncovered, over high heat, stirring a few times, until the pasta is tender but still firm to the bite.

Drain the pasta and place in the bowl. Sprinkle with additional cheese, if desired, and toss until the pasta and sauce are well combined. Taste, adjust the seasoning, and serve.

ZITI WITH PEPPERS AND CRISP BREAD CRUMBS

Ziti con Peperoni e Pane Tostato

SERVES 4 TO 6

In Italy today there seems to be a revival of rustic dishes. They can be found in *trattorie* and certainly in homes. Perhaps the reason is that they are healthy, economical, quick to prepare, pleasing to the eyes, and very, very good.

The bread crumbs here take the place of the cheese, since cheese was once too expensive for the farmers to use on a regular basis. The crispness of the fried bread crumbs makes this dish immensely appetizing.

3 medium red bell peppers
   (about 2 pounds), roasted
   (page 10)
½ cup extra-virgin olive oil
1 garlic clove, finely minced
2 tablespoons capers, rinsed
   and chopped
1 tablespoon chopped fresh
   parsley

Salt to taste
Chopped fresh red chili pepper
   or hot red pepper flakes to
   taste
1 pound ziti, penne, or rigatoni
½ cup loosely packed dry
   crumbs from crustless Italian
   bread

Cut the peppers into ¼-inch-thick strips and set aside.

Heat ⅓ cup of the oil in a large skillet over medium heat. Add the peppers and cook, stirring, for 4 to 5 minutes. Add the garlic and capers, and stir until the garlic begins to color, about 1 minute. Add the parsley, season with salt and chili pepper, and stir well. Turn the heat off under the skillet.

CONTINUED

Meanwhile, bring a large pot of water to a boil. Add 1 tablespoon of salt and the pasta. Cook, uncovered, over high heat until the pasta is tender but still a bit firm to the bite. Scoop up and reserve 1 cup of the pasta cooking water.

While the pasta is cooking, heat the remaining oil in a small skillet over medium-high heat and add the bread crumbs. Stir quickly until bread crumbs begins to color, about 1 minute. Turn the heat off under the skillet.

Drain the pasta and add it to the peppers. Season lightly with salt and put the heat back under the skillet. Add the fried bread crumbs and mix everything quickly over low heat until the pasta is well coated with the sauce. Add a few table-spoons of the reserved cooking water and a bit more oil if pasta looks too dry. Taste, adjust the seasoning, and serve.

TASTY VARIATIONS ON A RUSTIC THEME

Here are some of my favorite improvisations for this dish.

Stir in some cooked broccoli and cauliflower florets with the peppers.

Add some diced fresh tomatoes and sauté 4 to 5 minutes with the peppers.

Add a handful of thinly sliced black or green olives.

Chop 3 or 4 anchovies and add them when you add the garlic.

Omit the red bell peppers and make the dish with just oil, garlic, chili pepper, and bread crumbs.

ZITI WITH NEAPOLITAN PORK RAGÙ

Ziti con Ragù alla Napoletana

※

SERVES 4 TO 6

This is one of those legendary ragùs that Neapolitan mothers and grandmothers ritually prepared on Sundays. The dish generally was begun early in the morning, with the slow browning of the onion, pancetta, pork, and pork spareribs, in a mixture of oil and lard. Strong, scented tomato paste would be stirred into the pot and allowed to turn a rich, brown color. Wine would be added and reduced slowly, while the cook stirred and stirred so that nothing would stick to the bottom of the pot. Then water was added and the ragù would cook at the barest of a simmer for a few hours, until the meat would basically fall apart and the sauce would have a reddish brown color and a rich, aromatic flavor.

I was introduced to this beautiful dish by my mother-in-law, who was a wonderful regional cook. She tossed the sauce with spaghetti and served the meat afterward as a second course. Today this dish is somewhat lighter because the lard and pork spare ribs have been omitted. But the slow cooking, executed with tender loving care, is still there.

⅓ to ½ cup extra-virgin olive oil

2½ pounds center-cut pork loin roast or Boston butt

Salt and freshly ground black pepper to taste

2½ cups finely minced yellow onion

¼ pound pancetta, finely minced

1 cup medium-bodied red wine

1 cup tomato paste

3½ cups water

1 pound ziti, penne, or spaghetti

½ cup freshly grated Parmigiano-Reggiano cheese

Heat the oil in a large wide-bottomed saucepan over medium heat. Season the pork with salt and generously with pepper, and add to the pan. Cook until the pork has a nice golden color on all sides, 5 to 7 minutes. Transfer meat to a plate.

CONTINUED

Add the onion and pancetta to the pan and cook, stirring, until the onion is lightly golden and soft, 7 to 8 minutes. Raise the heat to high, add the wine, and stir until wine is almost all reduced, 4 to 5 minutes. Add the tomato paste and stir quickly and constantly until its color becomes dark red, 4 to 5 minutes. (Stir constantly or the paste will stick to the bottom of the pan.) Add the water, stir thoroughly into the sauce, and bring to a boil. Reduce the heat to low and return the meat to the pan. Cover the pan, leaving the lid slightly askew, and simmer, stirring occasionally, for 1½ to 2 hours. Add a bit more water if liquid reduces too much.

Remove meat from the pan and set aside until ready to use. (It can be served as a second course after the pasta.) Raise the heat to medium and let the sauce bubble gently uncovered, stirring, until it becomes thicker and darker, 5 to 6 minutes. Taste and adjust the seasoning. Keep sauce warm over very low heat.

Meanwhile, bring a large pot of water to a boil. Add 1 tablespoon of salt and the pasta. Cook, uncovered, over high heat until the pasta is tender but still a bit firm to the bite.

Drain the pasta and place in a large heated serving bowl. Add about half of the ragù and ¼ cup of the Parmigiano. Stir quickly and thoroughly until the pasta is well coated with the sauce. Add more sauce as needed. Taste, adjust the seasoning, and serve with the remaining Parmigiano.

A RICH SAUCE MADE RICHER

A little of this rich, full-bodied sauce goes a long way. So you needn't pour it on. Sometimes sausage is added and cooked slowly with the sauce. In that case, the sausage should be browned with the meat, then removed and added to the pan again when the sauce begins to simmer. If sausage is added, it is a good idea to make the sauce a day ahead and refrigerate it, so the next day you can remove some of the solid fat on top. However, don't remove all the fat or the sauce won't have that great rich taste.

SHELLS WITH PORCINI MUSHROOMS, SAUSAGE, AND CREAM
Conchiglie con Porcini, Salsiccia, e Panna

🦌

SERVES 4 TO 6

One of the most succulent dishes of Bologna is *gramigna con la salsiccia*. (*Gramigna* is a special local pasta that looks like thick, short strands of doughy spaghetti.) The traditional *gramigna* sauce is a rich blend of superlative local sausage, porcini mushrooms, butter, and cream. In this version, the sauce has sautéed finely minced vegetables, smoked ham (speck), and saffron, and is paired with shells or penne. This is not one of the lightest dishes in the world, but it is certainly one of the tastiest.

FOR THE SAUCE

1 ounce dried porcini
    mushrooms, soaked in 2 cups
    lukewarm water for
    20 minutes
¼ teaspoon powdered saffron
    (page 12)
2 tablespoons unsalted butter
2 tablespoons extra-virgin
    olive oil
¼ cup finely minced yellow
    onion
¼ cup finely minced carrot
¼ cup finely minced celery
½ pound mild Italian sausage,
    casings removed and finely
    chopped

2 ounces sliced speck or
    prosciutto, finely minced
½ cup dry white wine
1 cup heavy cream
Salt and white pepper to taste
1 to 2 tablespoons chopped
    fresh parsley

TO COMPLETE THE DISH

1 pound shells, penne, rigatoni,
    or fettuccine
½ cup freshly grated
    Parmigiano-Reggiano cheese

Prepare the sauce: Drain the porcini mushrooms and reserve the soaking water. Rinse the mushrooms well under cold running water and chop them roughly. Line a strainer with 2 paper towels and strain the water into a bowl to get rid of the sandy deposits. Stir the saffron into the mushroom water and set aside.

CONTINUED

Heat the butter and oil in a large skillet over medium heat. When the butter begins to foam, add the onion, carrot, and celery and cook, stirring, until the vegetables are lightly golden and soft, 5 to 6 minutes. Raise the heat to high and add the sausage. Stir with a large spoon to break up the sausage into small pieces, and cook until the sausage is golden, 5 to 6 minutes. Add the mushrooms and speck or prosciutto, and stir for a few minutes. Add the wine and reduce it almost completely. Add 1½ cups of the reserved porcini water and the cream. Season with salt and just a bit of white pepper. Bring the sauce to a gentle boil, then reduce the heat to medium-low and simmer, uncovered, until it has a medium-thick consistency, 3 to 4 minutes. Stir in the parsley, taste and adjust the seasoning, and turn the heat off under the skillet.

Meanwhile, bring a large pot of water to a boil. Add 1 tablespoon of salt and the pasta. Cook, uncovered, over high heat, stirring occasionally, until the pasta is tender but still a bit firm to the bite.

Drain the pasta and place it in the skillet with the sauce. Add half of the Parmigiano and mix everything quickly over low heat until the pasta and the sauce are well combined. If pasta looks dry, stir in a little of the remaining porcini soaking water. Serve at once with additional Parmigiano if desired.

La Spaghettata

(SPAGHETTI AT MIDNIGHT)

Spaghetti with Spicy White Tuna Sauce

Spaghetti with Fresh Tuna, Olive Paste, and Tomato Sauce

Spaghetti with Fresh Tomatoes, Pancetta, Cream,
and Worcestershire Sauce

Spaghetti with Tomatoes and Fresh Arugula

Spaghetti with Hot Anchovy Sauce

Spaghetti with Zucchini and Fresh Mint

Spaghetti with Mushrooms Carbonara

Spaghetti with Clams and Saffron

Spaghetti with Fried Bread Crumbs, Pancetta,
and Hot Pepper

Spaghetti with Squid, Tomatoes, and Mint

Spaghetti with Olive Pesto

Whole Wheat Spaghetti with Smoked Mussels

Spaghetti with Mozzarella and Fresh Herbs

Spaghetti with Mushrooms, Speck, and Cream

Spaghetti with Cauliflower, Pine Nuts, and Raisins

Spaghetti with Marinara Sauce

_S_paghetti! A word that immediately conjures up images of a sunny land, blue skies, tranquil seas, and exuberant people. Of the many types of Italian pasta, spaghetti is perhaps the most loved and revered, the least threatening, the most familiar, and the most immediate. In fact, it is spaghetti that many of us reach for when we want to prepare a quick, delicious pasta dish. The thought of a plate of spaghetti dressed with luscious chunks of fresh tomatoes, green basil, and shining green olive oil is enough to set your gastric juices in motion. The twirling of the spaghetti around the fork, and the few strands of spaghetti that fall off the fork in spite of your efforts, makes eating this pasta a joyous act.

The image of spaghetti has come a long way. Once a poor man's staple, spaghetti today is a dish for all occasions. It can be found in homey _trattorie,_ elegant restaurants, fast-food shops, and in the homes of Italians regardless of their place or origin or social status.

Because of its immediacy and the many quick sauces that pair so well with it, spaghetti is generally the pasta choice for impromptu get-togethers. _Ci facciamo una spaghettata?_ ("How about a nice plate of spaghetti?") _La spaghettata_ is an Italian ritual. It takes place generally after a movie, show, or sports event, at someone's home or in an unpretentious _trattoria._ The only rule is that the spaghetti be dressed with an appetizing sauce, that it get to the table quickly, and that it be enjoyed in a spirit of conviviality.

But a _spaghettata_ should not be relegated to those few times. It's perfect food for busy cooks who need to feed their family healthful food quickly and reasonably. Keep a well-stocked pantry at all times: canned tomatoes, anchovies, garlic, sun-dried tomatoes, olives, capers, canned tuna—these are ingredients that can be turned into delicious sauces in no time. Have some fresh vegetables in your refrigerator too: zucchini, tomatoes, and mushrooms can be quickly sautéed with some pancetta or prosciutto. Be adventurous; you have a whole world of possibilities stored on your pantry shelves and in the refrigerator.

In this short chapter every dish can be completed in the time it takes the water to come to a boil and cook the pasta. All these dishes were intended to be stress free. As you gather in the kitchen with your friends or family, you will be able to prepare these dishes as Italians do. Exuberantly and joyfully!

SPAGHETTINI WITH SPICY
WHITE TUNA SAUCE
Spaghettini con Intingolo di Tonno Piccante

This is the type of dish I love to cook on my day off, because it is incredibly quick and delicious. Don't be tempted to "jazz" this dish up with additional ingredients. Try it first as it is, and believe Italians when they say that what you leave out of a dish is probably just as important as what you put in.

1 (7-ounce) can white tuna packed in oil (see Note, below)

⅓ cup extra-virgin olive oil

1 to 2 tablespoons unsalted butter

⅓ cup finely minced yellow onion

3 anchovy fillets, chopped

2 garlic cloves, minced

½ cup dry white wine

2 tablespoons chopped fresh parsley

Salt to taste

Chopped fresh chili pepper or hot red pepper flakes to taste

1 tablespoon unsalted butter

1 pound spaghettini or spaghetti

Drain the tuna of its soaking oil, place on a cutting board, and chop very fine. Set aside.

Heat the oil and butter in a large skillet over medium heat. Add the onion and cook, stirring, until onion is lightly golden, 4 to 5 minutes. Add the anchovies and garlic, and stir for about 1 minute. Add the tuna and stir well into the savory base. Add the wine and cook until wine is almost all reduced. Add the parsley and season with salt and chili pepper. Stir the butter into the sauce and turn the heat off under the skillet.

Meanwhile, bring a large pot of water to a boil. Add 1 tablespoon of salt and the pasta. Cook, uncovered, over high heat, stirring occasionally, until the pasta is tender but still firm to the bite.

Just before you are ready to drain the pasta, scoop up about ½ cup of the cooking water, add to the sauce, and turn the heat on to medium. Drain the pasta and place in a large, heated serving bowl. Add the sauce and toss well until pasta and sauce are well combined. Taste, adjust the seasoning, and serve.

INDISPENSABLE CANNED TUNA

Canned tuna is an indispensable ingredient in the Italian pantry. It is practical, tasty, versatile, and in the hands of the skilled cook, becomes utterly irresistible. Of the many types of canned tuna available today, Italian predilection goes for the soft white tuna packed in oil.

In selecting a favored brand of canned tuna, make sure that its color is uniform without any dark parts in it. The aroma, which is influenced by the olive oil it is packed in, should be pleasantly aromatic, not strong or overpowering. If you have leftover tuna, remove it from the can, discard the oil, place it in a glass bowl, and cover with some fresh oil. Then wrap the bowl tightly with plastic wrap and refrigerate it for a few days.

SPAGHETTI WITH FRESH TUNA, OLIVE PASTE, AND TOMATO SAUCE

Spaghetti con Sugo di Tonno, Pesto di Olive, e Pomodori

SERVES 4 TO 6

Pasta with fresh tuna or swordfish is a standard preparation in Sicilian cooking. In this dish, small chunks of fresh tuna are paired with a quick sauce of tomatoes and olive paste. The pasta is then tossed with the sauce just long enough to absorb the fragrant flavor.

⅓ cup extra-virgin olive oil

1 large garlic clove, peeled and lightly crushed

1½-inch-thick tuna or swordfish steak (about 1 pound), cut into ½-inch cubes

½ cup dry white wine

1 tablespoon black olive paste (see A Simple Italian Pantry, page 221)

4 cups canned Italian plum tomatoes with their juice, put through a food mill to remove seeds

Salt and freshly ground black pepper to taste

2 tablespoons chopped fresh parsley

1 pound spaghetti

Heat the oil in a large skillet over medium heat. Add the garlic and cook until it is golden on all sides. Discard the garlic and add the tuna. Stir for a minute or two until tuna looses its raw color, 1 to 2 minutes. Add the wine and cook until it is reduced approximately by half, about 2 minutes. With a slotted spoon, scoop up the tuna and set aside on a plate.

Stir the olive paste into the remaining wine, then add the tomatoes. Season lightly with salt and generously with pepper, and bring the sauce to a fast simmer. Reduce the heat to medium-low and simmer the sauce, uncovered, 5 to 6 minutes. Return the tuna to the skillet, stir a few times, then add the parsley and turn the heat off under the skillet.

Meanwhile, bring a large pot of water to a boil. Add 1 tablespoon of salt and the spaghetti. Cook, uncovered, over high heat until the pasta is tender but still firm to the bite.

Drain the pasta and place in the skillet with the sauce. Toss everything quickly over low heat until pasta and sauce are well combined. Taste, adjust the seasoning, and serve.

A SIMPLE ITALIAN PANTRY

Olive paste, which can be found in Italian markets and specialty food stores, is an important item in the Italian pantry. With a bit of olive paste, some sun-dried tomatoes, garlic, and good extra-virgin olive oil, you have the basic elements of a quick pasta dish. Some olive pastes are made only with finely minced black or green olives and extra virgin olive oil; others contain anchovies and garlic.

Of the several brands on the market, my favorite is Ardoino. As you use the paste, add just enough oil to the jar to cover the remaining paste. Once the paste is opened, it should be kept tightly sealed in the refrigerator. To make your own olive paste, see Spaghetti with Olive Pesto on page 234.

SPAGHETTI WITH FRESH TOMATOES, PANCETTA, CREAM, AND WORCESTERSHIRE SAUCE
Spaghetti con Pomodori, Pancetta, Panna, e Salsa Worcester

❧

SERVES 4 TO 6

About ten years ago, pasta with vodka sauce became very popular in Italy and could be found all over the country. Today, another foreign ingredient has found its way into pasta dishes: Worcestershire sauce. This aromatic, hot, sweet-and-sour sauce seems to have captured the fancy of many Italian chefs. When I first tested this dish, I cautiously used only a few drops of the hot sauce to avoid overpowering the other ingredients. Then I added more until I found the right balance of flavors. Use Worcestershire sauce as you would salt and pepper. Go easy, taste, and add more if needed.

2 pounds ripe tomatoes, peeled and seeded (page 9)
⅓ cup extra-virgin olive oil
2 garlic cloves, peeled and lightly crushed
¼ pound thickly sliced pancetta, cut into ½-inch pieces

Salt and freshly ground black pepper to taste
¼ cup heavy cream
Worcestershire sauce to taste
1 pound spaghettini or spaghetti

Mince the tomatoes very fine and set aside with all their juices until ready to use.

Heat the oil in a large skillet over medium heat. Add the garlic and cook until it is golden on all sides. Discard the garlic and add the pancetta. Cook, stirring, until the pancetta is lightly golden, about 2 minutes. Add the tomatoes, season with salt and pepper, and cook, stirring occasionally, for 4 to 5 minutes. Add the cream and Worcestershire sauce, stir for a minute or so, and turn the heat off under the skillet.

Meanwhile, bring a large pot of water to a boil. Add 1 tablespoon of salt and the spaghetti. Cook, uncovered, over high heat until the pasta is tender but still a bit firm to the bite. Scoop up and reserve about 1 cup of the pasta cooking water.

Drain the pasta and place in the skillet with the sauce. Toss everything quickly over low heat until pasta and sauce are well combined. Add some of the reserved pasta water if pasta seems a bit dry. Taste, adjust the seasoning, and serve at once.

SPAGHETTI WITH TOMATOES AND FRESH ARUGULA

Spaghetti con Sugo di Pomodori e la Rucola

※

SERVES 4 TO 6

It was a cool fall day in the heart of the Chianti area of Tuscany. My husband and I were hungry, as we always seem to be when we are in Italy, and a *trattoria* had been recommended to us by the manager of our hotel. I wanted pasta, and so did my husband, but we wanted something simple to counteract the rich meal of the night before. So we opted for spaghetti with fresh arugula. It was such an amazing, delicious dish that the day after we went back to Trattoria alla Piazza in Castellina for more. The secret of the dish is quite simple: the best olive oil and the best plum tomatoes. Combine the sauce with the cooked spaghetti, then add the arugula and toss the pasta just like a salad. The arugula retains its distinctive taste and green color.

3 bunches fresh arugula (about 1 pound)

⅓ cup extra-virgin olive oil

1 large garlic clove, peeled and lightly crushed

1 tablespoon finely minced Italian sun-dried tomatoes

4 cups canned Italian plum tomatoes with their juice, put through a food mill to remove seeds

Salt to taste

Chopped fresh red chili pepper or hot red pepper flakes to taste

1 pound spaghetti or spaghettini

Detach the arugula leaves from the stems and tear the leaves into small pieces. Wash the arugula well under cold running water, pat dry, and set aside.

Heat the oil in a large skillet over medium-high heat. Add the garlic, brown on all sides, and discard it. Add the sun-dried tomatoes and stir quickly once or twice. Add the tomatoes and season with salt and hot pepper. Cook, stirring occasionally, until the sauce has a medium-thick consistency, 6 to 7 minutes.

Meanwhile, bring a large pot of water to a boil. Add 1 tablespoon of salt and the spaghetti. Cook, uncovered, over high heat until the pasta is tender but still firm to the bite.

Drain the pasta and place in the skillet with the sauce. Toss everything together over low heat until the pasta and sauce are well combined. Taste and adjust the seasoning. Turn the heat off and add the arugula liberally. Toss the pasta just like a salad and serve at once.

SPAGHETTI WITH HOT ANCHOVY SAUCE
Spaghetti alla Bagna Cauda

❧

SERVES 4 TO 6

One of the most celebrated dishes of Piemonte is *bagna cauda* ("hot bath"), a dip for vegetables made with sweet butter, olive oil, garlic, and lots of anchovies. The traditional way to serve this dish is with winter vegetables, which are dipped into the mixture. A nontraditional but highly enjoyable way to use *bagna cauda,* however, is as a sauce for spaghetti. This is what I call happy food. It has no pretense; it is hearty and highly flavorful, quick to prepare, and totally inexpensive. And the little bit of *peperoncino,* or hot red chili pepper, added to the hot sauce doesn't hurt, either.

¼ cup extra-virgin olive oil

3 tablespoons unsalted butter

1 garlic clove finely chopped

8 to 10 anchovy fillets, finely chopped

Salt to taste

1 pound spaghetti or spaghettini

Chopped fresh red chili pepper or hot red pepper flakes to taste

2 tablespoons chopped fresh parsley

Heat the oil and butter in a large skillet over medium-low heat. When the butter begins to foam, reduce the heat to low, add the garlic and anchovies, and season lightly with salt. Cook, stirring constantly with a wooden spoon, for about 10 minutes, making sure that the garlic does not color and the anchovies are cooked to a soft paste.

Meanwhile, bring a large pot of water to a boil. Add 1 tablespoon of salt and the spaghetti. Cook, uncovered, over high heat until the pasta is tender but still firm to the bite.

Drain the spaghetti and place in the skillet with the sauce. Add the hot pepper and parsley, and toss everything well over low heat until pasta and sauce are well combined. Taste, adjust the seasoning, and serve.

SPAGHETTI WITH ZUCCHINI AND FRESH MINT

Spaghetti con le Zucchine e Menta

❧

SERVES 4 TO 6

Pasta, fresh vegetables, and fresh herbs are the cornerstone of the Sicilian diet. In this dish, young zucchini are quickly browned in olive oil and tossed briefly with garlic and mint. The vital ingredient here is, of course, the mint. In its absence, use fresh basil, or that ever-present, wonderful standby, parsley.

2 pounds zucchini (the smallest you can find), sliced into thin rounds
1 pound spaghetti or spaghettini
⅓ to ½ cup extra-virgin olive oil
2 garlic cloves, finely minced

⅓ cup loosely packed shredded fresh mint leaves or a generous handful shredded fresh basil
Salt and freshly ground black pepper to taste

Bring a large pot of water to a boil. Add 1 tablespoon of salt and the spaghetti. Cook, uncovered, over high heat until the pasta is tender but still firm to the bite.

Meanwhile, heat the oil in a large skillet over medium-high heat. Add the zucchini, making sure not to crowd the skillet, and cook until zucchini are golden on both sides. (If necessary cook the zucchini in a couple of batches.) When zucchini are all sautéed, return to the skillet. Add the garlic and mint or basil and season with salt and generously with pepper and stir for about 1 minute.

Drain the pasta and add to the skillet. Season the pasta lightly with salt. Toss well over low heat until pasta and zucchini are well combined. Taste and adjust the seasoning.

SPAGHETTI WITH MUSHROOMS CARBONARA

Spaghetti alla Carbonara Arricchita

❧

SERVES 4 TO 6

Spaghetti alla carbonara is a delicious, much-loved traditional dish of Rome that combines spaghetti with olive oil, crisp golden pancetta, very fresh raw eggs, great Parmigiano-Reggiano cheese, and plenty of black pepper. In this contemporary preparation the classic *carbonara* is enriched with sautéed mushrooms, which bestow additional flavor on an already great dish.

3 egg yolks
1 large egg
⅓ cup heavy cream
Salt and freshly ground black
　　pepper to taste
⅓ cup extra-virgin olive oil
¼ pound thickly sliced pancetta,
　　cut into ½-inch dice

1 pound spaghetti or
　　spaghettini
¾ pound white cultivated
　　mushrooms, wiped clean
　　and thinly sliced
½ cup freshly grated
　　Parmigiano-Reggiano cheese

In a large, shallow serving dish that can later accommodate the pasta, beat the egg yolks and egg with the cream. Season with salt and generously with pepper and set aside.

Heat 2 tablespoons of the oil in a small skillet over medium heat. Add the pancetta and cook until it is golden. Set aside.

Bring a large pot of water to a boil. Add 1 tablespoon of salt and the spaghetti. Cook, uncovered, over high heat until the spaghetti is tender but still a bit firm to the bite.

While the pasta is cooking, heat the remaining 3 tablespoons oil in a large skillet over high heat. When the oil begins to smoke, add the mushrooms, making sure not to crowd the skillet, and cook until they are golden, 2 to 3 minutes. (If necessary, cook mushrooms in a couple of batches.) With a slotted spoon, transfer the mushrooms to a bowl.

Drain the spaghetti and place in the dish with the eggs. Add the pancetta and its cooking fat, the mushrooms, and about half of the Parmigiano and mix quickly and thoroughly until pasta is well coated with the sauce. Taste, adjust the seasoning, and serve with additional Parmigiano.

SPAGHETTI WITH CLAMS AND SAFFRON

Spaghetti con Vongole e Zafferano

❧

SERVES 4 TO 6

A plate of golden spaghetti laced with clams and dotted with red chili pepper and fresh parsley is, for me, one of the most beautiful of all Italian dishes. Make sure not to go overboard with the saffron—too much will overpower the dish.

½ cup extra-virgin olive oil
Juice of 1 large lemon
4 pounds manilla clams (or the smallest you can find), cleaned (page 11)
¼ teaspoon powdered saffron (page 12)
1 garlic clove, finely minced
Chopped fresh red chili pepper or hot red pepper flakes to taste

½ cup dry white wine
Salt to taste
1 pound spaghetti or spaghettini
1 to 2 tablespoons chopped fresh parsley

Put 2 tablespoons of the oil and the lemon juice in a large skillet and place over medium heat. Add the clams, cover the skillet, and cook until clams open. Transfer them to a bowl as they open. Toss out any clams that do not open. Detach the clam meat from the shells and place in a bowl. Line a small strainer with paper towels and strain the clam juices. Add the saffron to the juices, mix well, and set aside.

Wipe the skillet clean with paper towels, and put it over medium heat with the remaining olive oil. Add the garlic and chili pepper, and stir for less than a minute. Add the wine and cook until it is reduced approximately by half, 2 to 3 minutes. Add the reserved clam juices, season with salt, and stir for a minute or two until the juices begin to thicken. Add the clam meat, stir once or twice, then turn the heat off under the skillet.

Meanwhile, bring a large pot of water to a boil. Add 1 tablespoon of salt and the spaghetti. Cook, uncovered, over high heat until the pasta is tender but still a bit firm to the bite. Scoop up and reserve about 1 cup of the pasta cooking water.

Drain the pasta and add to the skillet. Add the parsley and season lightly with salt. Toss well over low heat until pasta and sauce are well combined. Add some of the reserved pasta water if pasta looks a bit dry. Taste, adjust the seasoning, and serve.

SPAGHETTI WITH FRIED BREAD CRUMBS, PANCETTA, AND HOT PEPPER
Spaghetti alla Carrettiera Arricchita

SERVES 4 TO 6

Some of my favorite pasta dishes are the ones rooted in the peasant tradition. Here, pancetta, anchovies, garlic, chili pepper, and bread crumbs are turned into a terrific sauce. The fried bread crumbs, used instead of the more expensive cheese, coat the pasta with a delightful crispness. The large amount of oil is necessary because the bread crumbs soak it up considerably. Do not add pasta water to this preparation, for it will make the bread crumbs soggy.

1 pound spaghetti or
spaghettini
½ cup extra-virgin olive oil
¼ pound thickly sliced
pancetta, cut into thin strips
3 anchovy fillets, finely
chopped
1 large garlic clove, finely
minced

Chopped fresh red chili pepper
or hot red pepper flakes to
taste
2 tablespoons plain bread
crumbs
2 tablespoons chopped fresh
parsley

Bring a large pot of water to a boil. Add 1 tablespoon of salt and the spaghetti. Cook, uncovered, over high heat until the spaghetti is tender but still firm to the bite.

Heat the oil in a large skillet over medium heat. Add the pancetta and cook, stirring, until it is lightly golden, about 2 minutes. Add the anchovies, garlic, and hot pepper and stir less than a minute. Raise the heat to high, add the bread crumbs, and stir quickly until the bread crumbs are lightly golden, 5 to 10 *seconds*. (Keep your eyes on the skillet because the bread crumbs will turn golden in no time at all.) Turn the heat off under the skillet.

Drain the spaghetti and place in the skillet with the sauce. Add the parsley and season the pasta lightly with salt. Toss everything well over low heat until pasta and sauce are well combined. Taste, adjust the seasoning, and serve.

SPAGHETTI WITH SQUID, TOMATOES, AND MINT

Spaghetti con Calamari, Pomodori, e Menta

꩜

SERVES 4 TO 6

This is a typical dish of southern Italy where a small amount of fish is used in conjunction with tomatoes and fresh herbs and turned into a most lively sauce for pasta. The distinctive touch here is the fresh mint which imparts a clean, fresh taste to the dish.

⅓ cup extra-virgin olive oil

1 large garlic clove, peeled and lightly crushed

⅓ cup finely chopped yellow onion

2 to 3 anchovy fillets, chopped

Chopped fresh red chili pepper or hot red pepper flakes to taste

4 cups canned Italian plum tomatoes with their juice, put through a food mill to remove seeds

Salt to taste

¾ pound whole squid, cleaned (page 12), or ½ pound cleaned squid, cut into ¼-inch rings

6 to 8 fresh mint leaves, chopped

1 tablespoon chopped fresh parsley

1 pound spaghetti or spaghettini

Heat the oil in a large skillet over medium heat. Add the garlic and brown on all sides. Discard the garlic and add the onion, anchovies, and chili pepper. Cook, stirring, until onion is lightly golden, 4 to 5 minutes. Add the tomatoes and season with salt. Cook, uncovered, stirring occasionally for 4 to 5 minutes. Add the squid, mint, and parsley. Reduce the heat to medium-low and simmer 2 to 3 minutes longer. Taste and adjust the seasoning.

Meanwhile, bring a large pot of water to a boil. Add 1 tablespoon of salt and the spaghetti. Cook, uncovered, stirring, occasionally, until the pasta is tender but still firm to the bite.

Drain the pasta and place in a skillet with the sauce. Toss over low heat until the pasta and sauce are well combined. Taste, adjust the seasoning, and serve.

⁂

NOTE

Do not cook the squid longer than a few minutes or they will become tough.

REPLACING TOMATOES WITH BREAD CRUMBS

Here's an interesting spin on this dish:

⁂ *Heat the oil and sauté the squid for less than 1 minute.*

⁂ *Add the garlic and chili pepper and stir a few times.*

⁂ *Add the bread crumbs and stir until they turn lightly golden, less than 1 minute.*

⁂ *Stir in the mint and the cooked spaghetti.*

⁂ *Add some of the spaghetti cooking water if needed.*

SPAGHETTI WITH OLIVE PESTO
Spaghetti al Pesto di Olive

❧

SERVES 4 TO 6

This simple but extremely flavorful dish has many variations. It is a dish that lets you play with flavorful ingredients, mixing and matching them to suite your taste. The spicy pecorino makes a terrific match but if it is too assertive, use Parmigiano-Reggiano.

FOR THE OLIVE PESTO

1 cup pitted black olives
3 anchovy fillets
2 tablespoons capers
1 garlic clove, peeled
1 tablespoon minced sun-dried tomatoes
½ cup extra-virgin olive oil
1 heaping tablespoon freshly grated pecorino Romano cheese or 3 tablespoons freshly grated Parmigiano-Reggiano cheese

Salt and freshly ground black pepper to taste

TO COMPLETE THE DISH

1 pound spaghetti or spaghettini
Salt and freshly ground black pepper to taste
1 to 2 tablespoons chopped fresh parsley

Prepare the olive pesto: Combine all the ingredients except the cheese and seasoning in a food processor and pulse the machine on and off until the ingredients are finely minced but not completely pureed. Transfer the pesto to a bowl, stir in the pecorino or Parmigiano, and season lightly with salt and pepper. Set aside. (Makes approximately 1½ cups pesto.)

Bring a large pot of water to a boil. Add 1 tablespoon of salt and the spaghetti. Cook, uncovered, over high heat until the spaghetti is tender but still a bit firm to the bite. Scoop up about 1 cup of the pasta cooking water and put half of it in a large skillet. Put the skillet over medium heat and let the water come to a full boil.

Drain the pasta and place in the skillet. Season with salt and pepper. Add the parsley and about 1 cup of the olive pesto. Toss everything quickly until pasta and sauce are well combined. Add a bit more reserved pasta water or pesto if needed. Taste, adjust the seasoning, and serve.

WHOLE WHEAT SPAGHETTI
WITH SMOKED MUSSELS
Spaghetti Integrali con Cozze Affumicate

🦐

SERVES 4 TO 6

I love the flavor and texture of smoked mussels paired with whole wheat pasta. Smoked scallops or smoked fish can also be used.

Today many supermarkets and specialty food stores carry fresh or frozen smoked mussels and scallops. These are excellent items to keep in your freezer so that you can whip up a great plate of pasta whenever you want it.

⅓ cup extra-virgin olive oil
1 pound ripe tomatoes, peeled, seeded, and diced (page 9)
1 tablespoon finely minced sun-dried tomatoes
1 garlic clove, finely minced
1 pound smoked mussels, each cut into 3 or 4 pieces

Salt and freshly ground black pepper to taste
1 pound spaghetti or spaghettini
2 tablespoons chopped fresh parsley

Heat the oil in a large skillet over medium heat. Add the fresh and dried tomatoes and cook, stirring, for 2 to 3 minutes. Add the garlic and stir once or twice. Add the smoked mussels, season with salt and pepper, and stir for a minute or two.

Meanwhile, bring a large pot of water to a boil. Add 1 tablespoon of salt and the spaghetti. Cook, uncovered, over high heat until spaghetti is tender but still a bit firm to the bite. Scoop up and reserve about 1 cup of the pasta cooking water.

Drain the spaghetti and place in the skillet with the sauce. Add the parsley and ½ cup of the reserved water, and season lightly with salt. Toss everything quickly over low heat until pasta and sauce are well combined. Add remaining pasta water if needed. Taste, adjust the seasoning, and serve.

SPAGHETTI WITH MOZZARELLA AND FRESH HERBS

Spaghetti con Mozzarella e Erbe Miste

❧

SERVES 4 TO 6

This dish was inspired by a great Roman appetizer of skewered bread and mozzarella brushed generously with garlic and anchovies. I reasoned that if those appetizing ingredients were good for the bread, they would be equally good with pasta. And they were.

After you have made this dish a few times, improvise. For example, add a few ripe, diced tomatoes to the garlic and anchovies; use smoked mozzarella instead of the fresh mozzarella; add some fresh red chili pepper; or omit the mozzarella and increase the amount of herbs.

1 pound spaghetti or spaghettini
⅓ to ½ cup extra-virgin olive oil
2 garlic cloves, minced
3 to 4 anchovy fillets, chopped
1 tablespoon minced sun-dried tomatoes
Salt and freshly ground black pepper to taste
⅓ to ½ cup loosely packed roughly chopped fresh herbs (basil, oregano, mint, thyme, and parsley)
½ pound fresh mozzarella, cut into small cubes

Bring a large pot of water to a boil. Add 1 tablespoon of salt and the spaghetti. Cook, uncovered, over high heat until the pasta is tender but still a bit firm to the bite. Scoop up and reserve about 1 cup of the pasta water.

Heat the oil in a large skillet over medium heat. Add the garlic, anchovies, and sun-dried tomatoes and stir for about 1 minute.

Drain the pasta and place it in the skillet. Season lightly with salt and generously with pepper. Add about ½ cup of the reserved pasta water and the fresh herbs. Stir well over low heat to combine. Add the mozzarella (see A Quick Melt, page 237) and a bit more pasta water if needed. Stir once or twice, taste, adjust the seasoning, and serve.

SPAGHETTI WITH MUSHROOMS, SPECK, AND CREAM

Spaghetti con Funghi, Speck, e Panna

SERVES 4 TO 6

Pasta, mushrooms, and smoked ham are an unbeatable combination. Any type of mushroom will do. If you live in a large city where unusual ingredients are easily available, look for porcini mushrooms, portobello, or shiitake. If not, use white cultivated mushrooms.

⅓ cup extra-virgin olive oil

½ pound mushrooms, wiped clean and thinly sliced (see **Preparing Portobellos,** page 238)

¼ pound thickly sliced speck or prosciutto, cut into small strips

1 garlic clove, finely minced

1 cup heavy cream

½ cup low-sodium canned chicken broth

Salt and freshly ground black pepper to taste

1 pound spaghetti or spaghettini

1 tablespoon unsalted butter

1 to 2 tablespoons chopped fresh parsley

⅓ to ½ cup freshly grated Parmigiano-Reggiano cheese

Heat the oil in a large skillet over high heat. When the oil begins to smoke, add the mushrooms, making sure not to crowd the skillet, and cook until golden, 1 to 2 minutes. (If necessary, cook mushrooms in a couple of batches.)

CONTINUED

Reduce the heat to medium and add the speck and garlic. Stir quickly a few times, then add the cream and broth. Season with salt and pepper, and simmer the sauce for about 2 to 3 minutes, or until it has a medium-thick consistency.

Meanwhile, bring a large pot of water to a boil. Add 1 tablespoon of salt and the spaghetti. Cook, uncovered, over high heat until the pasta is tender but still firm to the bite.

Drain the spaghetti and place in the skillet with the sauce. Add the butter and parsley, and toss everything quickly over low heat until pasta and sauce are well combined. If pasta seems a bit dry, add a bit more cream or broth. Taste, adjust the seasoning, and serve with a light sprinkling of freshly grated Parmigiano.

PREPARING PORTOBELLOS

If using portobello mushrooms, wipe clean with a moist towel. Remove the stems and the dark gills beneath the caps. Slice the mushrooms thinly and, if slices are too long, cut them in half.

SPAGHETTI WITH CAULIFLOWER, PINE NUTS, AND RAISINS
Spaghetti con i Broccoli Arriminati

SERVES 4 TO 6

This splendid pasta dish sets aside the notion that Sicilian food is perennially tinged with tomatoes and garlic. This traditional dish pairs pasta with an unusual sauce of cauliflower, onion, pine nuts, raisins, and saffron.

1 small head cauliflower (about
2 pounds), broken into small
florets
1 pound spaghetti or
spaghettini
¼ teaspoon powdered saffron
(page 12)
⅓ cup extra-virgin olive oil
⅓ cup finely minced yellow
onion
4 anchovy fillets, chopped
⅓ cup pine nuts
½ cup raisins, soaked in
lukewarm water to cover
until soft and drained

Salt and freshly ground black
pepper to taste
1 to 2 tablespoons chopped
fresh parsley
2 to 3 tablespoons freshly
grated pecorino Romano
cheese or ¼ cup freshly
grated Parmigiano-Reggiano
cheese

Bring a large pot of water to a boil. Wash the florets under cold running water, then add to the boiling water with 1 tablespoon of salt. Cook, uncovered, over high heat until tender, 7 to 10 minutes depending on size. With a large slotted spoon or a skimmer, scoop up the florets and place in a bowl.

Add the spaghetti to the boiling water and cook until tender but still firm to the bite. Scoop up about 1 cup of the cooking water. Mix the saffron with the water and set aside.

While the pasta is cooking, heat the oil in a large skillet over medium-low heat. Add the onion and anchovies, and cook, stirring occasionally, until the onion is lightly golden and soft, 6 to 7 minutes. Raise the heat to medium and add the pine nuts, raisins, and cauliflower florets. Season with salt and pepper. Cook for a minute or two, stirring and breaking down the florets into smaller pieces.

Drain the spaghetti and place in the skillet with the sauce. Season the pasta lightly with salt. Add about half of the reserved saffron water, the parsley, and the pecorino or Parmigiano. Toss everything over low heat until pasta and sauce are well combined. Add more saffron water if pasta seems a bit dry. Taste, adjust the seasoning, and serve.

SPAGHETTI WITH MARINARA SAUCE
Spaghetti alla Marinara

❧

SERVES 4 TO 6

A marinara sauce implies some type of seafood. Curiously, however, the typical marinara sauce is made with tomatoes, garlic, and lots of fresh oregano, without any trace whatsoever of seafood. There are many theories for this, from the need of sailors to make a quick sauce to toss with their pasta before going out to sea, to the fact that they needed the revenues from the sale of the fish they caught to survive. Whatever the reason, this marinara sauce is delicious and quick to prepare. Fresh oregano is the secret ingredient. If not available, use dried oregano with a light hand or double the amount of fresh basil.

⅓ cup extra-virgin olive oil
2 garlic cloves, finely minced
4 cups canned Italian plum tomatoes with their juice, put through a food mill to remove seeds
Salt and freshly ground black pepper to taste
Chopped fresh red chili pepper or hot red pepper flakes to taste (optional)

½ cup loosely packed fresh oregano leaves or 1 teaspoon dried
⅓ cup loosely packed fresh basil leaves, finely shredded
1 pound spaghetti or spaghettini

Heat the oil in a large skillet over medium heat. Add the garlic and stir just long enough for the garlic to begin to color, less than 1 minute. Add the tomatoes, season with salt and pepper, and add the chili pepper if using. As soon as the sauce comes to a boil, reduce the heat just a bit and cook the sauce at a lively simmer, stirring occasionally, until it has a medium-thick consistency, 8 to 10 minutes. Add the oregano and basil during the last few minutes of cooking.

Meanwhile, bring a large pot of water to a boil. Add 1 tablespoon of salt and the spaghetti. Cook, uncovered, over high heat until the spaghetti is tender but still firm to the bite. Drain the pasta and place in the skillet with the sauce. Toss well over low heat until the pasta and sauce are well combined. Serve hot.

Risotto and Rice Dishes

Risotto with Butter and Parmigiano-Reggiano

FISH RISOTTI

Risotto with Salmon and Lemon Zest
Risotto of the Fisherman
Risotto with Shrimp and Fresh Tomatoes
Risotto with Monkfish, Saffron, and Peas
Risotto with Mussels, Tomatoes, and Chili Pepper
Risotto with Squid
Risotto with Squid and Tomatoes
Risotto with Smoked Salmon and Mascarpone
Risotto with Clams, Mussels, and Spicy Broccoli
Risotto with Ligurian White Fish Sauce

VEGETABLE RISOTTI

Risotto with Roasted Red Bell Peppers
Milanese Risotto with Mushrooms
Risotto with Corn and Saffron
Risotto with Speck and Artichoke Hearts
Risotto with Butternut Squash and Peas
Risotto with Roasted Butternut Squash

Risotto with Cabbage and Pancetta
Risotto with Beans and Cabbage
Risotto with Mushrooms and Tomatoes
Risotto with Savory Tomato Sauce
Risotto with Fresh Tomatoes and Basil

CHEESE RISOTTI

Risotto with Tomatoes and Smoked Mozzarella
Risotto with Gorgonzola
Risotto with Three Cheeses

MEAT RISOTTI

Risotto with Sausage, Porcini, and Tomatoes
Risotto with Sausage, Beans, and Red Wine
Risotto with Pork Ragù
Risotto with Duck Ragù
Risotto with Lamb Ragù
Risotto with Pan-Roasted Quail
Risotto with Veal and Peas
Risotto with Veal and Porcini Mushrooms

Risotto with Blueberries

RICE TIMBALLOS AND SAVORY BOILED RICE DISHES

Rice with Sicilian Stewed Peppers
Rice with Fontina Cheese
Rice with Milk, Butter, and Parmigiano
Rice with Cauliflower
Saffron Risotto Timballo with Glazed Mushrooms
Risotto Timballo with Sausage Stew
Risotto Timballo with Eggplant and Zucchini

*R*isotto, a rice dish, is one of the most splendid of all Italian preparations. Riso—rice, not pasta—is the dominant staple of many northern Italian regions where it is cultivated, particularly Piedmont, Lombardy, and the Veneto.

Preparing risotto utilizes a cooking technique that is uniquely northern Italian. While most of the world boils or steams their rice, northern Italians braise it with savory ingredients in a flavorful broth which imparts wonderful color and flavor. The possibilities for the flavor base of risotto are endless. Savory meats, cheeses, vegetables, herbs, sausage, ragùs, shellfish, or game are added at different stages of the cooking process, giving risotto an ever-changing identity. It is one of the most versatile dishes in Italian gastronomy.

THE INGREDIENTS

Two ingredients always part of a risotto are rice and broth. To make a perfect risotto, you need the appropriate rice. Of the many varieties of rice that Italy grows, three lead the pack as favorite choices for risotto:

- *Arborio*—Its large, plump grain is rich in starch, which dissolves while cooking to give the rice a very creamy texture while retaining its firmness. Arborio is widely available in Italian markets and specialty food stores.
- *Vialone Nano*—A medium-grain rice with a resilient starch that does not dissolve as easily as Arborio rice does. This rice is very popular in the Veneto region.
- *Carnaroli*—Also rich in soft starch, like Arborio rice it dissolves easily in cooking while retaining an al dente quality. Carnaroli is often the choice of chefs and food professionals in Italy.

Another important ingredient in the cooking of risotto is the liquid, since it has the dual function of cooking the rice and adding flavor. Homemade meat broth, chicken broth, fish broth, and vegetable broth are used alternately in this chapter. A homemade broth has a richness of taste that no canned or instant broth will ever achieve. However, for those days when it is virtually impossible to prepare the real thing, I have added a quick broth (page 25), which can be whipped up in 20 minutes, as well as the substitutes of low-sodium canned chicken or beef broth.

THE COOKING TECHNIQUE

A risotto is begun by sautéing chopped onion in butter or, on occasion, in olive oil. This is the flavor base to which rice is added and quickly sautéed for a couple of minutes until it is coated with the fat in the pan. (The fat protects the rice from breaking.) This step is called *tostatura,* "toasting the rice."

Often a splash of wine is added to the rice and is quickly allowed to evaporate. Then the rice is cooked briskly with a small addition of hot broth and stirred constantly until all the broth has been absorbed. Then a bit more broth is added and the cooking process is repeated until the rice is done. This cooking technique allows the rice to slowly release its starch while absorbing the flavors of the other ingredients in the pan. The constant stirring of the rice is essential to avoid sticking and burning.

Butter and, except for seafood risotto, Parmigiano are stirred into the rice during the last few minutes of cooking. This step is called *mantecare,* meaning "to stir together," and it gives the steaming mass of risotto its velvety, creamy texture.

Regional cooking styles determine the consistency of a finished risotto. For example, in the Veneto, the finished risotto is always somewhat soft and a bit running—*all'onda,* or "with a wave." In my region of Emilia-Romagna, as well as in Piedmont and Lombardy, the finished risotto is tighter and not as soft. Needless to say, cooking risotto is a matter of preference.

When I was a cooking teacher years ago, I urged my students to begin their risotto cooking adventure with the simplest, purest of all risotti, *risotto alla Parmigiana* (page 247) so that they would get the method down before trying more complex preparations. I urged them to look into the pot and see the changes that occur during the cooking: the onion that becomes soft and pale yellow; the rice that changes from chalky white to translucent and is totally coated with the fat in the skillet; the metamorphosis of the rice as it grows, turning plumper and creamier until it swells into a large, soft mass. All these signs will teach more about the dish than a recipe ever can.

In this chapter, there is a wonderful assortment of risotti. Some are made with fresh vegetables and are light and delicate. Others are made with seafood and shellfish. (Try the one with clams, mussels, and spicy broccoli—it is divine. . . .) And others have the addition of meat ragùs or savory sauces, which make them perfect dishes for cold, wintry days.

When I was working on this chapter, I tested so many risotti that I developed a corn on the middle finger of my right hand because of all the stirring. However, the reward was that my husband, my kitchen crew, and I ate risotto almost daily. The following are what I call *I consigli del buon senso*—good, commonsense advice to guide you in cooking your first risotto.

MAKING RISOTTO AT HOME

First, the bad news. Risotto, like pasta, should not be prepared ahead of time or the rice will become overcooked and sticky when reheated. In an ideal world, a risotto should be made and served immediately after it is done. That is when the risotto looks and tastes best. Now for the details and tips.

- Sauté the onion. Add the rice and stir it for a couple of minutes until the rice is translucent and completely coated with the fat in the skillet. Turn the heat off under the skillet and cover it with a lid. You can prepare the rice up to this point a few hours ahead. Once the onion and rice are reheated and the first ladle of hot broth is added, it will take no longer than 15 to 18 minutes to complete the dish.

- The exact cooking time depends on the heat you are using, the size of your burner, the type of pot, and so on. I like to use a large, heavy skillet so that the rice has plenty of space to grow. When I am home, I use a Calphalon skillet; when I am at my restaurant, I use a heavy aluminum restaurant skillet or sauté pan.

- Make sure the broth for the risotto is hot, and always have a little more on hand. If you run out of broth, heat some water and use it in place of broth. Never use more liquid than called for.

- Be careful with salt. Keep in mind that the broth is already seasoned and most of the time the sauce or ragù that goes into the risotto will be seasoned as well.

- It is not necessary to wash the rice before using it.

- Prepare all the ingredients for the risotto in advance. Chop, mince, dice, and line up the ingredients on a tray in the order in which you will use them so that the actual cooking is effortless and relaxing.

- The most used word in a recipe for risotto is *stir*. You need to stir, stir, stir, or you won't have a risotto to speak of.

- Risotto is always cooked uncovered over medium heat. A risotto is never cooked in a double boiler or microwave oven. The look, taste, texture, and consistency of a risotto is achieved only by cooking the rice with the risotto technique.

🐜 During the last few minutes of cooking you need to watch the risotto like a newborn baby—very carefully. Be stingy with the amount of broth you add. Stir constantly and taste often so that you know when it is time to stop the cooking.

🐜 How long should a risotto cook? Well, that's debatable. Because there are so many variables and so many personal preferences, the best way to know is to taste. For me, the risotto is ready within 18 to 20 minutes. If you find the rice too firm for your taste, cook it a few more minutes.

Now that you have read this well-meaning advice, forget about it. Just get to the stove and start cooking. Perhaps your very first risotto will not go down in history, but I can assure you that practice makes perfect: the more risotto you cook, the better it will become.

OTHER RICE DISHES·

In this chapter you will also find several boiled rice dishes and timballos. There is a Rice with Milk, Butter, and Parmigiano (page 304\) that my mother prepared for us children and for my grandmother. (Rice boiled in milk is also popular in several other northern Italian regions.) There is a Rice with Fontina Cheese (page 303) that comes from Piedmont and one from Sicily that is tossed with stewed peppers. These are dishes that come in handy when you are in the mood for a quick and delicious rice dish. Then there is the timballo, an impressive molded rice dish that originated centuries ago in Arab countries. Of course, Italians use a great deal of rice in their soups as well, but that is another chapter altogether.

RISOTTO WITH BUTTER AND PARMIGIANO-REGGIANO

Risotto alla Parmigiana

᯽

SERVES 4 TO 6

This is perhaps the simplest and most basic of all risotti. It is the first risotto I taught my daughters because the sparseness of the ingredients allowed them to concentrate entirely on technique. If you have never made a risotto before, I urge you to begin with this one. Pay attention, however, to the ingredients, which must be of top quality. The Parmigiano-Reggiano should be the real McCoy. The butter should be unsalted, and the chicken broth should be homemade. Whatever effort you put into this dish will be highly rewarded.

6 cups Basic Chicken Broth (page 21) or low-sodium canned chicken broth

4 tablespoons unsalted butter

½ cup finely minced yellow onion

2 cups imported Arborio rice or other rice for risotto

½ cup dry white wine

½ cup freshly grated Parmigiano-Reggiano cheese

Heat the broth in a medium saucepan and keep warm over low heat.

Melt 3 tablespoons of the butter in a large skillet over medium heat. Add the onion and cook, stirring, until the onion is pale yellow and soft, 4 to 5 minutes. Add the rice and stir quickly for a minute or two until the rice is translucent and is well coated with the butter. Stir in the wine and keep stirring until it is almost all reduced. Add ½ cup of the simmering broth or just enough to barely cover the rice. Cook, stirring, until the broth has been absorbed almost completely. Continue cooking and stirring the rice in this manner, adding broth ½ cup or so at a time for about 18 minutes. Taste the rice to determine its doneness, which at this point should be tender but still a bit firm to the bite.

When the last addition of broth is almost all reduced, add the remaining tablespoon butter and ⅓ cup of the Parmigiano. Stir quickly until the butter and cheese are melted and the rice has a moist, creamy consistency. Taste, adjust the seasoning, and serve with a sprinkling of additional Parmigiano if desired.

CONTINUED

Fish Risotti

RISOTTO WITH SALMON AND LEMON ZEST

Risotto con Salmone e Limone

SERVES 4 TO 6

Every time I make a risotto I am fascinated by the way the plump grains of the rice absorb the liquid and grow in front of my eyes. This risotto, which has just a hint of lemon and is enriched by the Champagne, is as delicate as it is elegant. It is also one of the easiest risotti to make. You can substitute lobster or shrimp for the salmon. Cut the lobster or shrimp into ½-inch pieces and use as instructed in the recipe.

3 cups Basic Fish Broth
   (page 23) or low-sodium
   chicken broth mixed with
   3 cups water
4 tablespoons unsalted butter
⅓ cup finely minced shallots or
   ½ cup minced yellow onion
2 cups imported Arborio rice or
   other rice for risotto

1 cup medium-dry Champagne
   or dry white wine
¾ pound salmon fillet, cut into
   ½-inch pieces
Grated zest of 1 lemon
1 to 2 tablespoons chopped
   fresh parsley

Heat the broth in a medium saucepan and keep warm over low heat.

Melt 3 tablespoons of the butter in a large skillet over medium heat. When the butter foams, add the shallots or onion and cook, stirring, until pale yellow and soft, 4 to 5 minutes. Add the rice and stir quickly until it is well coated with the butter, 1 to 2 minutes. Add the Champagne or wine, and cook until it is almost all reduced. Add ½ cup of simmering broth or just enough to barely cover the rice. Cook and stir until the broth has been absorbed almost completely. Continue cooking and stirring the rice in this manner, adding the broth ½ cup at a time for 14 to 15 minutes.

Add the salmon and the grated lemon zest to the rice. Cook and stir for 3 to 4 minutes, adding a bit of broth as needed. Add the remaining tablespoon butter and the parsley, and stir until the rice has a moist, creamy consistency. Taste and adjust the seasoning and serve.

RISOTTO OF THE FISHERMAN

Risotto con Scampi, Vongole, e Cozze

❧

This risotto has many variations, and its identity changes depending on the area where it is made, on the type of fish or shellfish used, and on the whim of the cook. For this dish, select the freshest fish available. Do take the time to make the Basic Fish Broth, which will enrich the dish considerably. And be prepared to spend 18 to 20 minutes watching and stirring the rice. In return, you will be rewarded with a really beautiful dish.

FOR THE SHELLFISH

½ cup dry white wine

2 tablespoons olive oil

1½ pounds manilla clams (or the smallest you can get), cleaned (page 11)

1½ pounds medium mussels, cleaned (page 11)

3 cups Basic Fish Broth (page 23) or low-sodium chicken broth mixed with 3 cups water

18 medium shrimp, peeled and deveined

FOR THE RISOTTO

2 to 3 tablespoons extra-virgin olive oil

½ cup finely minced yellow onion

1 garlic clove, finely minced

2 cups imported Arborio rice or other rice for risotto

½ cup dry white wine

1 tablespoon unsalted butter

1 to 2 tablespoons chopped fresh parsley

Prepare the shellfish: Put the wine and oil in a large skillet and place over medium heat. Add the clams and mussels, and cover the skillet. Cook just until the clams and mussels open. Transfer them to a bowl as they open. Line a strainer with paper towels and strain the liquid into a bowl to get rid of the sandy deposits and set aside. (You should have approximately ½ to ¾ cup of liquid.) Detach the meat from the shells, place in a bowl, and pour in the strained liquid.

Bring the broth to a simmer in a medium saucepan. Add the shrimp and cook no longer than 1 minute. With a large slotted spoon, scoop up the shrimp and place in a bowl. As soon as the shrimp are cool enough to handle, cut them into bite-size pieces and return them to the bowl. Keep the broth warm over low heat.

Prepare the risotto: Heat the oil in a large skillet over medium heat. Add the onion and garlic, and cook, stirring, until the onion is pale yellow and soft, 4 to 5 minutes. Add the rice and stir quickly until it is well coated with the oil and onion, 1 to 2 minutes. Add the wine and cook until it is almost all reduced. Add ½ cup of simmering broth or just enough to barely cover the rice. Cook, stirring, until the broth has been absorbed almost completely. Continue cooking and stirring the rice in this manner, adding broth ½ cup at a time for 15 to 16 minutes.

When the last addition of broth is almost all reduced and the rice looks somewhat dry, add the shrimp, mussels, clams, and reserved cooking liquid. Cook, stirring quickly, until the liquid is almost all absorbed, 3 to 4 minutes. Swirl in the butter and parsley, and stir until the rice has a moist, creamy consistency. Taste, adjust the seasoning, and serve.

RISOTTO WITH SHRIMP AND FRESH TOMATOES

Risotto con Scampi e Pomodori

❧

SERVES 4 TO 6

This is a simple yet delicious preparation that can be made basically with any kind of firm-fleshed white fish. At La Mora, an excellent restaurant a few miles outside the city of Lucca, I had it with eels that were cut into small pieces. Knowing that eel is not too popular with Americans, I prepare it with lobster, monkfish, or shrimp. The shrimp can be left whole, as in this recipe, or they can be cut into smaller pieces.

FOR THE SHRIMP AND TOMATO SAUCE

3 to 4 tablespoons extra-virgin olive oil

24 medium shrimp (about 1¼ pounds), peeled and deveined

2 garlic cloves, minced

Chopped fresh red chili pepper or hot red pepper flakes to taste

1½ pounds fresh, ripe tomatoes, peeled, seeded, and diced (page 9)

Salt to taste

FOR THE RISOTTO

6 cups Vegetable Broth (page 24), or 3 cups low-sodium canned chicken broth mixed with 3 cups water

2 to 3 tablespoons extra-virgin olive oil

½ cup finely minced yellow onion

2 cups imported Arborio rice or other rice for risotto

½ cup dry white wine

6 to 8 fresh basil leaves, shredded, or 1 to 2 tablespoons chopped fresh parsley

1 tablespoon unsalted butter

Prepare the shrimp and tomato sauce: Heat the oil in a large skillet over medium heat. Add the shrimp and cook until they are golden on all sides, 1 to 2 minutes. Transfer shrimp to a plate. Add the garlic and chili pepper to the skillet and stir quickly once or twice. (Remember that the skillet is very hot and the garlic will color in no time at all.) Add the diced tomatoes and all their juices, and season with salt. Cook, stirring occasionally, until the tomatoes are soft and the juices have thickened, 4 to 6 minutes. Return the shrimp to the skillet, stir just long enough to mix them with the sauce, then turn the heat off under the skillet. (Makes approximately 3 cups sauce.)

Prepare the risotto: Heat the broth in a medium saucepan and keep warm over low heat.

Heat the oil in a large skillet over medium heat. Add the onion and cook, stirring, until the onion is pale yellow and soft, 4 to 5 minutes. Add the rice and stir quickly until it is well coated with the oil and onion, 1 to 2 minutes. Add the wine and cook, stirring, until it is almost all reduced. Now add ½ cup of simmering broth or just enough to barely cover the rice. Cook and stir until the broth has been absorbed almost completely. Continue cooking and stirring the rice in this manner, adding the broth ½ cup or so at a time for 14 to 15 minutes.

When the last addition of broth is almost all reduced and the rice looks somewhat dry, add about half of the shrimp sauce. Stir quickly for a minute or so until the sauce has been absorbed, then add the remaining shrimp sauce. Stir and cook until most of the sauce has been absorbed and the rice has a moist, creamy consistency. Stir in the basil or parsley and the butter, taste, adjust the seasoning, and serve.

A MOVABLE SAUCE

This sauce is delicious and extremely versatile. It can be used over spaghetti or linguine, or served as an appetizer or an entrée with a few slices of grilled polenta or grilled bread. It can also be enriched with clams and mussels and served as a great seafood stew for lunch or dinner.

RISOTTO WITH MONKFISH,
SAFFRON, AND PEAS

Risotto con Coda di Rospo,
Zafferano, e Piselli

❧

SERVES 4 TO 6

What a beautiful dish this is! Yellow with saffron, speckled with the bright green of the fresh peas and the lovely chunks of the fish. Monkfish can be substituted with any other white, firm-fleshed fish. Blanched asparagus tips or sautéed zucchini can be used instead of peas. By changing a few ingredients you will have created a new dish.

FOR THE MONKFISH

3 tablespoons extra-virgin
   olive oil
2 large garlic cloves, peeled and
   lightly crushed
¾ pound monkfish fillets, cut
   into ½-inch pieces
Salt to taste
½ cup dry white wine

FOR THE RISOTTO

3 cups Basic Fish Broth
   (page 23) or low-sodium
   canned chicken broth mixed
   with 3 cups water

¼ teaspoon powdered saffron
   (page 12)
4 tablespoons unsalted butter
½ cup finely minced yellow
   onion (optional)
2 cups imported Arborio rice or
   other rice for risotto
½ cup dry white wine
1 cup shelled fresh blanched
   peas or thawed frozen peas
Salt (optional)

Prepare the monkfish: Heat the oil in a medium skillet over medium heat. Add the garlic and cook until golden on both sides. Discard the garlic and add the fish to the skillet. Cook, stirring, just long enough for the fish to change color, about 1 minute. Season lightly with salt. Raise the heat to high and add the wine. Stir for a minute or two, until the wine and fish juices have reduced approximately by half. Turn the heat off under the skillet. (Makes approximately 2 cups sauce.)

Prepare the risotto: Heat the broth in a medium saucepan and keep warm over low heat. Place the saffron in a small bowl and add ½ cup of the hot broth. Mix well and set aside until ready to use.

Melt 3 tablespoons of the butter in a large skillet over medium heat. When the butter foams, add the onion and cook, stirring, until the onion is pale yellow and soft, 4 to 5 minutes. Add the rice and stir quickly until it is well coated with the butter and onion, 1 to 2 minutes. Stir in the wine and cook until almost all reduced. Add about ½ cup of simmering broth, or just enough to barely cover the rice. Cook, stirring, until the broth has been absorbed almost completely. Continue cooking and stirring the rice in this manner, adding the broth ½ cup at a time for about 15 minutes.

When the last addition of broth is completely reduced, add the broth with the dissolved saffron and stir until it has been absorbed. Add the peas and about half of the monkfish sauce. Stir quickly for a minute or so, then add remaining sauce and tablespoon butter. Cook, stirring, until most of the liquid has been absorbed and the rice has a moist, creamy consistency, 2 to 3 minutes. Taste, adjust the seasoning, and serve.

CREATING A NEW DISH

Here is a simplified variation on this risotto:

Omit the monkfish sauce.

Begin the risotto in the usual manner and cook it for 15 to 16 minutes.

Mix the saffron with a bit of broth and add that to the risotto.

Stir the raw fish and peas into the risotto and cook 2 to 3 minutes with small addition of broth.

Stir the butter into the risotto and serve.

RISOTTO WITH MUSSELS, TOMATOES, AND CHILI PEPPER

Risotto alle Cozze, Pomodori, e Peperoncino

❦

SERVES 4 TO 6

There was a time when I positively disliked mussels—until the day I tasted my first risotto with mussels on the Adriatic coast. The mussels were plump and fragrant from the sea, a delightful contrast to the bright red tomatoes. Here the tomatoes are added at the beginning of the cooking, rather than at the end, thus softening and breaking apart thoroughly, giving the risotto its red color.

FOR THE MUSSELS

½ cup dry white wine
2 tablespoons extra-virgin
    olive oil
2½ pounds mussels, cleaned
    (page 11)
Salt to taste

FOR THE RISOTTO

3 cups Basic Fish Broth
    (page 23) or low-sodium
    canned chicken broth mixed
    with 3 cups water
2 to 3 tablespoons extra-virgin
    olive oil

½ cup finely minced yellow
    onion
1 garlic clove, finely minced
1 pound ripe tomatoes, peeled,
    seeded, and diced (page 9)
Salt to taste
Chopped fresh red chili pepper
    or hot red pepper flakes to
    taste
2 cups imported Arborio rice or
    other rice for risotto
½ cup dry white wine
1 to 2 tablespoons chopped
    fresh parsley
1 tablespoon unsalted butter

Prepare the mussels: Put the wine and oil in a large skillet and place over medium heat. Add the mussels, season with a bit of salt, and cover the skillet. Cook just until the mussels open. Transfer them to a bowl as they open. Line a strainer with paper towels and strain the liquid into a bowl to get rid of the sandy deposits. Set aside. Detach the meat from the shells, cut the mussels into 2 or 3 pieces, and place in a small bowl.

Prepare the risotto: Heat the broth in a medium saucepan and keep warm over low heat.

Heat the oil in a large skillet over medium-low heat. Add the onion and garlic and cook, stirring, until pale yellow and soft, 4 to 5 minutes. Add the tomatoes, season with salt and chili pepper, and cook, stirring, for a minute or two. Add the rice and stir quickly for about 1 minute. Add the wine. Cook, stirring, until it is almost all reduced. Add ½ cup of simmering broth or just enough to barely cover the rice. Cook, stirring, until the broth has been absorbed almost completely. Continue cooking and stirring the rice in this manner, adding the broth ½ cup at a time for 15 to 16 minutes.

When the last addition of broth is almost all reduced and the rice looks somewhat dry, add the mussels, their reserved cooking liquid, the parsley, and the butter. Cook, stirring quickly, for a minute or two until the liquid has been absorbed and the rice has a moist, creamy consistency. Taste, adjust the seasoning, and serve.

RISOTTO WITH SQUID
Risotto con Calamari

❦

SERVES 4 TO 6

This is another risotto that begins with a preliminary "savory sauce," cooked very briefly to ensure that the squid remains tender.

FOR THE SQUID

1½ pounds squid (the smallest you can get), cleaned (page 12)

3 tablespoons extra-virgin olive oil

2 garlic cloves, minced

2 to 3 anchovy fillets, finely chopped

1 tablespoon chopped fresh parsley

Salt and freshly ground black pepper to taste

FOR THE RISOTTO

3 cups Basic Fish Broth (page 23) or low-sodium canned chicken broth mixed with 3 cups water

2 to 3 tablespoons extra-virgin olive oil

½ cup finely minced yellow onion

2 cups imported Arborio rice or other rice for risotto

½ cup dry white wine

1 tablespoon unsalted butter

Prepare the squid: Cut the squid into ½-inch rings. Heat the oil in a medium skillet over medium heat. Add the garlic, anchovies, parsley, and squid. Cook, stirring, until the squid turns chalky white, about 1 minute. Season with salt and pepper and turn the heat off under the skillet.

Prepare the risotto: Heat the broth in a medium saucepan and keep warm over low heat.

Heat the oil in a large skillet over medium heat. Add the onion and cook, stirring, until pale yellow and soft, 4 to 5 minutes. Add the rice and stir quickly until it is well coated with the oil, 1 to 2 minutes. Add the wine and cook until it is almost all reduced. Now add ½ cup of the simmering broth or just enough to barely cover the rice. Cook, stirring, until the broth has been absorbed almost completely. Continue cooking and stirring the rice in this manner, adding broth ½ cup at a time for 17 to 18 minutes.

When the last addition of broth is almost all reduced, add the squid and all its sauce to the rice. Add the butter and stir quickly until the butter melts and the rice has a moist, creamy consistency. Taste, adjust the seasoning, and serve.

RISOTTO WITH SQUID AND TOMATOES

Risotto con Calamari e Pomodori

✿

SERVES 4 TO 6

This risotto is a version of the recipe on page 258, with the addition of fresh tomatoes and chili pepper, which give the risotto a very appetizing look and a brand new identity.

FOR THE SQUID SAUCE

1½ pounds squid (the smallest you can get), cleaned (page 12)

3 tablespoons extra-virgin olive oil

2 garlic cloves, minced

2 to 3 anchovy fillets, finely chopped

⅓ cup loosely packed fresh oregano leaves or 1 tablespoon chopped fresh parsley

Chopped fresh red chili pepper or hot red pepper flakes to taste

Salt to taste

FOR THE RISOTTO

6 cups Basic Vegetable Broth (page 24), or 3 cups low-sodium chicken broth mixed with 3 cups water

2 to 3 tablespoons extra-virgin olive oil

½ cup finely minced yellow onion

1 pound ripe tomatoes, peeled, seeded, and diced (page 9)

2 cups imported Arborio rice or other rice for risotto

½ cup dry white wine

1 tablespoon unsalted butter

CONTINUED

Prepare the squid: Cut the squid into ½-inch rings. Heat the oil in a medium skillet over medium heat. Add the garlic, anchovies, oregano or parsley, chili pepper, and squid. Cook, stirring, until the squid turns chalky white, about 1 minute. Season with salt and turn the heat off under the skillet.

Prepare the risotto: Heat the broth in a medium saucepan and keep warm over low heat.

Heat the oil in a large skillet over medium heat. Add the onion and cook, stirring, until the onion is pale yellow and soft, 4 to 5 minutes. Add the tomatoes and stir for a few minutes. Add the rice and stir quickly for a minute or two. Add the wine and stir until it is almost all reduced. Now begin adding ½ cup of the simmering broth or just enough to barely cover the rice. Cook, stirring, until the broth has been absorbed almost completely. Continue cooking and stirring the rice in this manner, adding broth ½ cup at a time for 17 to 18 minutes.

When the last addition of broth is almost all reduced, add the squid and all its sauce to the rice. Add the butter and stir quickly until the butter melts and the rice has a moist, creamy consistency. Taste, adjust the seasoning, and serve.

RISOTTO WITH SMOKED SALMON AND MASCARPONE

Risotto con Salmone Affumicate e Mascarpone

SERVES 4 TO 6

If I have a dinner party at my house, this is the risotto I would choose. For me, the smokiness of the salmon and the sweetness of the mascarpone cheese is a heavenly combination. Just look into the pot when you add the mascarpone and see how it melts, coating every grain of rice. Taste, subtlety, and elegance—this dish has it all!

You can also use Champagne, which works so nicely with salmon, instead of wine, adding a couple of glasses a little at a time to the rice. In that case, you will need to use less broth.

6 cups Vegetable Broth
    (page 24), or 3 cups low-
    sodium canned chicken broth
    mixed with 3 cups of water
3 tablespoons unsalted butter
⅓ cup finely minced thoroughly
    washed leek, white part only
2 cups imported Arborio rice or
    other rice for risotto
½ cup dry white wine

3 to 4 ounces smoked salmon,
    cut into thin strips
2 to 3 tablespoons mascarpone
    cheese
1 tablespoon chopped fresh
    parsley

Heat the broth in a medium saucepan and keep warm over low heat.

Heat the butter in a large skillet over medium heat. When the butter foams, add the leek and cook, stirring, until leek is pale yellow and quite soft, 8 to 10 minutes. Add the rice and stir quickly for a minute or two until it is well coated with the butter. Add the wine and stir until wine is almost all reduced. Add ½ cup of the simmering broth or just enough to barely cover the rice. Cook, stirring, until the broth has been absorbed almost completely. Continue cooking and stirring the rice in this manner for 16 to 17 minutes.

When the last addition of broth is almost all reduced, add the salmon and stir for a minute or two. Add the mascarpone and the parsley. Stir quickly until the cheese is melted and the rice has a moist, creamy consistency. Taste, adjust the seasoning, and serve.

RISOTTO WITH CLAMS, MUSSELS, AND SPICY BROCCOLI

Risotto con Vongole, Cozze, e Broccoli Piccanti

❧

SERVES 4 TO 6

I love Rome and Roman cooking; it is direct, colorful, boisterous, and satisfying. Occasionally, however, one encounters a restaurant that dances to its own tune, and Alberto Ciarla is such a place. The food of this beautiful, sophisticated restaurant is both traditional and innovative. This risotto is an adaptation of one I had there several years back. It can be made with one or several types of shellfish. Make sure to cook the broccoli until almost mushy, so that when it is cooked with the rice, it practically melts, giving the risotto a beautiful light green color.

FOR THE MUSSELS AND CLAMS

2 tablespoons extra-virgin olive oil

½ cup water

1½ pounds mussels, cleaned (page 11)

1½ pounds manilla clams (or the smallest you can get), cleaned (page 11)

FOR THE RISOTTO

3 cups Basic Fish Broth (page 23) or Vegetable Broth (page 24) or low-sodium canned chicken broth mixed with 3 cups water

1 bunch fresh broccoli (about 1½ pounds)

¼ cup extra-virgin olive oil

½ cup finely minced yellow onion

2 garlic cloves, finely minced

Chopped fresh red chili pepper or hot red pepper flakes to taste

2 ounces pancetta, finely minced

2 cups imported Arborio rice or other rice for risotto

½ cup dry white wine

Prepare the mussels and clams: Put the oil and the water in a large skillet and place over medium heat. Add the mussels and clams, and cover the skillet. Cook just long enough for the mussels and clams to open. Transfer them to a bowl as they open. Line a strainer with paper towels and strain the pan liquid into a bowl to get rid of sandy deposits. Detach the meat from the shells, cut them into 2 to 3 pieces, and place them in the bowl with the strained liquid. (If you wish, leave some in their shells to use for decoration.)

Prepare the risotto: Heat the broth in a medium saucepan and keep warm over low heat.

Separate the broccoli florets from the stalks and cook the florets in salted boiling water until very tender. Drain and set aside.

Heat the oil in a large skillet over medium heat. Add the onion, garlic, chili pepper, and pancetta. Cook, stirring, until the onion is pale yellow and the pancetta lightly golden, 4 to 5 minutes. Add the broccoli and stir well for a few minutes. Add the rice and stir for a minute or two. Stir in the wine and cook until it is almost all reduced. Add ½ cup of the simmering broth or just enough to barely cover the rice. Cook, stirring, until the broth has been absorbed almost completely. Continue cooking and stirring the rice in this manner, adding the broth ½ cup or so at a time for 17 to 18 minutes.

When the last addition of broth is almost all reduced, add the shellfish and their liquid. Cook and stir until most of the liquid has been absorbed, 1 to 2 minutes. Taste, adjust the seasoning, and serve.

RISOTTO WITH LIGURIAN
WHITE FISH SAUCE

Risotto con Sugo di Pesce Ligure

❧

SERVES 4 TO 6

Seafood and fresh herbs are two dominant ingredients in the cooking of Liguria. This risotto is enriched by a lovely traditional Ligurian sauce which has the addition of porcini mushrooms.

FOR THE FISH SAUCE

¼ cup extra-virgin olive oil

⅓ cup finely minced yellow onion

⅓ cup finely minced celery

1 garlic clove, minced

2 anchovy fillets, chopped (optional)

1 tablespoon chopped fresh parsley

½ ounce dried porcini mushrooms, reconstituted, (page 10) and minced

1 pound mixed fish fillets and shellfish (orange roughy, halibut, scallops, prawns), cut into ½-inch cubes

Salt and freshly ground black pepper to taste

¼ cup dry white wine

½ cup Basic Fish Broth (page 25) or Vegetable Broth (page 24) or low-sodium canned chicken broth

FOR THE RISOTTO

4 to 5 cups Basic Fish Broth (page 23) or Vegetable Broth (page 24), or 3 cups low-sodium canned chicken broth mixed with 1 to 2 cups water

2 tablespoons extra-virgin olive oil

2 cups imported Arborio rice or other rice for risotto

½ cup dry white wine

8 to 10 fresh basil leaves, finely shredded

1 tablespoon unsalted butter

Prepare the fish sauce: Heat the oil in a medium, wide-bottomed saucepan over medium heat. Add the onion, celery, garlic, anchovies, if using, and parsley and cook, stirring, until the vegetables are soft, 6 to 7 minutes. Raise the heat to high and add the mushrooms. Stir for a minute or two. Add the diced fish, season with salt and pepper, and cook, stirring, until the fish loses its raw color, 2 to 3 minutes. Add the wine and stir until wine is almost all reduced. Add the broth and reduce the heat to low. Simmer the sauce, uncovered, for 4 to 5 minutes. (Makes approximately 2 to 2½ cups sauce.)

Prepare the risotto: Heat the broth in a medium saucepan and keep warm over low heat.

Heat the oil in a large skillet over medium heat. Add the rice and stir quickly for a minute or two until the rice is well coated with the oil. Add the wine and cook until it is almost all reduced. Add ½ cup of simmering broth or just enough to barely cover the rice. Cook, stirring, until the broth has been absorbed almost completely. Continue cooking and stirring the rice in this manner, adding the broth ½ cup or so at a time, for about 15 to 16 minutes.

When the last addition of broth is almost all reduced and the rice looks somewhat dry, add half of the fish sauce. Cook and stir until most of the fish juices have been absorbed. Add the remaining sauce, the basil, and the butter. Cook and stir until the fish juices have been absorbed and the rice has a moist, creamy consistency. Taste, adjust the seasoning, and serve.

☙

NOTE

When the fish is sautéed, it releases a lot of its natural juices. Resist the temptation to cook down the juices completely, because in doing so you will overcook the fish. Think of those juices as a flavorful ingredient that enriches the risotto.

Vegetable Risotti

RISOTTO WITH ROASTED
RED BELL PEPPERS
Risotto con Peperoni Arrosti

❧

SERVES 4 TO 6

Most vegetable risottos are light, delicate, and colorful. I love the look of this risotto, with its rosy color. Yellow and red peppers can also be added for color and taste.

For a Risotto Primavera, or springtime risotto, use any spring vegetables, such as peas, asparagus, small zucchini, or baby carrots. Dice the vegetables and quickly blanch them, then add to the risotto during the last 5 minutes of cooking.

2 large red bell peppers, roasted and peeled (page 10)

6 cups Vegetable Broth (page 24) or low-sodium canned chicken broth

4 tablespoons unsalted butter

½ cup finely minced yellow onion

2 cups imported Arborio rice or other rice for risotto

½ cup dry white wine

5 to 6 basil leaves, finely shredded, or 1 tablespoon chopped fresh parsley

⅓ cup freshly grated Parmigiano-Reggiano cheese

Cut the peppers into thin strips, then dice the strips. Place the peppers in a bowl, cover, and set aside until ready to use.

Heat the broth in a medium saucepan and keep warm over low heat.

Melt 3 tablespoons of the butter in a large skillet over medium heat. When the butter foams, add the onion and cook, stirring, until the onion is pale yellow and soft, 4 to 5 minutes. Add the rice and stir quickly until it is well coated with the butter and onion, 1 to 2 minutes Add the peppers and all the juices to the rice and stir once or twice. Add the wine and cook, stirring, until it is almost all reduced. Add ½ cup of the simmering broth or just enough to barely cover the rice. Cook and stir until the broth has been absorbed almost completely. Continue cooking and stirring the rice in this manner, adding the broth ½ cup at a time for 16 to 17 minutes.

When the last addition of broth is almost all reduced, add the basil or parsley, the remaining tablespoon butter, and the Parmigiano to the rice. Stir quickly for a minute or two until the butter and cheese melt and the rice has a moist, creamy consistency. Taste, adjust the seasoning, and serve.

MILANESE RISOTTO
WITH MUSHROOMS
Risotto alla Milanese con Funghi

❧

SERVES 4 TO 6

Views on how to make a traditional *risotto alla Milanese* sow discord. Some sources insist on a few tablespoon of roast gravy; others opt for beef marrow or some other savory fat product, such as pancetta; still others omit all of these and add a glass of white or red wine to the rice after it has been stirred with the butter and onion. I am sure that those versions are valid, but since it is almost impossible to find two Italian cooks who will agree on everything, I leave the debate to food historians.

I first tasted this risotto in Milano at Casa Fontana, a restaurant that serves over thirty types of risottos. I did not inquire about this risotto's pedigree because I was just too busy enjoying it.

CONTINUED

1 ounce dried porcini
 mushrooms, reconstituted,
 (page 10) and minced
6 cups Basic Meat Broth
 (page 20) or low-sodium
 canned beef or chicken broth
⅓ teaspoon powdered saffron
 (page 12)

4 tablespoons unsalted butter
½ cup finely minced yellow
 onion
2 cups imported Arborio rice or
 other rice for risotto
½ cup dry white wine
⅓ cup freshly grated
 Parmigiano-Reggiano cheese

Reserve 1 cup of the porcini soaking water. Heat the broth in a medium saucepan and keep warm over low heat. Place the saffron in a small bowl and add ½ cup of the hot broth. Mix well and set aside until ready to use.

Melt 3 tablespoons of the butter in a large skillet over medium heat. When the butter foams, add the onion and cook, stirring, until pale yellow and soft, 4 to 5 minutes. Add the rice and stir quickly until it is well coated with the butter and onion, 1 to 2 minutes. Add the mushrooms and stir a few times. Stir in the wine and cook until it is almost all reduced. Add the reserved porcini water and cook, stirring, until it has been absorbed almost completely. Now, begin adding the hot broth ½ cup or so at a time, or just enough to barely cover the rice. Cook, stirring, until the broth has been absorbed almost completely. Continue cooking and stirring the rice in this manner, adding the broth ½ cup at a time for about 15 minutes.

Add the reserved broth with the saffron to the rice, and stir for a minute or two. Add the remaining tablespoon butter and the Parmigiano and stir quickly until the butter and cheese melt and the rice has a moist, creamy consistency. Taste, adjust the seasoning, and serve.

RISOTTO WITH CORN AND SAFFRON

Risotto con Granturco e Zafferano

❧

SERVES 4 TO 6

As if saffron were not enough to give this risotto a bright golden color, the corn kernels make it absolutely sunny.

6 cups Basic Chicken Broth (page 21) or low-sodium canned chicken broth
⅓ teaspoon powdered saffron (page 12)
4 tablespoons unsalted butter
½ cup finely minced yellow onion

2 cups imported Arborio rice or other rice for risotto
1 cup fresh corn kernels (from 1 cob)
½ cup dry white wine
⅓ cup freshly grated Parmigiano-Reggiano cheese

Heat the broth in a medium saucepan and keep warm over low heat.

Place the saffron in a small bowl and add ½ cup of the hot broth. Mix well and set aside until ready to use.

Melt 3 tablespoons of the butter in a large skillet over medium heat. When the butter foams, add the onion and cook, stirring, until the onion is pale yellow and soft, 4 to 5 minutes. Add the rice and stir quickly until it is well coated with the butter and onion, 1 to 2 minutes. Add the corn and stir once or twice. Add the wine and stir until it is almost all reduced. Now begin adding the hot broth ½ cup or so at a time, or just enough to barely cover the rice. Cook, stirring, until the broth has been absorbed almost completely. Continue cooking and stirring the rice in this manner, adding the broth ½ cup at a time for about 15 minutes.

Add the reserved broth with the saffron to the rice, and stir for a minute or two. Add the remaining tablespoon butter and the Parmigiano, and stir quickly until the butter and cheese melt and the rice has a moist, creamy consistency. Taste, adjust the seasoning, and serve.

RISOTTO WITH SPECK AND ARTICHOKE HEARTS

Risotto con Speck e Carciofini

❦

SERVES 4 TO 6

As is often the case in Italian cooking, there are many variations to a dish. In many parts of Tuscany, the artichokes are sliced thin and sautéed together with the onion. Then they are cooked with the rice until the risotto is completed. In Siena, the artichokes are cooked separately from the risotto, generally with the addition of prosciutto, pancetta, or speck, as I have done in this recipe. I like this second version better because the *intingolo* (savory sauce) of artichokes adds lots more flavor to the risotto.

FOR THE ARTICHOKES

- 1¼ pounds baby artichokes, cleaned and cooked (page 9)
- 2 tablespoons extra-virgin olive oil
- ¼ pound speck or prosciutto, cut into ⅛-inch-thick slices and diced
- 1 garlic clove, minced
- 1 tablespoon chopped fresh parsley
- Salt and freshly ground black pepper to taste

FOR THE RISOTTO

- 6 cups Vegetable Broth (page 24) or Basic Chicken Broth (page 21) or low-sodium canned chicken broth
- 4 tablespoons unsalted butter
- ½ cup finely minced yellow onion
- 2 cups imported Arborio rice or other rice for risotto
- ½ cup dry white wine
- ⅓ cup freshly grated Parmigiano-Reggiano cheese

Prepare the artichokes: Cut the artichokes into thin wedges and set aside. Heat the oil in a medium skillet over medium heat. Add the speck or prosciutto, garlic, and parsley and cook, stirring, until the garlic turns lightly golden, about 1 minute. Add the artichokes. Season with salt and pepper, stir for a minute or two, and turn the heat off under the skillet.

Prepare the risotto: Heat the broth in a medium saucepan and keep warm over low heat.

Melt 3 tablespoons of the butter in a large skillet over medium heat. When the butter foams, add the onion. Cook, stirring, until the onion is pale yellow and soft, 4 to 5 minutes. Add the rice and stir quickly until it is well coated with the butter and onion, 1 to 2 minutes. Add the wine and cook until it is almost all reduced. Add ½ cup of the simmering broth or just enough to barely cover the rice. Cook and stir until the broth has been absorbed almost completely. Continue cooking and stirring the rice in this manner, adding the broth ½ cup at a time for about 10 minutes.

Add the artichokes and all their sauce to the rice. Cook and stir, adding more broth as needed, until the rice is tender but still firm to the bite, 7 to 8 minutes. Add the remaining tablespoon butter and the Parmigiano, and stir until butter and cheese melt and the rice has a moist, creamy consistency. Taste, adjust the seasoning, and serve.

ARTICHOKE SAUCE OTHER WAYS

This lovely artichoke sauce also can be used as a great side dish; it can be tossed with pasta such as penne or shells; or you can use it as a topping for bruschetta.

RISOTTO WITH BUTTERNUT SQUASH AND PEAS

Risotto con la Zucca e Piselli

❦

SERVES 4 TO 6

Squash takes a place of honor in the cooking of several northern Italian regions. It becomes the filling of incomparable stuffed pasta in Emilia-Romagna. It is turned into golden risotti and velvety soups in Lombardy, and into hardy soups in the Veneto. This risotto has fresh peas, which add taste and color to the dish.

6 cups Vegetable Broth (page 24) or Basic Chicken Broth (page 21) or low-sodium canned chicken broth
4 tablespoons unsalted butter
½ cup finely minced yellow onion
2 pounds butternut squash, peeled, seeded, and diced

2 cups imported Arborio rice or other rice for risotto
½ cup dry white wine
1 cup cooked fresh peas or thawed frozen peas
⅓ cup freshly grated Parmigiano-Reggiano cheese

Heat the broth in a medium saucepan and keep warm over low heat.

Melt 3 tablespoons of the butter in a large skillet over medium heat. When the butter foams, add the onion and squash. Cook, stirring, for 5 to 6 minutes until the squash and onion are lightly colored. Add the rice and stir quickly for a minute or two. Add the wine and stir until it is almost all reduced. Now begin adding the hot broth ½ cup or so at a time or just enough to barely cover the rice. Cook, stirring, until the broth has been absorbed almost completely. Continue cooking and stirring the rice in this manner, adding broth ½ cup at a time for 16 to 17 minutes.

Add the peas and stir for a minute or so, then add the remaining tablespoon butter and the Parmigiano. Add a touch more broth if needed. Stir quickly until the cheese melts and the rice has a moist, creamy consistency. Taste, adjust the seasoning, and serve.

RISOTTO WITH ROASTED
BUTTERNUT SQUASH
Risotto con la Zucca al Forno

⚜

SERVES 4 TO 6

One of the most popular dishes at my restaurant in Sacramento is tortelli with butternut squash, a specialty of my region of Emilia-Romagna. One day while I was making the tortelli, I had a sudden craving for a butternut squash risotto. So I made a risotto using the roasted butternut squash I had at hand, instead of the raw squash that the traditional recipe calls for. With the addition of a dash of freshly grated nutmeg this dish has a deeper, more seasoned flavor.

2 pounds butternut squash

6 cups Basic Chicken Broth
  (page 21) or low-sodium
  canned chicken broth

4 tablespoons unsalted butter

½ cup finely minced yellow
  onion

2 cups imported Arborio rice or
  other rice for risotto

½ cup dry white wine

⅓ cup freshly grated
  Parmigiano-Reggiano cheese

½ teaspoon freshly grated
  nutmeg

Preheat the oven to 400° F.

Cut the squash lengthwise and, with a tablespoon, scoop out the seeds. Wrap the squash in foil and place in the oven. Bake 1½ hours, or until tender. Cool the squash, then unwrap it. With a tablespoon, scoop out the pulp from the shells and place in a bowl. Set aside, covered, until ready to use. (Makes about 2 cups cooked squash pulp.)

Heat the broth in a medium saucepan and keep warm over low heat.

Melt 3 tablespoons of the butter in a large skillet over medium heat. When the butter foams, add the onion and cook, stirring, until the onion is pale yellow and soft, 4 to 5 minutes. Add the rice and stir quickly until it is well coated with the butter, 1 to 2 minutes. Add the wine and stir until it is almost all reduced. Now begin adding the hot broth ½ cup or so at a time or just enough to barely cover the rice. Cook, stirring, until the broth has been absorbed almost completely.

CONTINUED

Risotto and Rice Dishes • 273

Continue cooking and stirring the rice in this manner, adding broth a bit at a time for about 12 minutes.

Add the squash to the rice in a couple of batches and stir well after each addition. Cook and stir, adding small additions of broth, until the squash is totally blended with the rice, 5 to 6 minutes. Add the remaining tablespoon butter, the Parmigiano, and the nutmeg. Stir quickly until the cheese melts and the rice has a moist, creamy consistency. Taste, adjust the seasoning, and serve.

RISOTTO WITH CABBAGE
AND PANCETTA
Risotto con Verza e Pancetta

SERVES 4 TO 6

Rice is without any doubt the most important ingredient of the Veneto region. How lucky for us, because it is in the Veneto that one could practically eat a different risotto every day for months. This is one of the splendid risotti of the region that, unusually enough, is not made with seafood, but with a hearty combination of cabbage and pancetta.

If you're in the mood for fennel, try replacing the cabbage with one fennel bulb, stalks trimmed. Discard the fennel stalks, dice the bulb very fine, then follow the recipe below.

6 cups Vegetable Broth (page 24) or Basic Chicken Broth (page 21) or low-sodium canned chicken broth

½ pound Savoy cabbage

⅓ cup extra-virgin olive oil

½ cup finely minced yellow onion

1 garlic clove, minced

3 to 4 ounces pancetta, cut into ⅛-inch-thick slices and diced

2 cups imported Arborio rice or other rice for risotto

½ cup dry white wine

1 tablespoon unsalted butter

⅓ cup freshly grated Parmigiano-Reggiano cheese

Heat the broth in a medium saucepan and keep warm over low heat.

Remove and discard the bruised outer leaves of the cabbage. Slice the cabbage in half and remove the inner core. Cut the cabbage into thin strips and the strips into small pieces.

Heat the oil in a large skillet over medium heat. Add the onion, garlic, and pancetta and cook, stirring, until the pancetta turns lightly golden, 2 to 3 minutes. Add the cabbage. Cook and stir for 2 to 3 minutes, then reduce the heat to low, cover the skillet, and let the cabbage sweat 5 to 6 minutes longer. Stir the cabbage a few times during cooking.

Remove the lid and raise the heat to medium again. Add the rice. Stir quickly for a minute or two, then add the wine. When the wine is almost all reduced, begin adding the hot broth ½ cup or so at a time or just enough to barely cover the rice. Cook, stirring, until the broth has been absorbed almost completely. Continue cooking and stirring the rice in this manner, adding broth a bit at a time for about 18 minutes.

When the last addition of broth is almost all incorporated, add the butter and the Parmigiano. Stir quickly until the cheese is melted and the rice has a moist, creamy consistency. Taste, adjust the seasoning, and serve.

A SAVORY PASTA SAUCE

The savory base of cabbage and pancetta can also become a great pasta sauce. If you want to use it as a sauce, you need to cook the cabbage over low heat 15 to 20 minutes longer or until it is completely soft. This sauce is great over whole wheat pasta.

RISOTTO WITH BEANS
AND CABBAGE

Risotto con Fagioli e Verza

❧

SERVES 4 TO 6

Much peasant cooking made do with what was grown in the fields. Simple, everyday ingredients were transformed into no-nonsense dishes that fed large families. Cabbage, beans, onions, and carrots would be turned into thick aromatic soups or hearty risotti. In northern Italy, there are many variations on this peasant dish. Some contain meats while others are made only with vegetables.

With the same ingredients in larger proportions, you can prepare the splendid Bean, Cabbage, and Rice Soup on page 30.

½ cup dried cranberry beans, soaked (page 11)

6 cups Basic Meat Broth (page 20), or 3 cups low-sodium canned beef broth mixed with 3 cups water

½ pound Savoy cabbage

⅓ cup extra-virgin olive oil

½ cup finely minced yellow onion

½ cup finely minced carrot

1 tablespoon chopped fresh parsley

1 garlic clove, minced

Salt and freshly ground black pepper to taste

2 cups imported Arborio rice or other rice for risotto

1 tablespoon unsalted butter

½ cup freshly grated Parmigiano-Reggiano cheese

Drain and cook the beans, making sure not to overcook them; they should retain a slight bite. Set aside until ready to use. Heat the broth in a medium saucepan and keep warm over low heat. (For preparing beans ahead, see page 154.)

Remove and discard the bruised outer leaves of the cabbage. Slice the cabbage in half and remove the inner core. Cut the cabbage into thin strips and chop it roughly.

Heat the oil in a large skillet over medium heat. Add the onion, carrot, parsley, and garlic and cook, stirring, until the vegetables are soft, 5 to 6 minutes. Add the cabbage and season with salt and pepper. Cook and stir for 2 to 3 minutes, then reduce the heat to low, cover the skillet, and let the cabbage sweat 5 to 6 minutes. Stir the cabbage a few times during cooking.

Raise the heat to medium again and add the rice. Stir quickly for a few minutes and add the beans. Now begin adding the hot broth, ½ cup or so at a time or just enough to barely cover the rice. Cook, stirring, until the broth has been absorbed almost completely. Continue cooking and stirring the rice in this manner, adding broth a little at a time for about 18 minutes.

When the last addition of broth is almost all incorporated, add the butter and the Parmigiano. Stir quickly until the cheese is melted and the rice has a moist, creamy consistency. Taste, adjust the seasoning, and serve.

RISOTTO WITH MUSHROOMS
AND TOMATOES

Risotto con Intingolo di Funghi e Pomodori

❧

SERVES 4 TO 6

In the Ligurian region the sauce for this risotto is made with fresh porcini mushrooms. Since fresh porcini are not easy to find here, I have made it using a mixture of fresh shiitake and dried porcini. While the shiitake provide the texture of the fresh mushroom, the dried porcini add their intense flavor to the sauce.

This mushroom sauce is also terrific served over penne, rigatoni, or boiled or steamed rice.

FOR THE SAUCE

1 ounce dried porcini
    mushrooms, reconstituted
    (page 10) and minced
3 tablespoons extra-virgin
    olive oil
2 garlic cloves, peeled and
    lightly crushed
¼ pound portobello, shiitake, or
    cultivated white mushrooms,
    wiped clean and thinly sliced
2 tablespoons chopped fresh
    parsley
2 cups canned Italian plum
    tomatoes with their juice, put
    through a food mill to
    remove seeds
Salt and pepper to taste

FOR THE RISOTTO

4 cups Basic Chicken Broth
    (page 21) or low-sodium
    canned chicken broth
3 tablespoons unsalted butter
½ cup finely minced yellow
    onion
2 cups imported Arborio rice or
    other rice for risotto
½ cup dry white wine
⅓ cup freshly grated
    Parmigiano-Reggiano cheese
Salt and freshly ground black
    pepper to taste

Prepare the sauce: Reserve 1 cup of the porcini soaking water. Set aside.

Heat the oil in a medium skillet over medium heat. Add the garlic, brown on all sides, then discard it. Add the fresh mushrooms to the skillet and cook, stirring, until they are lightly golden, about 2 minutes. Add the minced porcini and the parsley, and stir briefly. Add the porcini soaking water and cook over high heat until the water is reduced by half. Stir in the tomatoes, season with salt and pepper, then reduce the heat to low and simmer the sauce, stirring occasionally, for 8 to 10 minutes. Set aside.

Prepare the risotto: Heat the broth in a medium saucepan and keep warm over low heat.

Melt the butter in a large skillet over medium heat. When the butter foams, add the onion and cook, stirring, until the onion is pale yellow and soft, 4 to 5 minutes. Add the rice and stir quickly until it is well coated with the butter, 1 to 2 minutes. Add the wine and stir until it is almost all reduced. Now begin adding the hot broth ½ cup or so at a time or just enough to barely cover the rice. Cook, stirring, until the broth has been absorbed almost completely. Continue cooking and stirring the rice in this manner, adding broth a bit at a time for 12 to 13 minutes.

When the last addition of broth has been absorbed and the rice looks somewhat dry, add about one third of the sauce. Stir for a minute or two until the sauce has been absorbed. Keep cooking the rice, adding the sauce a little at a time, until all sauce has been used up, about 5 minutes. Add the Parmigiano and stir quickly until the cheese is melted and the rice has a moist, creamy consistency. Taste, adjust the seasoning, and serve.

THE SAUTÉED VERSION

If you want to make a Risotto with Sautéed Fresh Mushrooms only, sauté ½ pound of mixed mushrooms in oil until golden. Add a bit of chopped garlic and parsley, stir for about 1 minute, and set aside. Prepare the risotto as instructed and cook it for about 18 minutes. Add the mushrooms to the risotto, stir for a minute or two, and serve.

RISOTTO WITH SAVORY
TOMATO SAUCE
Risotto con Intingolo di Pomodori

❧

SERVES 4 TO 6

A good tomato sauce has many uses. It can be prepared with fresh or canned tomatoes and just a bit of seasoning, or it can be enriched with vegetables and herbs. This tomato sauce was standard in our house in Bologna. My mother would serve it over pasta or boiled rice, or stirred into a risotto.

FOR THE TOMATO SAUCE

2 tablespoons extra-virgin
    olive oil
⅓ cup minced yellow onion
¼ cup minced celery
¼ cup minced carrot
1 tablespoon chopped fresh
    parsley
2 cups canned Italian plum
    tomatoes with their juice, put
    through a food mill to
    remove seeds
Salt to taste

FOR THE RISOTTO

4 to 5 cups Basic Chicken Broth
    (page 21) or low-sodium
    canned chicken broth
4 tablespoons unsalted butter
2 cups imported Arborio rice or
    other rice for risotto
½ cup dry white wine
⅓ cup freshly grated
    Parmigiano-Reggiano cheese

Prepare the tomato sauce: Heat the oil in a medium saucepan over medium heat. Add the vegetables and parsley and cook, stirring, until vegetables are soft, 7 to 8 minutes. Add the tomatoes and season lightly with salt. Reduce the heat to medium-low and simmer, uncovered, stirring from time to time, until the sauce has a medium-thick consistency, 8 to 10 minutes. Set aside.

Prepare the risotto: Heat the broth in a medium saucepan and keep warm over low heat.

Heat 3 tablespoons of the butter in a large skillet over medium heat. When the butter foams, add the rice and stir quickly until it is well coated with the butter, 1 to 2 minutes. Add the wine and stir until it is almost all reduced. Add ½ cup of the simmering broth or just enough to barely cover the rice. Cook, stirring, until the broth has been absorbed almost completely. Continue cooking and stirring the rice in this manner, adding the broth ½ cup or so at a time for 12 to 13 minutes.

When the last addition of broth has been absorbed and the rice looks somewhat dry, add about one third of the sauce. Stir for a minute or two until the sauce has been absorbed. Keep cooking the rice, adding the sauce a little at a time, until all the sauce has been used, 5 to 6 minutes. Add the remaining tablespoon butter and the Parmigiano, and stir quickly until the butter and cheese are melted and the rice has a moist, creamy consistency. Taste, adjust the seasoning, and serve.

LIGHTER OR RICHER RISOTTO

For a light, fresh-tasting risotto, omit the Parmigiano.
For a rich, creamy risotto, stir the Parmigiano
into the rice.

RISOTTO WITH FRESH TOMATOES AND BASIL

Risotto con Pomodori Freschi e Basilico

❦

SERVES 4 TO 6

When I prepare dishes like this risotto that are so utterly simple and straight-forward, and yet so immensely pleasing, I understand why Italian food is one of the most loved foods in the world! It was on the Ligurian Riviera that I first tasted this—a creamy concoction of rice, bright fresh red tomatoes, and aromatic Ligurian basil, blended together in a meltingly delicious dish.

6 cups Basic Chicken Broth
    (page 21) or low-sodium
    canned chicken broth
3 tablespoons olive oil
2 garlic cloves, peeled and
    lightly crushed
½ cup finely minced yellow
    onion
1½ pounds ripe tomatoes,
    peeled, seeded, and diced
    (page 9)

Salt to taste
2 cups imported Arborio rice or
    other rice for risotto
½ cup dry white wine
8 to 10 large fresh basil leaves,
    finely shredded
1 tablespoon unsalted butter
⅓ cup freshly grated
    Parmigiano-Reggiano cheese
    (optional)

Heat the broth in a medium saucepan and keep warm over low heat.

Heat the oil in a large skillet over medium heat. Add the garlic and cook until golden on both sides. Discard the garlic and add the onion. Cook, stirring, until the onion is pale yellow and soft, 4 to 5 minutes. Add the tomatoes and all their juices, season with salt, and stir for a minute or two. Add the rice and stir for a few minutes. Add the wine and cook until it is almost all reduced. Add ½ cup of the simmering broth or just enough to barely cover the rice. Cook, stirring, until the broth has been absorbed almost completely. Continue cooking and stirring the rice in this manner, adding broth ½ cup at a time for about 18 minutes.

When the last addition of broth is almost all reduced, add the basil, butter, and Parmigiano, if using it. Stir quickly until the butter and cheese are melted and the rice has a moist, creamy consistency. Taste, adjust the seasoning, and serve.

Cheese Risotti

RISOTTO WITH TOMATOES AND SMOKED MOZZARELLA
*Risotto ai Pomodori
e Mozzarella Affumicata*

❦

SERVES 4 TO 6

One of the dishes we do at my restaurant is pasta or gnocchi topped with a traditional sauce of tomatoes and smoked mozzarella. One day as I was tasting the sauce I thought it would be delicious combined into a risoto. It worked beautifully.

FOR THE SAUCE

2 tablespoons extra-virgin
    olive oil
1 large garlic clove, peeled and
    lightly crushed
2 cups canned Italian plum
    tomatoes with their juice, put
    through a food mill to
    remove seeds
2 ounces smoked mozzarella,
    grated

FOR THE RISOTTO

4 to 5 cups Basic Chicken Broth
    (page 21) or low-sodium
    canned chicken broth
3 tablespoons unsalted butter
½ cup finely minced yellow
    onion
2 cups imported Arborio rice or
    other rice for risotto
½ cup dry white wine
Salt if needed

Prepare the sauce: Heat the oil in a medium saucepan over medium heat. Add the garlic and cook until it is golden on both sides. Discard the garlic, add the tomatoes, and simmer for 6 to 7 minutes. Add the mozzarella, stir for less than 1 minute, and turn the heat off under the skillet. (Makes approximately 1½ cups sauce.)

Prepare the risotto: Heat the broth in a medium saucepan and keep warm over low heat.

CONTINUED

Heat the butter in a large skillet over medium heat. When the butter foams, add the onion and cook, stirring, until the onion is pale yellow and soft, 4 to 5 minutes. Add the rice and stir quickly until it is well coated with the butter and onion, 1 to 2 minutes. Add the wine and cook until it is almost all reduced. Add ½ cup of the simmering broth or just enough to barely cover the rice. Cook, stirring, until the broth has been absorbed almost completely. Continue cooking and stirring the rice in this manner, adding the broth ½ cup or so at a time for 12 to 13 minutes.

Now add a small ladle of the sauce and cook, stirring, until the sauce has been absorbed. Keep cooking the rice, adding the sauce a little at a time, until all the sauce has been used up and the rice has a moist, creamy consistency, about 5 minutes. Taste, adjust the seasoning, and serve.

NOTE

This risotto doesn't need Parmigiano or butter added at the last moment, since the mozzarella binds the rice. Keep in mind that smoked mozzarella is quite salty, and very probably this risotto will not need additional salt.

WITHOUT TOMATOES

For a Risotto with Smoked Mozzarella, but without the tomatoes, prepare the risotto and cook it for 18 minutes. Add the cubed mozzarella directly to the risotto, stir quickly to melt the cheese, and serve.

RISOTTO WITH GORGONZOLA
Risotto al Gorgonzola

❧

SERVES 4 TO 6

This is one of the simplest of all risotti. Its outstanding taste is courtesy of Gorgonzola, one of Italy's most glorious cheeses. Even though Gorgonzola is a table cheese, it is also widely used in cooking. When buying Gorgonzola, check it for freshness: it should have a white or light creamy color, and should be soft, creamy, and even a bit runny. Mediocre, old, or overassertive Gorgonzola will ruin this dish. You can also try this with 4 ounces of mild fontina cheese instead of the strong-tasting Gorgonzola.

6 cups Basic Chicken Broth (page 21) or low-sodium canned chicken broth	½ cup dry white wine
3 tablespoons unsalted butter	2 to 3 ounces mild Gorgonzola cheese
½ cup finely minced yellow onion	1 to 2 tablespoons chopped fresh parsley
2 cups imported Arborio rice or other rice for risotto	

Heat the broth in a medium saucepan and keep warm over low heat.

Melt the butter in a large skillet over medium heat. When the butter foams, add the onion and cook, stirring, until the onion is pale yellow and soft, 4 to 5 minutes. Add the rice and stir quickly until it is well coated with the butter and onion, 1 to 2 minutes. Add the wine and stir until it is almost all reduced. Now begin adding the hot broth ½ cup or so at a time, or just enough to barely cover the rice. Cook, stirring, until the broth has been absorbed almost completely. Continue cooking and stirring the rice in this manner, adding broth ½ cup at a time for 16 to 17 minutes.

When the last addition of broth is almost all incorporated, break the Gorgonzola into several small pieces and add to the rice together with the parsley. Stir quickly until the cheese melts and the rice has a moist, creamy consistency. Taste, adjust the seasoning, and serve.

RISOTTO WITH THREE CHEESES
Risotto ai Tre Formaggi

꽃

SERVES 4 TO 6

This is not one of the lightest risotti in the world, but it certainly is one of the most voluptuous. At the point when the cheeses are added to the rice and they slowly begin to melt, look at how the cheese and rice bind together in blissful, fragrant union.

6 cups Basic Chicken Broth (page 21) or low-sodium canned chicken broth
3 tablespoons unsalted butter
½ cup finely minced yellow onion

2 cups imported Arborio rice or other rice for risotto
½ cup dry white wine
4 ounces 3 combined cheeses, such as fontina, mozzarella, Gorgonzola, or taleggio, diced

Heat the broth in a medium saucepan and keep warm over low heat.

Melt the butter in a large skillet over medium heat. When the butter foams, add the onion and cook, stirring, until the onion is pale yellow and soft, 4 to 5 minutes. Add the rice and stir quickly until it is well coated with the butter and onion, 1 to 2 minutes. Add the wine and stir until it is almost all reduced. Now begin adding the hot broth ½ cup or so at a time or just enough to barely cover the rice. Cook, stirring, until the broth has been absorbed almost completely. Continue cooking and stirring rice in this manner, adding broth ½ a cup at a time for 17 to 18 minutes.

When the last addition of broth is almost all incorporated, add the cheeses. Stir quickly until the cheeses melt and the rice has a moist, creamy consistency. Add a touch more broth if rice seems a bit dry. Taste, adjust the seasoning, and serve.

Meat Risotti

RISOTTO WITH SAUSAGE, PORCINI, AND TOMATOES

Risotto con Intingolo di Salsiccia, Porcini, e Pomodori

🐝

SERVES 6

Make a nice ragù or savory sauce—one night you serve it over fettuccine, penne, or a soft steaming polenta and the next time what is left can be stirred into a simple risotto. This is the type of food that is always on the menu of the good cook. This is how Italian women cook.

FOR THE SAUCE

1 ounce dried porcini
  mushrooms, reconstituted
  (page 10) and minced
2 to 3 tablespoons olive oil
¼ pound mild Italian sausage,
  casings removed, finely
  chopped
1 garlic clove, minced
1 tablespoon chopped fresh
  sage or 1 teaspoon
  crumbled dried
1½ cups canned Italian plum
  tomatoes with their juice,
  put through a food mill to
  remove seeds
Salt and freshly ground black
  pepper to taste

FOR THE RISOTTO

4 to 5 cups Basic Meat Broth
  (page 20) or low-sodium
  canned beef broth or
  chicken broth
3 tablespoons unsalted butter
½ cup finely minced yellow
  onion
2 cups imported Arborio rice or
  other rice for risotto
½ cup full-bodied red wine,
  such as Barbera or Zinfandel
⅓ cup freshly grated
  Parmigiano-Reggiano cheese

CONTINUED

Prepare the sauce: Reserve 1 cup of the porcini soaking water and set aside.

Heat the oil in a small saucepan over medium heat. Add the sausage and cook, breaking it apart with a large wooden spoon until it begins to lose its raw color. Add the garlic, sage, and porcini mushrooms and stir for about 1 minute. Add the reserved porcini water and cook until it is almost all reduced. Stir in the tomatoes, season with salt and pepper, and simmer the sauce for 8 to 10 minutes, stirring occasionally. Then turn the heat off under the pan. (Makes approximately 2 cups sauce.)

Prepare the risotto: Heat the broth in a medium saucepan and keep warm over low heat.

Melt the butter in a large skillet over medium heat. Add the onion and cook, stirring, until onion is pale yellow and soft, 4 to 5 minutes. Add the rice and stir quickly until it is well coated with the butter and onion, 1 to 2 minutes. Add the wine and cook until it is almost all reduced. Now add ½ cup of the simmering broth or just enough to barely cover the rice. Cook, stirring, until the broth has been absorbed almost completely. Continue cooking and stirring the rice in this manner, adding broth ½ cup or so at a time for about 12 to 13 minutes.

When the last addition of broth is almost all reduced and the rice looks some-what dry, add about one third of the sauce. Stir for a minute or two until the sauce has been absorbed. Keep cooking the rice, adding the sauce a little at a time until all the sauce has been used up, about 5 minutes. Stir in a little more broth if needed. Add the Parmigiano and stir quickly until the cheese is melted and the rice has a moist, creamy consistency. Taste, adjust the seasoning, and serve.

RISOTTO WITH SAUSAGE, BEANS, AND RED WINE
Risotto alla Pavese

༜

SERVES 4 TO 6

One of the most venerable restaurants in Milan is the Gran San Bernardo. Eating here takes you back in time. The restaurant is old-fashioned, the service is slow and relaxed, and the food is classic of the area. This is one of their wonderful risotti.

½ cup dried cranberry beans, soaked, drained, and cooked (page 11)

5 cups Basic Meat Broth (page 20) or low-sodium canned beef broth or chicken broth

2 tablespoons olive oil

2 tablespoons unsalted butter

½ cup finely minced yellow onion

¼ pound fresh mild Italian sausage, casings removed and finely chopped (see The Importance of Ingredients, page 290)

2 cups imported Arborio rice or other rice for risotto

2 cups full-bodied red wine, such as a Barbera, Barolo, or Zinfandel (see The Importance of Ingredients, page 290)

⅓ cup freshly grated Parmigiano-Reggiano cheese

Drain the beans and set aside. Heat the broth in a medium saucepan and keep warm over low heat. (For preparing the beans ahead, see page 154.) Do not use canned beans for this dish.

Heat the oil with 1 tablespoon of the butter in a large skillet over medium heat. Add the onion and cook, stirring, until the onion is pale yellow and soft, 4 to 5 minutes. Add the sausage and cook, breaking it apart with a large wooden spoon, until it begins to lose its raw color. Add the rice and stir quickly until it is well coated with the fat in the skillet, 1 to 2 minutes. Add ½ cup of wine and stir until it is almost all reduced. Add the remaining wine ½ cup at a time, stirring constantly until it is all absorbed.

Now begin adding the hot broth ½ cup or so at a time or just enough to barely cover the rice. Cook, stirring, until the broth has been absorbed almost completely. Continue cooking and stirring the rice in this manner, adding broth a bit at a time for 14 to 15 minutes.

Add the beans. Cook and stir, adding broth as needed, for 3 to 4 minutes. Add the remaining tablespoon butter and the Parmigiano. Stir quickly until the cheese melts and the rice has a moist, creamy consistency. Taste, adjust the seasoning, and serve.

THE IMPORTANCE OF INGREDIENTS

By now we all know that good ingredients are vital to the sucess of a dish, so make sure

- *To choose a good quality wine to cook with and serve with the meal.*
- *That the sausage is fresh and mild. A spicy sausage or one that is loaded with fennel or dried herbs will not be appropriate for this dish.*
- *That the beans, fresh or dried, are freshly cooked for this dish.*

Even though canned beans are convenient, they will not do justice to this dish.

RISOTTO WITH PORK RAGÙ

Risotto con Ragù di Maiale alla Modenese

❧

SERVES 6 TO 8

This homey but fresh-tasting ragù comes from Modena, one of the gastronomically rich cities of the Emilia-Romagna region. The flavorful base of vegetables, paired with the sweetness of pork and long, slow cooking, produces a delicate ragù that enriches an otherwise simple risotto. To me this is a great example of uncontrived home cooking.

FOR THE PORK RAGÙ

1 tablespoon unsalted butter
2 tablespoons olive oil
⅓ cup finely minced yellow onion
⅓ cup finely minced carrot
⅓ cup finely minced celery
½ pound lean ground pork
2 ounces pancetta, finely minced
2 tablespoons tomato paste mixed with 2 cups Basic Chicken Broth (page 21) or low-sodium canned chicken broth

Salt and freshly ground black pepper to taste
2 tablespoons milk

FOR THE RISOTTO

6 cups Basic Chicken Broth (page 21) or low-sodium canned chicken broth
3 tablespoons unsalted butter
2 cups imported Arborio rice or other rice for risotto
½ cup dry white wine
½ cup freshly grated Parmigiano-Reggiano cheese

Prepare the ragù: Heat the butter and oil in a medium saucepan over medium heat. Add the onion, carrot, and celery and cook, stirring, until the vegetables are lightly golden and soft, 5 to 6 minutes. Add the pork and pancetta. Cook, stirring to break up the meat with a large spoon, until the meat loses its raw color, 4 to 5 minutes. Add the tomato paste mixture and season with salt and pepper. Cook, uncovered, over low heat for about 1 hour, stirring the sauce a few times. Add the milk and simmer 5 minutes longer. At this point the sauce should have a thick consistency. Set aside until ready to use. (Makes approximately 2 cups sauce.)

CONTINUED

Prepare the risotto: Heat the broth in a medium saucepan and keep warm over low heat.

Melt the butter in a large skillet over medium heat. When the butter foams, add the rice and stir quickly until it is well coated with the butter, 1 to 2 minutes. Add the wine and stir until it is almost all reduced. Now begin adding the hot broth ½ cup or so at a time or just enough to barely cover the rice. Cook, stirring, until the broth has been absorbed almost completely. Continue cooking and stirring the rice in this manner, adding broth a little at a time for 12 to 13 minutes.

When the last addition of broth has been absorbed and the rice looks somewhat dry, add about one third of the sauce. Stir for a minute or two until the sauce has been absorbed. Keep cooking the rice, adding the sauce a little at a time, until all sauce has been used up, about 5 minutes. Add a bit of additional broth if rice seems too dry. Stir ⅓ cup of the Parmigiano into the rice and keep stirring until the cheese is melted and the rice has a moist, creamy consistency. Taste, adjust the seasoning, and serve with a sprinkle of additional Parmigiano if desired.

DOUBLE YOUR PLEASURE

As in other risotti with ragùs or meat sauces, it is a good idea to double the ragù recipe. Use what you need for the risotto and refrigerate or freeze what is left. What a bonus to come home from work and have this great sauce ready to be tossed with tagliatelle, fettuccine, penne, rigatoni, or shells.

RISOTTO WITH DUCK RAGÙ

Risotto con Ragù di Anatra

🦆

SERVES 6 TO 8

In and around the city of Ferrara, this dish is prepared with whole wild duck. Since wild duck is not exactly a staple at our supermarkets, I have simplified the dish by using duck breast. While the traditional preparation puts the duck sauce *over* the risotto, I have integrated the sauce into the risotto for an easier presentation.

FOR THE DUCK RAGÙ

3 to 4 tablespoons extra-virgin olive oil

4 skinless, boneless half duck breasts (about 1¼ pounds), cut into ½-inch pieces

1 garlic clove, minced

1 tablespoon chopped fresh sage, or ½ tablespoon finely crumbled dried

½ cup dry white wine

1½ pounds ripe tomatoes, peeled, seeded, and minced (page 9), or 2 cups canned Italian tomatoes with their juice, put through a food mill to remove seeds

½ cup Basic Chicken Broth (page 21) or low-sodium canned chicken broth

Salt and freshly ground black pepper to taste

FOR THE RISOTTO

5 cups Basic Chicken Broth (page 21) or low-sodium canned chicken broth

3 tablespoons unsalted butter

½ cup finely minced yellow onion

2 cups imported Arborio rice or other rice for risotto

½ cup dry white wine

½ cup freshly grated Parmigiano-Reggiano cheese

CONTINUED

Prepare the sauce: Heat the oil in a medium saucepan over medium heat. Add the duck and cook, stirring, until the meat begins to color, 2 to 3 minutes. Add the garlic and sage, and stir less than a minute. Add the wine and cook over high heat until it is almost all reduced. Add the tomatoes and broth, and season with salt and pepper. Reduce the heat to low and simmer the sauce, uncovered, stirring occasionally, for 25 to 30 minutes. At the end of cooking, the sauce should have a medium-thick consistency. Add a bit more broth or water if needed. Set aside until ready to use. (Makes approximately 2 to 2½ cups of sauce.)

Prepare the risotto: Heat the broth in a medium saucepan and keep warm over low heat.

Heat the butter in a large skillet over medium heat. When the butter foams, add the onion and cook, stirring, until the onion is pale yellow and soft, 4 to 5 minutes. Add the rice and stir quickly until it is well coated with the butter, 1 to 2 minutes. Add the wine and stir until it is almost all reduced. Now begin adding the hot broth ½ cup or so at a time or just enough to barely cover the rice. Cook, stirring, until the broth has been absorbed almost completely. Continue cooking and stirring the rice in this manner, adding the broth a bit at a time for 12 to 13 minutes.

When the last addition of broth has been absorbed and the rice looks some-what dry, add about one third of the sauce. Stir for a minute or two until the sauce has been absorbed. Keep cooking the rice, adding the sauce a little at a time, until all sauce has been used up, about 5 minutes. Add a bit of additional broth if rice seems a too dry. Add ⅓ cup of the Parmigiano and stir quickly until the cheese is melted and the rice has a moist, creamy consistency. Taste, adjust the seasoning, and serve with a bit of additional Parmigiano if desired.

RISOTTO WITH LAMB RAGÙ
Risotto con Ragù di Agnello

꙰

SERVES 6

This lamb ragù comes from Umbria. It is generally served over pici, a local homemade pasta, or pappardelle, the widest of all the noodles. I use it interchangeably over pasta and incorporated into a risotto. In preparing the risotto, I omit the onion. The rice is stirred directly into the hot butter, cooked halfway with the broth, then finished with a small addition of the sauce. This is a satisfyingly hearty and flavorful dish. There's more sauce in this recipe than you'll need. Leftover sauce will taste terrific over rigatoni or penne.

FOR THE LAMB RAGÙ

4 tablespoons olive oil
½ cup finely minced yellow
   onion
½ cup finely minced carrot
½ cup finely minced celery
   stalk, white part only
1 pound lamb shoulder, cut
   into ¼-inch dice
1 tablespoon chopped fresh
   rosemary, or 1 teaspoon dried
1 bay leaf
½ cup dry white wine
1 pound ripe tomatoes, peeled,
   seeded, and minced
   (page 9)

Salt and freshly ground black
   pepper to taste

FOR THE RISOTTO

5 cups Basic Meat Broth
   (page 20) or low-sodium
   canned beef broth
3 tablespoons unsalted butter
2 cups imported Arborio rice or
   other rice for risotto
½ cup dry white wine
½ cup freshly grated
   Parmigiano-Reggiano cheese

Prepare the lamb ragù: Heat the oil in a medium saucepan over medium heat. Add the vegetables and cook, stirring, until they are lightly golden and soft, 5 to 6 minutes. Add the lamb, rosemary, and bay leaf. Cook, stirring, until the lamb has lost its raw color, 4 to 5 minutes. Raise the heat to high and add the wine. Cook, stirring, until the wine is almost all reduced. Add the tomatoes and their juices and season with salt and pepper. Simmer the ragù, uncovered, over low heat, 40 to 45 minutes. Stir occasionally and add a bit of water or broth if the sauce thickens too much. At the end of cooking, you should have a thick but moist sauce. Taste, adjust the seasoning, and set aside until ready to use. (Makes 3 to 3½ cups sauce.)

Prepare the risotto: Heat the broth in a medium saucepan and keep warm over low heat.

Melt the butter in a large skillet over medium heat. When the butter foams, add the rice and cook, stirring for a minute or two, until the rice is well coated with the butter. Add the wine and stir until it is almost all reduced. Add ½ cup or so of the hot broth or just enough to barely cover the rice. Cook, stirring, until the broth has been absorbed almost completely. Continue cooking and stirring the rice in this manner, adding broth a little at a time for 12 to 13 minutes.

When the last addition of broth has been absorbed and the rice looks somewhat dry, add about 1 cup of the lamb sauce. Stir for a minute or two until the sauce has been absorbed. Keep cooking the rice, add another cup of sauce a little at a time (for a total of 2 cups) until all the sauce has been absorbed, about 5 minutes. Stir ⅓ cup of Parmigiano into the rice and mix quickly until the cheese is melted and the rice has a moist, creamy consistency. Taste, adjust the seasoning, and serve with a sprinkling of additional Parmigiano if desired.

RISOTTO WITH
PAN-ROASTED QUAIL
Risotto con le Quaglie in Tegame

※

SERVES 6

This dish can be eaten as a first course *or* as an entree. It belongs to several northern Italian regions. A few years back I enjoyed it at Trattoria dei Binari in Milan, where it was served over a bed of saffron risotto and the quail had not been deboned.

Luckily for us, we don't have to hunt quail and neither do we have to pluck and bone them. Most specialty markets sell them already boned. The only drawback is that they might become a bit dry. For this reason, I wrap them with slices of pancetta, which gives taste and added moisture to the little birds.

Pan roasting is a typical Italian way of roasting meats that renders them moist and flavorful. It allows the cook to keep a watchful eye on the progress of the dish and to regulate the heat and the amount of liquid in the pan. As an alternative, see the oven method given below.

6 boned quail (about 2 pounds)
Salt and freshly ground black
   pepper to taste
12 slices pancetta (about
   ½ pound)
⅓ to ½ cup extra-virgin
   olive oil

1 cup dry Marsala wine, such as
   Florio or Pellegrino
1 recipe Risotto with Butter
   and Parmigiano-Reggiano
   (page 247)

Wash the quail inside out and pat dry with paper towels. Season lightly with salt and pepper. Wrap 2 slices of pancetta tightly around the body and wings of each quail, trying to give the quail a round shape. Leave the legs free. Secure the pancetta with wooden picks.

Heat the oil in a large skillet over medium heat. Add the quail, breasts side down, and cook, turning them gently as needed, until they are golden brown all over, 5 to 7 minutes. Off the heat, carefully tilt the skillet and remove as much fat as possible. Put the skillet back over medium heat and add half of the Marsala wine. Stir briefly until the wine begins to bubble. Then reduce the heat to low, cover the pan, and cook gently for about 10 minutes. Check the birds a few times during cooking, adding a bit of water or wine if the liquid in the pan reduces too much. At the end of cooking, there should be 2 to 3 tablespoons of pan juices left in the skillet. Turn the heat off under the skillet. (The quails can be prepared an hour or so ahead and kept at room temperature, tightly covered.)

While the quail are cooking, prepare the risotto. When done after 18 to 20 minutes, spoon it onto individual flat serving dishes, spreading it lightly on the plates.

Reheat the quail gently, if necessary, and place over the rice in the center of each dish. Put the skillet back on high heat, add the remaining wine, and bring the pan juices to a fast simmer. Cook, stirring and scraping the bottom with a wooden spoon, until the sauce is thick and glazy, about 1 minute. Pour a bit of sauce over each quail and serve.

AL FORNO

Preheat the oven to 375° F. Brown the quail in an ovenproof skillet on top of the stove. Discard the fat and add half of the wine. Place in the oven and roast, uncovered, 8 to 10 minutes. Place quail over the risotto and complete the sauce as instructed.

RISOTTO WITH VEAL AND PEAS
Risotto Ricco alla Padovana

※

SERVES 6 TO 8

Even though the majority of risotti from the Veneto region are made with fish, shellfish, or vegetables, the meat risotti can be equally outstanding. In this dish lean, ground veal is cooked gently with the vegetables. Then the rice is added and the dish is finished in the traditional way with a small addition of hot broth. The amount of meat and peas might seem a bit excessive, but they are the reason this risotto is called *ricco,* or rich.

7 cups Basic Chicken Broth (page 21) or low-sodium canned chicken broth
3 tablespoons unsalted butter
2 tablespoons olive oil
1 cup finely minced yellow onion
½ cup finely minced celery

1 pound ground veal shoulder
2 cups imported Arborio rice or other rice for risotto
1 cup dry white wine
2 cups cooked fresh peas or thawed frozen peas
½ cup freshly grated Parmigiano-Reggiano cheese

Heat the broth in a medium saucepan and keep warm over low heat.

Heat 2 tablespoons of the butter and the oil in a large skillet over medium heat. Add the onion and celery and cook, stirring, until the vegetables are lightly golden and soft, 5 to 6 minutes. Add the veal and cook, stirring to break up the meat with a large spoon, until the meat loses its raw color, 4 to 5 minutes. Add the rice, stir for a minute or two, then add the wine. Cook, stirring, until the wine is almost all reduced.

Add ½ cup of the hot broth or just enough to barely cover the rice. Cook, stirring, until the broth has been absorbed almost completely. Continue cooking and stirring the rice in this manner, adding broth a little at a time for 15 to 16 minutes.

Add the peas and stir for a minute or two. Add the remaining tablespoon butter and ⅓ cup of the Parmigiano. Cook, stirring quickly, until the cheese is melted and the rice has a moist, creamy consistency. Taste, adjust the seasoning, and serve with a bit more Parmigiano if desired.

RISOTTO WITH VEAL AND PORCINI MUSHROOMS

Risotto Ricco alla Padovana con Porcini

※

SERVES 6 TO 8

As is always the case, there are several versions of a traditional dish. This variation on Risotto with Veal and Peas (page 299) uses dried porcini mushrooms instead of peas. Paired with chicken liver, the mushrooms add character and intense flavor to the risotto.

1 ounce dried porcini mushrooms, reconstituted (page 10) and minced	1 cup finely minced yellow onion
	½ cup finely minced celery
7 cups Basic Chicken Broth (page 21) or low-sodium canned chicken broth	1 pound ground veal shoulder
	2 chicken livers, finely minced
3 tablespoons unsalted butter	2 cups imported Arborio rice or other rice for risotto
2 tablespoons olive oil	½ cup freshly grated Parmigiano-Reggiano cheese

Reserve 1 cup of the porcini soaking water.

Heat the broth in a medium saucepan and keep warm over low heat.

Heat 2 tablespoons of the butter and the oil in a large skillet over medium heat. Add the onion and celery and cook, stirring, until the vegetables are lightly golden and soft, 5 to 6 minutes. Add the veal and chicken livers. Cook, stirring, to break up the meat with a large spoon until the meat loses its raw color, 4 to 5 minutes. Add the porcini mushrooms and stir once or twice. Add the rice, stir for a minute or two, then add the reserved mushroom water. Cook, stirring, until the water is almost all reduced.

Add ½ cup of hot broth or just enough to barely cover the rice. Cook, stirring, until the broth has been absorbed almost completely. Continue cooking and stirring the rice in this manner, adding broth a little at a time for 17 to 18 minutes.

Add the remaining tablespoon butter and the Parmigiano. Cook, stirring quickly, until the cheese is melted and the rice has a moist, creamy consistency. Taste, adjust the seasoning, and serve with a sprinkle of additional Parmigiano if desired.

RISOTTO WITH BLUEBERRIES
Risotto con Mirtilli

※

SERVES 4 TO 6

If anyone had told me years ago that I would have eaten and *really enjoyed* a risotto with blueberries, I would have laughed. But times change and we change along with them. I had my first risotto with blueberries in the fall of 1996 at Ristorante Sadler in Milan. My husband, who knows my preference goes toward classic food, dared me to order it. I did and to my surprise I loved it. It was light and delicate, with just a bit of sweetness given by the blueberries. It was also very pretty to look at. Who knows? Maybe in a few years I will try a risotto with strawberries.

2 pints fresh blueberries

6 cups Basic Chicken Broth (page 21) or low-sodium canned chicken broth

4 tablespoons unsalted butter

⅓ cup finely minced shallots or yellow onion

2 cups imported Arborio rice or other rice for risotto

1 cup medium-dry Champagne or dry white wine

¼ cup heavy cream

Clean the blueberries and set aside.

Heat the broth in a medium saucepan and keep warm over low heat.

Melt 3 tablespoons of the butter in a large skillet over medium heat. When the butter foams, add the shallots or onion and cook, stirring, until pale yellow and soft, 4 to 5 minutes. Add the rice and stir quickly until it is well coated with the butter and onion, 1 to 2 minutes. Add the Champagne or wine, and cook until almost all reduced. Add ½ cup of the simmering broth or just enough to barely cover the rice. Cook and stir until the broth has been absorbed almost completely.

Continue cooking and stirring the rice in this manner, adding broth ½ cup at a time for about 15 minutes.

Add the blueberries and cook for 3 to 4 minutes. Add the remaining tablespoon butter and the cream, and stir until the rice has a moist, creamy consistency. Taste, adjust the seasoning, and serve.

Rice Timballos and Savory Boiled Rice Dishes

RICE WITH SICILIAN STEWED PEPPERS
Riso con Peperonata alla Siciliana

❧

SERVES 4

The people of Sicily cook multicolored peppers, sweet onion, and ripe tomatoes gently with a bit of garlic, some olives, and a few capers until everything is meltingly tender and intensely aromatic. Traditionally, this dish is served as a vegetable, but with a little bit of *fantasia* (creativity) it can become a healthy, delicious first course.

⅓ cup extra-virgin olive oil

2 pounds red, yellow, and green bell peppers, seeded and cut into ½-inch pieces

1 large yellow onion, thinly sliced

1 garlic clove, minced

8 to 10 small green pitted olives, quartered

1 to 2 tablespoons capers, rinsed

1 pound ripe tomatoes, peeled, seeded, and finely minced (page 9)

Salt and freshly ground black pepper to taste

8 to 10 fresh basil leaves, shredded, or 1 tablespoon chopped fresh parsley

1½ cups imported Arborio rice

Heat the oil in a large skillet over medium heat. Add the peppers and cook, stirring, until they begin to color, 5 to 6 minutes. Add the onion and cook until onion and peppers are lightly golden, 5 to 6 minutes. Add the garlic, olives, and capers and stir once or twice. Add the tomatoes and season with salt and pepper. Reduce the heat to low and partially cover the skillet. Simmer the vegetables, stirring occasionally, until they are soft and tender and the juices in the skillet have thickened, 35 to 40 minutes. Stir in the basil or parsley. Remove from heat and set aside until ready to use.

Bring a medium saucepan of water to a boil over high heat. Add 1 tablespoon of salt and the rice, and stir briefly with a wooden spoon. Reduce the heat to low and simmer, uncovered, stirring occasionally, until the rice is tender but still firm to the bite, 13 to 15 minutes.

Drain the rice, making sure to leave it a bit wet, and place it in a warm serving bowl. Add the pepper mixture to the rice and mix well. Taste, adjust the seasoning, and serve.

RICE WITH FONTINA CHEESE
Riso con la Fontina

🌿

SERVES 4

This is perhaps one of the most basic, uncomplicated, economically sound ways to feed a family and one of the most delicious. In regions such as Piedmont, Lombardy, and the Veneto, where rice is a very important staple, preparations like this are on many tables. The rice is boiled in water or milk and, while still hot, is tossed with butter and locally produced cheese.

Salt to taste
1½ cups imported Arborio rice
4 tablespoons unsalted butter,
  at room temperature

¼ pound Italian fontina cheese,
  shredded or minced

Bring a medium pot of water to a boil over high heat. Add 1 tablespoon of salt and the rice, and stir briefly with a wooden spoon. Reduce the heat to low and simmer, uncovered, stirring occasionally, until the rice is tender but still firm to the bite, 13 to 15 minutes.

Drain the rice, making sure to leave it a bit wet, and place it in a warm serving bowl. Add the butter and the cheese, and mix quickly until the butter and cheese are melted and coat the rice. Taste, adjust the seasoning, and serve at once.

RICE WITH MILK, BUTTER, AND PARMIGIANO
Riso al Latte

❧

SERVES 4

My mother used to prepare this delicious dish of rice boiled in milk, which was tossed with sweet butter and Parmigiano and served piping hot, because she considered it "light, nutritious, and perfect for children of any age." Needless to say, when my daughters were young, I did the same for them.

8 cups whole or low-fat milk
1½ cups imported Arborio rice
Salt to taste

4 tablespoons unsalted butter
⅓ cup freshly grated
Parmigiano-Reggiano cheese

Place the milk in a medium saucepan and bring it to a gentle boil over medium heat. Add the rice, season with salt, and reduce the heat to low. Simmer, uncovered, stirring occasionally for the first 7 to 8 minutes. As the rice cooks and the milk reduces, the rice needs to be stirred constantly or it will stick to the bottom of the pot. Cook and stir until the rice is very tender and most of the milk has been absorbed, about 8 minutes. At this point the rice should have a moist consistency.

Turn the heat off under the pan. Add the butter and Parmigiano, and stir well to incorporate. Taste, adjust the seasoning, and serve at once.

MANGIARE IN BIANCO

Italians turn to mangiare in bianco, *eating something white when they are a bit under the weather, when they want to lighten up on their diet, or when they have partied a bit too much the night before. It is believed that a plate of pasta or rice, dressed only with a bit of fresh butter and cheese, restores body and mind. Indeed, a bowl of hot rice tossed with butter and cheese is a basic comfort food.*

RICE WITH CAULIFLOWER
Riso con Cavolfiore

This unassuming dish comes from Verona. It speaks of simple home cooking with an abundance of taste. Some cooks brown a whole garlic clove in oil, then discard it. Others omit the anchovies. It is all up to personal preference.

1 head cauliflower (about 1½ pounds), broken into very small florets
¼ cup extra-virgin olive oil
1 garlic clove, minced
2 to 3 anchovy fillets, minced
1½ pounds ripe tomatoes, peeled, seeded, and minced (page 9)

Salt and freshly ground black pepper to taste
1½ cups imported Arborio rice
1 tablespoon unsalted butter
⅓ cup freshly grated Parmigiano-Reggiano cheese

Wash the cauliflower florets under cold running water. Bring a medium pot of water to a boil over medium heat. Add 1 teaspoon of salt and the florets. Cook, uncovered, until the florets are very tender, 4 to 6 minutes depending on size. Drain the florets and set aside.

Heat the oil in a large skillet over medium heat. Add the garlic and anchovies, and cook until the garlic begins to color, about 1 minute. Add the tomatoes and cook, stirring, for 4 to 5 minutes. Add the florets, then season with salt and several grinds of pepper. Cook and stir until the florets begin to break into smaller pieces, 3 to 4 minutes. Taste, adjust the seasoning, and turn the heat off under the skillet.

Bring a medium pot of water to a boil over high heat. Add 1 tablespoon of salt and the rice, and stir briefly. Reduce the heat to low and simmer, uncovered, stirring occasionally, until the rice is tender but still a bit firm to the bite, 13 to 15 minutes.

Put the skillet with the vegetables back over medium heat. Drain the rice and add it to the vegetables. Add the butter and Parmigiano, and mix well until the butter and cheese are melted and the vegetables are well incorporated. Serve hot.

SAFFRON RISOTTO TIMBALLO
WITH GLAZED MUSHROOMS

Timballo di Risotto alla Zaffrano con Funghi

❧

SERVES 6

Timballo is a molded dish that originated in Arab countries, where the dish was called *atabal,* or "drum," because the mold used for the dish was shaped like a drum. Originally the rich filling of the Italian timballos were enclosed by pastry dough. Today, most Italian timballos are made of rice and occasionally of pasta, and their shape changes according to the type of mold used.

In this preparation, the classic saffron risotto is turned into an elegant timballo enriched with sautéed mixed mushrooms. Serve it hot as a first course of an elegant dinner party or as a main course of a more casual gathering.

FOR THE RISOTTO

5 cups Basic Chicken Broth
   (page 21) or low-sodium
   canned chicken broth
⅓ teaspoon powdered saffron
   (page 12)
4 tablespoons unsalted butter
½ cup finely minced yellow
   onion
2⅓ cups imported Arborio rice
   or other rice for risotto
1 cup dry white wine
½ cup freshly grated
   Parmigiano-Reggiano cheese

FOR THE MUSHROOMS

⅓ to ½ cup olive oil
2 garlic cloves, peeled and
   lightly crushed
1½ pounds mixed mushrooms,
   such as white cultivated,
   chanterelles, shiitake, or
   brown mushrooms, wiped
   clean and thinly sliced
½ cup dry white wine
⅓ cup heavy cream
1 tablespoon chopped fresh
   parsley
Salt and freshly ground pepper
   to taste

Prepare the risotto: Heat the broth in a medium saucepan and keep warm over low heat. Dissolve the saffron in ½ cup of the hot broth, mix well, and set aside until ready to use. Butter a 4-cup ring mold generously and set aside.

Preheat the oven to 400° F.

Melt 3 tablespoons of the butter in a large skillet over medium heat. When the butter foams, add the onion and cook, stirring, until the onion is pale yellow and soft, 4 to 5 minutes. Add the rice and stir quickly until it is well coated with the butter and onion, 1 to 2 minutes. Stir in the wine and cook until it is almost all reduced. Add ½ cup of the simmering broth or just enough to barely cover the rice and cook, stirring, until it has been absorbed. Continue cooking and stirring the rice in this manner, adding the broth ½ cup or so at a time for about 12 minutes. Add the reserved broth with the saffron and stir until it is all incorporated. Add the remaining tablespoon butter and the Parmigiano, and stir quickly until the butter and cheese melt and the rice has a moist, creamy consistency. At this point the rice should still be quite firm since its total cooking time did not exceed 15 minutes. Taste and adjust the seasoning.

Spoon the risotto into the mold and fill it to the rim. Press the risotto into the mold lightly with a spatula or a spoon, making sure there are not empty spaces left in the mold. (It is important that the rice be packed tightly all the way up the rim of the mold or it might fall apart as it is unmolded.) Put the mold on a baking sheet and place the sheet on the middle rack of the oven. Bake for 10 to 12 minutes, then cover the rice with a large sheet of aluminum foil or parchment paper to prevent the rice from becoming crisp, and bake 10 minutes longer.

Prepare the mushrooms: Heat ⅓ cup of the oil in a large skillet over high heat. Add the garlic cloves and cook until they are lightly golden on both sides. Discard the garlic and add just enough mushrooms to fit comfortably in the skillet. (Do not crowd the mushrooms or they won't brown properly.) Cook, stirring, until mushrooms are lightly golden. With a slotted spoon, pick up the mushrooms and place on paper towels to drain. Add another batch of mushrooms to the skillet, and a bit more oil if needed, and sauté them until all mushrooms are done. Transfer them to paper towels to drain. (Makes approximately 2½ cups cooked mushrooms.)

Discard the oil left in the skillet and put the skillet back over high heat. Add the wine and cream, and stir quickly until the liquid begins to thicken and is reduced approximately by half. Return the mushrooms to the skillet, add the parsley, and season with salt and pepper. Cook and stir for a minute or two until the mushrooms are well coated with the thick, glazy sauce. Taste, adjust the seasoning, and turn the heat off under the skillet.

Remove the mold from the oven and let stand for about 10 minutes. Using a knife, gently detach the rice from the sides of the mold. Place the mold on a kitchen towel carefully because the mold is still quite hot, and place a large, warm round platter over the mold. Holding the bottom of the mold with the towel, invert it over the platter. Pat gently all around the mold to loosen the rice, then unmold it over the platter.

Reheat the mushrooms briefly if necessary, then pile them into the empty cavity of the rice. Bring the dish to the table and serve it.

VERSATILE MUSHROOMS

🍄 *This delicious glazed mushroom preparation can also be used as a sauce for fettuccine or tagliatelle.*

🍄 *It can be added to risotto alla Parmigiana during the last 3 or 4 minutes of cooking.*

🍄 *It can be stirred into boiled or steamed rice.*

🍄 *It can be served as a vegetable next to grilled or roasted meats or used as a topping for crostini or bruschetta.*

RISOTTO TIMBALLO WITH SAUSAGE STEW

Timballo di Risotto con Intingolo di Salsiccia

⁂

SERVES 6

Humble elegance. Here the elegance of a rice timballo is combined with an unassuming but delicious sausage stew. As with most timballos, this one can be served in small portions as a first course or as the whole meal for a casual dinner.

The stew can also be served simply by itself enriched with potatoes or beans.

FOR THE STEW

1 ounce dried porcini
  mushrooms, reconstituted
  (page 10)
1 pound mild Italian sausage
1 to 2 tablespoons extra-virgin
  olive oil
½ cup minced yellow onion
½ cup minced carrot
½ cup minced celery
1 garlic clove, minced
1 tablespoon chopped fresh
  parsley
1½ cups canned Italian plum
  tomatoes with their juices,
  put through a food mill to
  remove seeds
Salt and freshly ground black
  pepper to taste

FOR THE RISOTTO

5 cups Basic Chicken Broth
  (page 21) or low-sodium
  canned chicken broth
4 tablespoons unsalted butter
½ cup finely minced yellow
  onion
2⅓ cups imported Arborio rice
  or other rice for risotto
½ cup dry white wine
½ cup freshly grated
  Parmigiano-Reggiano cheese

Prepare the stew: Reserve 1 cup of the porcini soaking water and set aside. Put about 1 cup of water in a large skillet and bring to a boil over medium heat. Prick the sausage skin in several places with a fork and add it to the skillet. Cook, uncovered, turning the sausage a few times while it cooks, until all water in the skillet is evaporated, 12 to 14 minutes, and only the sausage fat is left in the skillet. Brown the sausage on all sides in its own fat, adding a little additional oil if needed, then transfer it to a dish.

Put the skillet back over medium heat, add a bit of the oil if needed, and stir in the onion, carrot, and celery. Cook, stirring, until vegetables are golden and begin to soften, 5 to 6 minutes. Add the porcini mushrooms, the garlic, and parsley and stir for a minute or two. Meanwhile, cut the sausage into 1-inch pieces and return it to the skillet. Stir briefly, then add the reserved mushroom soaking water and the tomatoes. Season with salt and pepper. Bring the sauce to a fast simmer, then reduce the heat to low and partially cover the skillet. Simmer 15 to 20 minutes, stirring a few times, until the sauce has a thick consistency. Taste, adjust the seasoning, and turn the heat off under the skillet. (Makes approximately 4 cups of sauce.) (The sausage stew can be prepared up to 2 days ahead, refrigerated tightly covered, or frozen for a month.)

Prepare the risotto using the ingredients listed above and following the instructions for Saffron Risotto Timballo on page 306. Butter a 4-cup mold generously and place the risotto in the buttered mold.

Preheat the oven to 400° F. Put the mold on a baking sheet and place the sheet in the middle rack of the oven. Bake 10 to 12 minutes, then cover the rice with a large sheet of aluminum foil or parchment paper to prevent the rice from becoming crisp and bake 10 minutes longer.

Remove the mold from the oven and let stand for 10 minutes. Using a knife, gently detach the rice from the sides of the mold. Place the mold on a kitchen towel carefully, because the mold is still quite hot, and place a large, warm round platter over the mold. Holding the bottom of the mold with the towel, invert it over the platter. Pat gently all around the mold to loosen the rice, then unmold it over the platter.

Reheat the sausage stew briefly if necessary, then pile it into the hollow cavity of the rice. Bring the dish to the table and serve.

RISOTTO TIMBALLO WITH EGGPLANT AND ZUCCHINI

Timballo di Risotto con Melanzane e Zucchine al Funghetto

❧

SERVES 4 TO 6

In Italy, a preparation of eggplant, mushrooms, and other vegetables cooked with olive oil, garlic, and parsley is called *al funghetto*. This delicious and versatile dish is traditionally served as a vegetable, but I also love it as a topping for crostini or bruschetta or paired with rice and pasta.

FOR THE RISOTTO

5 cups Basic Chicken Broth
   (page 21) or low-sodium
   canned chicken broth
4 tablespoons unsalted butter
½ cup finely minced yellow
   onion
2⅓ cups imported Arborio rice
   or other rice for risotto
1 cup dry white wine
½ cup freshly grated
   Parmigiano-Reggiano cheese

FOR THE VEGETABLES

½ cup olive oil
3 medium zucchini (about
   1 pound), cut into rounds
1 medium eggplant (about
   1 pound), purged (page 10)
   and cut into ½-inch cubes
2 garlic cloves, minced
2 tablespoons capers, rinsed
¼ cup fresh oregano leaves, or
   1 tablespoon chopped
   fresh parsley
Salt and freshly ground black
   pepper to taste

Prepare the risotto using the ingredients listed and following the instructions for Saffron Risotto Timballo on page 306. Butter a 4-cup mold generously and place the risotto in the buttered mold.

Preheat the oven to 400° F., put the mold on a baking sheet, and place the sheet on the middle rack of the oven. Bake for 10 to 12 minutes, then cover the rice with a large sheet of aluminum foil or parchment paper to prevent the rice from becoming crisp, and bake 10 minutes longer.

CONTINUED

Prepare the vegetables: Heat ⅓ cup of oil in a large skillet over high heat. Add the zucchini and cook, stirring, until golden, 4 to 5 minutes. With a slotted spoon, transfer the zucchini to paper towels. Add the eggplant and remaining oil if needed to the skillet and cook, stirring, for 2 to 3 minutes until the eggplant turns lightly colored and soft.

Return the zucchini to the skillet. Add the garlic, capers, and oregano or parsley. Season with salt and pepper. Cook and stir for a minute or two. Taste, adjust the seasoning, and turn the heat off under the skillet. (Makes approximately 3½ cups of cooked vegetables.)

Remove the mold from the oven and let stand for about 10 minutes. Using a knife, gently detach the rice from the sides of the mold. Place the mold on a kitchen towel carefully because the mold is still quite hot, and place a large, warm round platter over the mold. Holding the bottom of the mold with the towel, invert it over the platter. Pat gently all around the mold to loose the rice, then unmold it onto the plate. Reheat the vegetables briefly if necessary, then pile them into the cavity of the rice. Bring the dish to the table and serve.

Gnocchi

Basic Potato Gnocchi

Basic Ricotta Gnocchi

Chestnut Flour Gnocchi with Pancetta, Roasted Pine Nuts, and Sage

Sweet Chestnut-Potato Gnocchetti with Butter and Sage

Butternut Squash–Potato Gnocchi with Fresh Tomatoes and Basil

Beet Gnocchi with Lemon Cream Sauce

Spinach-Potato Gnocchi with Fish Sauce

Saffron Gnocchi with Mushrooms, Prosciutto, Asparagus,
and Cream Sauce

Swiss Chard–Ricotta Gnocchi with Tomato-Vegetable Sauce

Ricotta-Saffron Gnocchi with Shrimp, Leeks, and Peas

Spinach-Ricotta Gnocchi with Walnut-Gorgonzola Sauce

Buckwheat Gnocchi with Belgian Endive and Pancetta

Buckwheat Gnocchi with Clams and Bitter Greens

Potato Gnocchi with Sausage and Beans

Potato Gnocchi with Osso Buco Sauce

Potato Gnocchi with Bolognese Meat Ragù

Potato Gnocchi with White Amatriciana Sauce

Potato Gnocchi Baked with Taleggio Cheese

Baked Semolina Gnocchi with Smoked Mozzarella

Bread Dumplings with Porcini Mushrooms

When the potato, after a long journey from its place of origin in the Andes mountains, was brought across the Atlantic and arrived in Italy around the middle of the 1500s, it was looked upon with suspicion and was grown only as an ornamental plant. It wasn't until much later that people began to understand its gastronomical possibilities. Italian creativity prepared the humble potato in splendid new ways, one of which was the potato gnocchi. The first recipe for potato gnocchi appeared in a Genovese cookbook in the early 1800s. Later on, potato gnocchi became popular in several other northern Italian regions.

I, like many other northern Italians, grew up on potato gnocchi. In leaner times a plate of gnocchi would become "dinner." In more affluent times, the gnocchi would be dressed with a rich, mouthwatering sauce and served as the first course of a multicourse meal.

The original potato gnocchi was prepared by mixing pureed cooked potatoes with flour, kneading it into a basic dough, and shaping the dough into delicious little dumplings. Varieties of gnocchi have expanded dramatically. Today they are made with ricotta, semolina, spinach, bread, whole wheat flour, chestnut flour, squash, and buckwheat flour. They can be flavored with saffron or with beets. They can be round, flat, or oblong. They might have ridges or they can be smooth. They might be dressed with rich meat or game ragù or simply with a bit of butter and fresh sage.

The best place to experiment with gnocchi making is at home. Begin with a simple batch of ricotta gnocchi, which for me are the easiest to make, then go on and try other varieties. Potato gnocchi are perhaps the trickiest to handle because of the amount of moisture in the potatoes and their starchy quality. Make sure to read the tips that follow. Don't get discouraged if your first attempts are not satisfactory. Try again and remember that practice makes perfect!

GENERAL TIPS FOR GNOCCHI

The flour. The amount of flour needed for gnocchi varies according to the moisture of the other ingredients. When you mix flour with the other ingredients, start with a bit less than the recipe suggests, and add more as needed, as you go along.

The dough. The dough for gnocchi doesn't need to be kneaded more than a few minutes. The longer the dough is kneaded, the more flour it will absorb, resulting in heavier gnocchi. A perfect dough should be compact but moist, and it should roll easily on the board.

Testing the gnocchi. Before you prepare a whole batch of gnocchi, test a few to determine their consistency. Drop them in boiling water. If the gnocchi fall apart in the water, knead in a bit more flour. If they are too hard, you have probably added too much flour.

Boiling the gnocchi. Use a large, broad pan that will accommodate 5 to 6 quarts of water. The broader the pan, the more space the gnocchi will have to float around and the less the chance they will stick together.

Precooking the gnocchi. Gnocchi made with potatoes, squash, or other ingredients that contain a large amount of moisture tend to become soft and somewhat sticky if made to wait overnight, since they will release some of their moisture. The ideal solution is to make and cook them within a few hours. When this is not possible, the next best thing is to lightly precook the gnocchi. In that instance, drop the gnocchi in plenty of salted boiling water. As soon as they begin to come to the surface of the water, scoop them up and lay them on a large platter, making sure that they don't touch each other. Allow to cool, then refrigerate, uncovered, for several hours or overnight. When you are ready to use them, drop the gnocchi again in boiling water. As they come to the surface of the water, remove them immediately and toss them with the sauce.

Freezing. Frozen gnocchi are available in the market. However, when cooked, frozen gnocchi lose their texture and consistency and become soft and mushy.

BASIC POTATO GNOCCHI
Gnocchi di Patate

✣

SERVES 4 TO 6

4 large russet potatoes
(about 2 pounds)
2 teaspoons salt

1½ to 2 cups unbleached
all-purpose flour

Preheat the oven to 375° F.

Wash and dry the potatoes. With a large knife, make a deep incision length-wise in each potato. Put the potatoes in the oven and bake until they are tender, about 1 hour.

Let potatoes cool slightly, but peel them while they are still quite warm and put them through a potato ricer or mash them with a fork. (Do not mash them in a food processor.) Put potatoes into a large bowl and season with salt. Add 1½ cups of the flour, a little at a time, and mix well with your hands until the flour and the potatoes stick together into a rough dough.

Transfer the mixture to a wooden board and knead lightly, gradually adding the remaining flour if the dough sticks heavily to the board and to your hands. Knead the dough for 2 to 3 minutes until it is smooth, pliable, and just a bit sticky.

Divide the dough into several equal pieces about the size of an orange. Flour your hands lightly. (Do not flour the working area or the dough will not slide smoothly.) Using both hands, roll out each piece of dough with a light back-and-forth motion into a roll of about the thickness of your index finger. Cut each roll into 1-inch pieces.

Hold a fork with its tines against a work board, the curved part of the fork facing away from you. Starting from

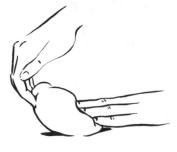

the curved outside bottom of the fork, press each piece of dough with your index finger firmly upward along the length of the tines. Let the gnocchi fall back onto the work surface. Repeat with remaining pieces of dough until all gnocchi have been formed. Place the gnocchi on a lightly floured platter or cookie sheet. They can be cooked immediately or kept in the refrigerator, uncovered, for several hours or overnight.

❦

NOTE

For shaping gnocchi with a cheese grater, see the Note in Basic Ricotta Gnocchi recipe (page 319).

BASIC RICOTTA GNOCCHI
Gnocchi di Ricotta

✤

SERVES 4 TO 6

1 pound whole-milk ricotta
⅓ cup freshly grated
   Parmigiano-Reggiano cheese
1 to 1½ cups unbleached all-
   purpose flour

2 teaspoons salt
1 large egg, lightly beaten in a
   small bowl

In a large bowl, combine all the ingredients except ½ cup of the flour. With your hands mix everything until the ricotta and flour are evenly incorporated and the mixture sticks together as a dough. Put the dough on a wooden board and knead it lightly for 2 to 3 minutes, adding a bit of the reserved flour if the dough sticks heavily to the board and your hands. When the dough is soft, pliable, smooth, and just a bit sticky, divide it into several large pieces of equal size.

Flour your hands lightly. Using both hands, roll out each piece of dough with a light back and forth motion, stretching it lightly sideways into a roll about the thickness of your index finger. Cut each roll into 1-inch pieces.

Hold a fork with its tines against a work board, the curved part of the fork facing away from you. Starting from the curved outside bottom of the fork, press each piece of dough with your index finger firmly upward along the length of the tines. With this action, the gnocchi will have the ridges of the fork on one side and the hollow indentation of your finger on the other side, which will allow the sauce to cling. Let the gnocchi fall back onto the work surface. Repeat with remaining pieces of dough until all the gnocchi have been formed.

Place the gnocchi on a lightly floured platter or cookie sheet. They can be cooked immediately or can be kept in the refrigerator, uncovered, for several hours or overnight.

NOTE

A cheese grater can also be used to form the indentations on the gnocchi. Pull the gnocchi up along the small-hole side of the cheese grater with your index finger, and let the gnocchi fall back onto the work surface. The gnocchi will have the hollow imprint of your finger on one side and the tiny imprint of the grater on the other. The imprints will hold the sauce beautifully.

CHESTNUT FLOUR GNOCCHI WITH PANCETTA, ROASTED PINE NUTS, AND SAGE

Gnocchi di Farina di Castagne con Pancetta, Pignoli, e Salvia

❧

SERVES 4 TO 6

The hills of Italy are covered with chestnut trees. My mother made delicious chestnut fritters for us kids and a great chestnut cake called *castagnaccio.* She also roasted the chestnuts in the old, heavy, black chestnut pan that had belonged to my grandmother. Somehow the long, cold winters of Bologna didn't seem so bad when we huddled around the large, heavy kitchen stove and happily munched on Mamma's delicacies.

Rustic chestnut gnocchi are perfect winter food. To appreciate the pronounced nutty taste of the chestnut flour, I have kept this sauce as simple and clean tasting as possible. You could also dress these gnocchi with unsalted butter, fresh sage, and Parmigiano.

FOR THE CHESTNUT FLOUR GNOCCHI

¾ cup chestnut flour

¾ cup unbleached all-purpose flour

1 pound ricotta

2 teaspoons salt

1 large egg, lightly beaten in a small bowl

FOR THE SAUCE

¼ cup pine nuts

2 tablespoons olive oil

1 garlic clove, peeled and lightly crushed

2 ounces thickly sliced pancetta, cut into ½-inch dice

3 tablespoons unsalted butter

5 to 6 fresh sage leaves

Salt and freshly ground black pepper to taste

½ cup freshly grated Parmigiano-Reggiano cheese

Prepare the gnocchi: In a large bowl, combine the chestnut flour and ½ cup of the white flour. Add all the other ingredients and make the dough and roll out the gnocchi as instructed for Basic Ricotta Gnocchi (pages 318–319).

Prepare the sauce: Preheat the oven to 350°. Place the pine nuts on a lightly oiled baking sheet and bake until golden, 2 to 3 minutes. Set aside.

Heat the oil in a large skillet over medium heat. Add the garlic and allow to brown on all sides. Discard the garlic. Add the pancetta and cook until it is golden, approximately 2 minutes. Off the heat, discard most of the fat in the skillet. Put the skillet back over medium-low heat and add the butter, sage, and pine nuts. Season with salt and pepper, stir for about 1 minute, then turn the heat off under the skillet.

While you are making the sauce, bring a large pot of water to a boil. Add 1 tablespoon of salt and the gnocchi. Cook, uncovered, over high heat until the gnocchi rise to the surface of the water, about 2 minutes. Scoop up and reserve about ⅓ cup of the gnocchi cooking water. Remove the gnocchi with a large slotted spoon or a skimmer, draining off the excess water against the side of the pot.

Place the gnocchi in the skillet with the sauce. Add the reserved cooking water and about half of the Parmigiano and mix well over low heat until the gnocchi and sauce are well combined. Taste, adjust the seasoning, and serve with remaining Parmigiano.

SWEET CHESTNUT-POTATO GNOCCHETTI WITH BUTTER AND SAGE

Gnocchetti Dolci di Castagne al Burro e Salvia

❧

SERVES 4 TO 6

This dish, which also utilizes the abundance of chestnuts in the mountains regions, came about at Christmas 1996, when I decided to create a first course that reflected the season and mood of the holiday. This dish takes its inspiration from the traditional squash tortelli of my region of Emilia-Romagna. It's an unusual, engagingly sweet dish that needs only hot golden butter, fresh sage, and freshly grated Parmigiano to be outstanding. Gnocchetti are gnocchi that are smaller in size than regular gnocchi.

FOR THE GNOCCHETTI

2 large boiling potatoes
    (about 1 pound), baked and
    put through a potato ricer
    (page 316)
6 ounces sweet chestnut puree
    (see Chestnuts, page 323)
1½ cups unbleached all-purpose
    flour
2 teaspoons salt
1 medium egg, lightly beaten in
    a small bowl

FOR THE SAUCE

3 to 4 tablespoons unsalted
    butter
8 to 10 fresh sage leaves,
    shredded
Salt to taste
½ cup freshly grated
    Parmigiano-Reggiano cheese

Prepare the gnocchi: In a large bowl, combine all the ingredients except ½ cup of the flour. Proceed to make the dough and roll out the gnocchi as instructed for Basic Potato Gnocchi (pages 316–317).

Bring a large pot of water to a boil. Add 1 tablespoon of salt and the gnocchi. Cook, uncovered, over high heat until the gnocchi rise to the surface of the water, about 2 minutes.

Prepare the sauce: While the gnocchi are cooking, heat the butter in a large skillet over medium heat. As soon as the butter turns lightly golden, add the sage and stir a few times. Turn the heat off under the skillet. (Make sure not to let butter become too dark.) Remove the gnocchi with a large slotted spoon or skimmer, draining off the excess water against the side of the pot.

Place the gnocchi in the skillet with the butter, season lightly with salt, and add a small handful of the Parmigiano. Toss well over low heat until gnocchi and sauce are well combined. Add a bit of the gnocchi cooking water if needed. Taste, adjust the seasoning, and serve with additional Parmigiano.

CHESTNUTS

Sweet chestnut puree in heavy syrup, imported from Italy or France, is available in jars or cans from specialized food stores. A wonderful substitute is roasted or boiled fresh chestnuts mixed with honey, but any one of the following would also work: roasted chestnuts sold in jars, canned whole chestnuts packed in water, or vacuum-packed chestnuts imported from Italy or France. (The vacuum-packed chestnuts are the sweetest and are moister.) If you are making gnocchi with any of these products, puree 6 ounces of chestnuts together with the potatoes, then add ¼ cup of honey, 1½ cups of flour, the salt, and the egg, then proceed as instructed in the recipe.

BUTTERNUT SQUASH–POTATO GNOCCHI WITH FRESH TOMATOES AND BASIL

Gnocchi di Zucca e Patate con Sugo di Pomodoro

❧

SERVES 4 TO 6

Sweet orange squash is a very popular vegetable in northern Italy, especially in Lombardy, Veneto, and Emilia-Romagna. Il Cigno Trattoria, in Mantova, uses squash as a filling for tortelli and mixes it with potatoes for unbelievably delicate gnocchi. These gnocchi taste best when tossed only with melted butter and fresh sage, or with ripe, fresh tomatoes and basil.

FOR THE GNOCCHI

2 large boiling potatoes (about 1 pound)
1 pound butternut squash (half of a 2-pound squash)
1¾ cups unbleached all-purpose flour
1 large egg, lightly beaten in a small bowl
2 teaspoons salt

FOR THE SAUCE

⅓ cup extra-virgin olive oil
⅓ cup finely minced shallots or yellow onion

1 pound ripe tomatoes, peeled, seeded, and diced (page 9)
Salt and freshly ground black pepper to taste
6 to 8 fresh basil leaves, finely shredded
1 tablespoon unsalted butter
⅓ cup freshly grated Parmigiano-Reggiano cheese

Prepare the gnocchi: Preheat the oven to 375° F. Wash and dry the potatoes. With a large knife, make an incision lengthwise in the potatoes and place on a baking sheet. Cut the squash lengthwise and place alongside the potatoes, cut part facing up. Bake until tender, 1 to 1½ hours.

As soon as you are able to handle them, peel the potatoes and the squash, put them through a potato ricer or mash them with a fork, and put them in a large bowl. Add 1½ cups of the flour, the egg, and salt. Proceed to make the dough and roll out the gnocchi as instructed for Basic Potato Gnocchi on pages 316–317.

Prepare the sauce: Heat the oil in a large skillet over medium-low heat. Add the shallots or onion and cook, stirring occasionally, until pale yellow and very soft, 6 to 7 minutes. Raise the heat to high and add the tomatoes. Season with salt and pepper. Cook, stirring, until the tomatoes are very soft, 5 to 6 minutes. Add the basil and the butter, stir once or twice, and turn the heat off under the skillet.

Meanwhile, bring a large pot of water to a boil. Add 1 tablespoon of salt and the gnocchi. Cook, uncovered, over high heat until the gnocchi rise to the surface of the water, about 2 minutes. Remove gnocchi with a large slotted spoon or a skimmer, draining off the excess water against the side of the pot.

Place the gnocchi in the skillet and mix well over low heat until gnocchi and sauce are well combined. Taste, adjust the seasoning, and serve with a sprinkling of the freshly grated Parmigiano.

BEET GNOCCHI WITH LEMON
CREAM SAUCE

Gnocchi di Bietole con Panna e Limone

❧

SERVES 4 TO 6

This is such a pretty dish that one almost hesitates to eat it. The first time I had a pasta dish with lemon sauce was in Bologna many years ago, at Ristorante Notai. It was served over thin, homemade angel hair, and was absolutely delicious. And this classic, simple sauce is the departing point for many other variations. A bit of prosciutto or smoked ham can be added. Cooked fresh peas, thin asparagus tips, or thinly sliced sautéed mushrooms can also be added. As always, a bit of cooking tradition and creativity make the cook's life in the kitchen wonderfully stimulating.

FOR THE BEET GNOCCHI

1 pound ricotta
⅓ cup freshly grated
   Parmigiano-Reggiano cheese
2 teaspoons salt
2 tablespoons finely pureed
   freshly cooked or canned
   beet
1½ to 2 cups unbleached
   all-purpose flour

FOR THE SAUCE

3 tablespoons unsalted butter
¾ cup heavy cream
½ cup Basic Chicken Broth
   (page 21) or low-sodium
   canned broth
Grated zest of 1 lemon
Salt to taste
½ cup freshly grated
   Parmigiano-Reggiano cheese

Prepare the gnocchi: Put the ricotta, Parmigiano, salt, and pureed beet in the bowl of a food processor and pulse the machine on and off until the beet is evenly blended with the ricotta. Transfer the mixture to a large bowl and add 1½ cups of the flour. Proceed to make the dough and roll out the gnocchi as instructed for Basic Ricotta Gnocchi on pages 318–319.

Bring a large pot of water to a boil. Add 1 tablespoon of salt and the gnocchi. Cook, uncovered, over high heat until gnocchi rise to the surface of the water, about 2 minutes.

Prepare the sauce: While the gnocchi are cooking, heat the butter in a large skillet over medium heat. As soon as the butter begins to foam, add the cream, broth, and lemon zest. Season with salt. Simmer the sauce, stirring, for a few minutes.

Remove the gnocchi with a large slotted spoon or a skimmer, draining off the excess water against the side of the pot. Place the gnocchi in the skillet with the sauce. Add about half of the Parmigiano, and mix well over low heat until gnocchi and sauce are well combined and the sauce clings to the gnocchi. Taste, adjust the seasoning, and serve with additional Parmigiano if desired.

SPINACH-POTATO GNOCCHI
WITH FISH SAUCE

Gnocchi di Spinaci e Patate
con Sugo di Pesce

❧

SERVES 4 TO 6

Potato gnocchi take very well to a large variety of sauces, from meat to fish sauces, to vegetable sauces, tomato sauces, or simply butter and cheese. This quick, fresh-tasting sauce can be prepared in 10 minutes. As it cooks, you should stir it often, breaking down any large pieces of fish or tomato so that in the end the sauce will be crumbly. Choose a soft, delicate fish such as sole, mahi mahi, halibut, or orange roughy.

FOR THE SPINACH-POTATO GNOCCHI

¼ cup very finely chopped
  cooked fresh or frozen
  spinach mixed with 1 large
  beaten egg
4 large boiling potatoes
  (about 2 pounds), baked and
  put through a potato ricer
  (page 316)
2 teaspoons salt
1½ to 2 cups unbleached
  all-purpose flour

FOR THE FISH SAUCE

1 pound ripe tomatoes, peeled
  and seeded (page 9)
⅓ cup extra-virgin olive oil
⅓ cup finely minced yellow
  onion

1 garlic clove, minced
1 tablespoon chopped fresh
  thyme or oregano
½ pound fillet of sole, orange
  roughy, or halibut, cut into
  ½-inch pieces
½ cup dry white wine
1 cup canned Italian plum
  tomatoes with their juice, put
  through a food mill to
  remove seeds
Salt and freshly ground black
  pepper to taste
¼ cup loosely packed finely
  shredded basil, or
  1 tablespoon chopped
  fresh parsley

Prepare the gnocchi: In a large bowl, combine all the ingredients except for ½ cup of the flour. Proceed to make the dough and roll out the gnocchi as instructed for Basic Potato Gnocchi on pages 316–317.

Prepare the sauce: Chop the tomatoes very fine, then collect the pulp and juices in a bowl and set aside until ready to use.

Heat the oil in a large skillet over medium heat. Add the onion, garlic, and thyme or oregano, and cook, stirring, until the onion is lightly golden, 4 to 5 minutes. Add the fish, and cook, stirring for a minute or two. Raise the heat to high and add the wine. Cook, stirring constantly, until the wine and fish juices are have reduced approximately by half, about 2 minutes. Add the fresh and canned tomatoes and season with salt and pepper. As soon as the tomatoes come to a boil, reduce the heat to medium-low and simmer, stirring occasionally, until the sauce has a medium-thick consistency and the fish is breaking apart and becomes an integral part of the sauce, 6 to 8 minutes. Add the basil or parsley, stir once or twice, and turn the heat off under the skillet.

Meanwhile, bring a large pot of water to a boil. Add 1 tablespoon of salt and the gnocchi. Cook, uncovered, over high heat, until gnocchi rise to the surface of the water, 1 to 2 minutes. Remove gnocchi with a large slotted spoon or a skimmer, draining off the excess water against the side of the pot.

Place the gnocchi in the skillet with the sauce and mix well over low heat until gnocchi and sauce are well combined. Taste, adjust the seasoning, and serve.

SAFFRON GNOCCHI WITH MUSHROOMS, PROSCIUTTO, ASPARAGUS, AND CREAM SAUCE

Gnocchi allo Zafferano con Funghi, Prosciutto, Asparagi, e Panna

❦

SERVES 4 TO 6

There are several variations on this lovely traditional northern Italian sauce, which uses prosciutto, mushrooms, asparagus, cream, and Parmigiano. The combination of golden saffron gnocchi with this mouthwatering sauce is simply blissful.

FOR THE SAFFRON GNOCCHI

1 pound whole-milk ricotta
⅓ cup freshly grated
　Parmigiano-Reggiano
　cheese
1 to 1½ cups unbleached
　all-purpose flour
2 teaspoons salt
⅛ teaspoon powdered saffron
　(page 12) beaten with
　1 large egg

FOR THE SAUCE

½ pound fresh asparagus tips
　(from 2½ to 3 pounds)

¼ cup extra-virgin olive oil
½ pound white cultivated
　mushrooms, wiped clean and
　thinly sliced
2 ounces thickly sliced
　prosciutto, diced
1 cup heavy cream
½ cup Basic Chicken Broth
　(page 21) or low-sodium
　canned chicken broth
Salt and freshly ground black
　pepper to taste
1 tablespoon unsalted butter
½ cup freshly grated
　Parmigiano-Reggiano cheese

Prepare the gnocchi: In a large bowl, combine all the ingredients except ½ cup of the flour. Proceed to make the dough and roll out the gnocchi as instructed for Basic Ricotta Gnocchi on pages 318–319.

Prepare the sauce: Bring a small saucepan of water to a boil. Add the asparagus tips and a pinch of salt, and cook until tender but still firm to the bite, 1 to 2 minutes depending on size. Drain the asparagus and set aside.

Heat the oil in a large skillet over high heat. When the oil begins to smoke, add the mushrooms and cook, stirring, until they are golden brown, 2 to 3 minutes. Add the prosciutto and stir once or twice. Add the cream and broth, then season with salt and pepper. Bring the cream to a boil, then reduce the heat to medium and add the asparagus tips. Cook, stirring, until the sauce has a medium-thick consistency, 3 to 4 minutes.

Meanwhile, bring a large pot of water to a boil. Add 1 tablespoon of salt and the gnocchi. Cook, uncovered, over high heat until the gnocchi rise to the surface of the water, 1 to 2 minutes. Remove gnocchi with a large slotted spoon or skimmer, draining off the excess water against the side of the pot.

Place gnocchi in the skillet with the sauce. Add the butter and about half of the Parmigiano. Toss well over low heat until gnocchi and sauce are well combined. Add a few tablespoons of the gnocchi cooking water if sauce seems a bit dry. Taste, adjust the seasoning, and serve with additional Parmigiano if desired.

SWISS CHARD–RICOTTA GNOCCHI WITH TOMATO-VEGETABLE SAUCE

Gnocchi di Biete e Ricotta con Salsa di Pomodoro

❧

SERVES 4 TO 6

In the fall of 1996 my husband and I spent a much anticipated vacation in the heart of Tuscany. Our only agenda was to rest and to dine in as many local restaurant and *trattorie* as was humanly possible. La Cantoniera, a lovely country restaurant near Radda in Chianti, served some of the best food we had in Tuscany. It was straightforward, rustic, and homey. This is one of their dishes.

FOR THE SWISS CHARD–RICOTTA GNOCCHI

¼ cup very finely chopped cooked fresh or frozen Swiss chard leaves or spinach, mixed with 1 large beaten egg

1 pound whole-milk ricotta

⅓ cup freshly grated Parmigiano-Reggiano cheese

1 to 1½ cups unbleached all-purpose flour

2 teaspoons salt

FOR THE TOMATO-VEGETABLE SAUCE

⅓ cup extra-virgin olive oil

⅓ cup finely minced yellow onion

¼ cup finely minced carrot

¼ cup finely minced celery

2 ounces pancetta, finely chopped

3 cups canned Italian plum tomatoes with their juice, put through a food mill to remove seeds

Salt and freshly ground black pepper to taste

10 to 12 fresh basil leaves, shredded, or 2 tablespoons chopped fresh parsley

½ cup freshly grated Parmigiano-Reggiano cheese

Prepare the gnocchi: In a large bowl, combine all the ingredients except for ½ cup of the flour. Proceed to make the dough and roll out the gnocchi as instructed for Basic Ricotta Gnocchi on pages 318–319.

Prepare the sauce: Heat the oil in a large skillet over medium heat. Add the vegetables and cook, stirring, until they are lightly golden and soft, about 6 minutes. Add the pancetta. Cook until pancetta has a nice golden color, 1 to 2 minutes. Add the tomatoes and season with salt and pepper. As soon as the sauce begins to bubble, reduce the heat to medium-low and simmer, uncovered, until sauce has a medium-thick consistency, 6 to 7 minutes. Add the fresh basil or parsley, and set aside until ready to use.

Meanwhile, bring a large pot of water to a boil. Add 1 tablespoon of salt and the gnocchi. Cook, uncovered, over high heat until gnocchi rise to the surface of the water, 1 to 2 minutes. Remove the gnocchi with a large slotted spoon or skimmer, draining off the excess water against the side of the pot.

Place gnocchi in the skillet with the sauce. Mix briefly over low heat until gnocchi and sauce are well combined. Taste, adjust the seasoning, and serve with the Parmigiano.

SAVORING THE SAUCE

Don't overcook the sauce or it will become too dense.

If you can get your hands on some fresh porcini mushrooms, slice them thinly and sauté in oil until golden. Add them to the sauce during the last minute or two of cooking.

To lighten a bit the color of the sauce and add shine and creaminess, stir a pat of unsalted butter into the sauce just before tossing it with the gnocchi.

RICOTTA-SAFFRON GNOCCHI
WITH SHRIMP, LEEKS, AND PEAS
Gnocchi di Ricotta e Zafferano
con Scampi, Porri, e Piselli

❧

SERVES 4 TO 6

I love ricotta gnocchi because they are lighter than the more traditional potato gnocchi. When I make ricotta gnocchi, I try to pair them with equally light ingredients. These gnocchi have a nice golden color from the saffron in the dough. The sauce is as delicious as it is quick to prepare, and the finished dish is colorful and inviting.

FOR THE RICOTTA-SAFFRON GNOCCHI

1 pound whole-milk ricotta
¼ cup freshly grated
   Parmigiano-Reggiano cheese
1 to 1½ cups unbleached all-
   purpose flour
2 teaspoons salt
⅛ teaspoon powdered saffron
   (page 12) beaten with
   1 large egg

FOR THE SAUCE

1 cup shelled fresh peas or
   thawed frozen peas
1 medium leek
¼ cup extra-virgin olive oil
½ pound medium shrimp,
   peeled, deveined, and cut
   into ½-inch pieces
Salt and freshly ground black
   pepper to taste
½ cup dry white wine
1 tablespoon unsalted butter

Prepare the gnocchi: In a large bowl, combine all the ingredients except for ½ cup of the flour, and proceed to make the dough and roll out the gnocchi as instructed for Basic Ricotta Gnocchi on pages 318–319.

Prepare the sauce: If using fresh peas, bring a small saucepan of water to a boil. Add a pinch of salt and the peas. Boil the peas on medium heat until they are tender, 5 to 10 minutes depending on size. Drain and set aside until ready to use.

Cut off the root of the leek and most of its green stalk. Cut leek in half lengthwise and slice it thinly. Place the leek in a colander and wash well under cold running water, making sure to remove all dirt.

Heat the oil in a large skillet over medium heat. Add the leek and cook, stirring, until pale yellow and soft, 7 to 8 minutes. Raise the heat to high, add the shrimp, and cook until shrimp begin to color, about 1 minute. Season with salt and pepper. Add the wine. Cook until wine is reduced almost by half, 1 to 2 minutes. Add the peas and stir until peas are heated through.

Meanwhile, bring a large pot of water to a boil. Add 1 tablespoon of salt and the gnocchi. Cook, uncovered, over high heat until the gnocchi rise to the surface of the water, 1 to 2 minutes. Remove the gnocchi with a large slotted spoon or skimmer, draining off the excess water against the side of the pot.

Place the gnocchi in the skillet with the sauce. Scoop up about ⅓ cup of the gnocchi cooking water and add to the skillet. Add the butter and mix briefly over low heat until gnocchi and sauce are well combined. Taste, adjust the seasoning, and serve.

SPINACH-RICOTTA GNOCCHI WITH WALNUT-GORGONZOLA SAUCE

Gnocchi di Spinaci e Ricotta con Salsa di Noci e Gorgonzola

✤

SERVES 4 TO 6

Gorgonzola is one of my favorite cheeses. I love it at the end of a meal, accompanied by pears and walnuts. Gorgonzola also becomes a sinfully delicious sauce when slowly simmered with cream and roasted walnuts. Freshly made, delicate gnocchi tossed with this sauce is an absolute delight.

Fresh Gorgonzola should have a rich white color and a soft, creamy consistency.

FOR THE SPINACH-RICOTTA GNOCCHI

¼ cup very finely chopped cooked fresh or frozen spinach mixed with 1 large beaten egg

1 pound whole-milk ricotta

⅓ cup freshly grated Parmigiano-Reggiano cheese

1 to 1½ cups unbleached all-purpose flour

2 teaspoons salt

FOR THE SAUCE

⅓ cup shelled walnuts

3 tablespoons unsalted butter

¾ cup heavy cream

3 ounces mild, sweet Gorgonzola cheese, cut into small pieces

Salt to taste

Prepare the gnocchi: In a large bowl, combine all the ingredients except for ½ cup of the flour. Proceed to make the dough and roll out the gnocchi as instructed for Basic Ricotta Gnocchi on pages 318–319.

Prepare the sauce: Preheat the oven to 375° F. Put the walnuts on a lightly oiled cookie sheet and place in the oven. Roast until walnuts have a light, golden color, 3 to 4 minutes. Remove from oven and place in the bowl of a food processor. Pulse the machine on and off until walnuts are finely chopped. Transfer to a bowl until ready to use.

Heat the butter in a large skillet over medium heat. When the butter begins to foam, add the walnuts and stir once or twice. Add the cream and Gorgonzola. Season lightly with salt. Reduce the heat to medium-low and simmer, stirring occasionally, until sauce has a medium-thick consistency, 3 to 4 minutes.

Meanwhile, bring a large pot of water to a boil. Add 1 tablespoon of salt and the gnocchi. Cook, uncovered, over high heat, until gnocchi rise to the surface of the water, 1 to 2 minutes. Remove them with a large slotted spoon or skimmer, draining off the excess water against the side of the pot.

Place the gnocchi in the skillet with the sauce. Mix briefly over low heat until gnocchi and sauce are well combined. Add some of the gnocchi cooking water if gnocchi seem a bit dry. Taste, adjust the seasoning, and serve.

BUCKWHEAT GNOCCHI WITH BELGIAN ENDIVE AND PANCETTA

Gnocchi di Grano Saraceno con Indivia Belga e Pancetta

❧

SERVES 4 TO 6

The idea of making buckwheat gnocchi came to me while I was eating a hardy, appetizing plate of short, broad buckwheat noodles, or *pizzoccheri*. After a few attempts with different flour proportions, I found the right formula and was able to produce lovely, taupe gnocchi. Buckwheat gnocchi are great tossed simply with butter and fresh sage, or with butter, cream, and fontina cheese. And they are absolutely wonderful paired with soft, slightly bitter endive and crisp, golden pancetta.

FOR THE GNOCCHI

⅓ cup buckwheat flour mixed with ½ cup unbleached all-purpose flour
1 pound ricotta (see Moist Dough, page 339)
¼ cup freshly grated Parmigiano-Reggiano cheese
2 teaspoons salt

FOR THE SAUCE

1 pound Belgian endive
⅓ cup extra-virgin olive oil
3 ounces thickly sliced pancetta, diced
1 tablespoon unsalted butter
Salt and freshly ground black pepper to taste
½ cup freshly grated Parmigiano-Reggiano cheese

Prepare the gnocchi: In a large bowl, combine all the ingredients and proceed to make the dough and roll out the gnocchi as instructed for Basic Ricotta Gnocchi on pages 318–319.

Prepare the sauce: Discard any wilted or bruised leaves from the Belgian endive. Detach the leaves and wash well under cold running water. Pat dry with paper towels. Stack the leaves one over the other and cut them into thin strips. Set aside.

Heat the oil in a large skillet over medium-high heat. Add the pancetta and cook, stirring, until lightly golden, 1 to 2 minutes. Add the endive and stir for a minute or two. Reduce the heat to low and cover the skillet. Let the endive cook and sweat until soft and almost wilted, 7 to 8 minutes. Add the butter, season with salt and pepper, and stir once or twice, then turn the heat off under the skillet.

Meanwhile, bring a large pot of water to a boil. Add 1 tablespoon of salt and the gnocchi. Cook, uncovered, over high heat until gnocchi rise to the surface of the water, 1 to 2 minutes. Remove the gnocchi with a large slotted spoon or skimmer, draining off the excess water against the side of the pot.

Place the gnocchi in the skillet with the sauce. Scoop up about ⅓ cup of the gnocchi cooking water and add to the skillet. Turn the heat to medium and mix well until gnocchi and sauce are well combined. Taste, adjust the seasoning, and serve with the Parmigiano.

MOIST DOUGH

If the ricotta is not creamy and moist, add a few tablespoons of milk to the gnocchi mixture, then work it into a dough and proceed as instructed.

BUCKWHEAT GNOCCHI WITH CLAMS AND BITTER GREENS
Gnocchi di Grano Saraceno con Vongole e Erbette

🐛

SERVES 4 TO 6

Every restaurant and *trattoria* in Italy serves bitter greens: arugula, Swiss chard, broccoli rabe, and puntarelle (wild chicory). These greens are served boiled with oil and lemon as a topping for pasta, or mixed raw with cultivated greens for salads. In this dish, wholesome buckwheat gnocchi are combined with small, tender clams and bitter greens in a most appetizing dish. Of course, this sauce is equally wonderful paired with dried pasta, such as cavatelli, orecchiette, or spaghettini.

FOR THE GNOCCHI

⅓ cup buckwheat flour mixed with ½ cup unbleached all-purpose flour
1 pound ricotta
¼ cup freshly grated Parmigiano-Reggiano cheese
2 teaspoons salt

3 pounds manilla clams (or the smallest you can get), cleaned (page 11)
⅓ cup extra-virgin olive oil
2 garlic cloves, minced
Salt and freshly ground black pepper to taste
1 tablespoon unsalted butter

FOR THE SAUCE

1 pound bitter greens (mustard greens, turnip tops, broccoli rabe, or Swiss chard)

Prepare the gnocchi: In a large bowl, combine all the ingredients and proceed to make the dough and roll out the gnocchi as instructed for Basic Ricotta Gnocchi on pages 318–319.

Prepare the sauce: Remove any bruised leaves and thick stems from the greens and soak in cold water. Wash the greens well in several changes of water, making sure to remove all dirt attached to the leaves. Tear the leaves into smaller pieces.

Bring a large saucepan of water to a boil. Add about 1 teaspoon of salt and the greens. Cook until tender. Drain well, making sure to remove as much water as possible, chop the greens roughly, and set aside until ready to use.

Put a large skillet over medium heat. Add the clams and cover the skillet. Cook just until the clams open. Transfer them to a bowl as they open. Line a strainer with paper towels and strain the clam juices into a bowl. Detach the clams from the shells and place in the bowl with their juices. If clams are large, cut in 2 or 3 pieces.

Heat the oil in a large skillet over medium heat. Add the garlic and stir until it begins to color, about 1 minute. Add the greens, and stir for about 1 minute until they are well coated with the oil. Add the clams and their juices. Season with salt and generously with pepper. Add the butter and stir for a minute or two or until the juices in the skillet have thickened. Turn the heat off under the skillet.

Meanwhile, bring a large pot of water to a boil. Add 1 tablespoon of salt and the gnocchi. Cook, uncovered, over high heat until the gnocchi rise to the surface of the water, 1 to 2 minutes. Remove the gnocchi with a large slotted spoon or a skimmer, draining off the excess water against the side of the pot.

Place the gnocchi in the skillet with the sauce. Mix briefly over low heat until gnocchi and sauce are well combined and the pan juices are thick. If gnocchi look a bit dry, add a few tablespoons of their cooking water to the skillet and stir quickly. Taste, adjust the seasoning, and serve.

POTATO GNOCCHI WITH
SAUSAGE AND BEANS
Gnocchi di Patate con Sugo
di Salsiccia e Fagioli

❧

SERVES 4 TO 6

This is a robust, unaffected dish that speaks the language of *la buona cucina casalinga,* or good home cooking. My mother had a great skill for this type of sauce, which she would combine with gnocchi, tagliatelle, or rigatoni. She also used such sauces as the savory base for soups or stews. I love this dish in winter, when the need for comfort food is deeply felt.

1 recipe Basic Potato Gnocchi
  (page 316)
½ cup dried cannellini beans,
  picked over and soaked
  overnight (page 11)
⅓ cup extra-virgin olive oil
⅓ cup finely minced yellow
  onion
1 link mild Italian sausage
  (about ¼ pound), casing
  removed and finely chopped
2 ounces pancetta, finely
  chopped

1 garlic clove, minced
4 to 5 leaves fresh sage,
  chopped
1 tablespoon chopped fresh
  parsley
2 tablespoons tomato paste
  diluted in 2 cups Basic
  Chicken Broth (page 21) or
  low-sodium canned broth
Salt and freshly ground black
  pepper to taste
½ cup freshly grated
  Parmigiano-Reggiano cheese

Prepare the gnocchi, place on a cookie sheet, and refrigerate, uncovered, for several hours or overnight, until ready to use.

Cook the beans and set aside. (For preparing beans ahead, see page 154.)

Heat the oil in a large skillet over medium heat. Add the onion and cook until it is lightly golden, 4 to 5 minutes. Add the sausage and pancetta. Cook, stirring, breaking down the sausage with a wooden spoon, until sausage and pancetta have a nice golden color, 3 to 4 minutes. Add the garlic, sage, and parsley, stir for about a minute, then add the diluted tomato paste. Season with salt and pepper. Bring the sauce to a gentle boil, then reduce the heat to low and simmer, uncovered, for 4 to 5 minutes. Add the beans and cook, stirring occasionally, until the sauce has a medium-thick consistency, 10 to 12 minutes. Keep warm.

Bring a large pot of water to a boil. Add 1 tablespoon of salt and the gnocchi. Cook, uncovered, over high heat until the gnocchi rise to the surface of the water, 1 to 2 minutes. When gnocchi begin to rise to the surface of the water after 1 to 2 minutes, remove them with a large slotted spoon or a skimmer, draining off the excess water against the side of the pot.

Place gnocchi in the skillet, add about half of the Parmigiano, and mix well over low heat until gnocchi and sauce are well combined. Taste, adjust the seasoning, and serve with the remaining Parmigiano.

POTATO GNOCCHI WITH OSSO BUCO SAUCE

Gnocchi di Patate con Sugo dell'Osso Buco

❧

SERVES 4 TO 6

Braising, a slow-cooking technique that produces tender, succulent meats and outstanding sauces, is used widely in great Italian cooking. When I make osso buco at my restaurant in Sacramento, I always double the amount of sauce so that we can serve it over gnocchi, pasta, or polenta. If you add also some of the meat, finely diced, to the sauce, you will have a richer, more interesting sauce.

1 recipe Basic Potato Gnocchi (page 316)

2 medium veal shanks (about 1 pound), cut 2 inches thick

½ cup all-purpose flour evenly spread over a sheet of aluminum foil

2 tablespoons olive oil

½ cup finely minced yellow onion

⅓ cup finely minced carrot

⅓ cup finely minced celery

1 to 2 ounces pancetta, diced (optional)

½ cup dry Marsala wine or white wine

1½ cups Basic Meat Broth (page 20) or low-sodium canned meat broth

2 cups canned Italian plum tomatoes with their juice, put through a food mill to remove seeds

Salt and freshly ground black pepper to taste

1 tablespoon chopped fresh parsley

1 to 2 tablespoons unsalted butter

½ cup freshly grated Parmigiano-Reggiano cheese

Prepare the gnocchi, place on a cookie sheet, and refrigerate, uncovered, for several hours or overnight, until ready to use.

Dredge the veal shanks in flour and shake off any excess. Heat the oil in a medium, heavy skillet over medium heat. Add the veal shanks and cook until golden on both sides, 5 to 6 minutes. Transfer the shanks to a dish. Add the onion, carrot, and celery to the skillet and cook, stirring, until they begin to color, 4 to 5 minutes. Add the pancetta if using, and cook for a minute or so.

Return the meat to the skillet, raise the heat to high, and add the wine. Cook until wine is almost all reduced, 3 to 4 minutes. Add the broth and tomatoes, season with salt and pepper, and bring to a gentle boil. Reduce the heat to low, cover the skillet leaving it slightly askew, and cook until the meat is tender and it begins to fall away from the bone, about 1½ hours. Stir and baste the meat a few times during cooking. Stir in the parsley, and set aside to cool slightly. When the meat is cool, cut it into small pieces (about the size of peas), put it back into the skillet, and mix well with the sauce. Taste, adjust the seasoning, and set aside until ready to use. (Osso buco can be prepared several hours or a day ahead.)

Bring a large pot of water to a boil. Add 1 tablespoon of salt and the gnocchi. Cook, uncovered, over high heat until gnocchi rise to the surface of the water, 1 to 2 minutes. When gnocchi begin to rise to the surface of the water after 1 to 2 minutes, remove them with a large slotted spoon or a skimmer, draining off the excess water against the side of the pot.

Put a large skillet over medium heat and add the butter. Place the gnocchi in the skillet and toss them quickly with the butter. Add about half of the sauce and ¼ cup of the Parmigiano, and mix well until gnocchi and sauce are well combined. Serve with a bit of additional sauce and Parmigiano if desired.

SLOW-COOKING TENDERNESS

The secret of a very tender osso buco is very slow cooking. Make sure to stir and baste the meat a few times during cooking. If the liquid in the pan reduces too much while simmering, add a bit more broth or tomatoes.

POTATO GNOCCHI WITH BOLOGNESE MEAT RAGÙ

Gnocchi di Patate con Ragù di Carne

※

SERVES 4 TO 6

Potato gnocchi pair extremely well with almost any type of meat sauce. My mother made terrific potato gnocchi, which she dressed with Bolognese meat ragù or a light tomato sauce. When you make a meat sauce, double or triple the recipe. Use what you need, and freeze what is left in several small containers so you will have an instant sauce for gnocchi.

1 recipe Basic Potato Gnocchi (page 316)	Salt to taste
	1 tablespoon unsalted butter
1 recipe Bolognese Meat Ragù (page 113)	½ cup freshly grated Parmigiano-Reggiano cheese

Prepare the gnocchi, place on a cookie sheet, and refrigerate, uncovered, for several hours or overnight, until ready to use.

Prepare the ragù and keep it warm over low heat. (The ragú can be prepared several hours or a day ahead.)

Bring a large pot of water to a boil. Add 1 tablespoon of salt and the gnocchi. Cook, uncovered, over high heat until the gnocchi rise to the surface of the water, 1 to 2 minutes. Remove the gnocchi with a large slotted spoon or a skimmer, draining off the excess water against the side of the pot.

Place the gnocchi in a large heated bowl. Add about half of the sauce, the butter, and ¼ cup of the Parmigiano. Mix everything well until gnocchi and sauce are well combined. Add more sauce if needed. Serve with additional Parmigiano.

POTATO GNOCCHI WITH WHITE AMATRICIANA SAUCE

Gnocchi di Patate all'Amatriciana

❧

SERVES 4 TO 6

One of the most famous of all Roman dishes is bucatini with white amatriciana sauce: thick, hollow spaghetti with a piquant sauce of onion, pancetta, garlic, chili pepper, and pecorino Romano cheese. In this dish, the fluffy potato gnocchi take the place of the bucatini, and Parmigiano-Reggiano replaces the more assertive pecorino Romano.

1 recipe Basic Potato Gnocchi
   (page 316)
⅓ cup extra-virgin olive oil
⅓ cup finely minced yellow
   onion
Chopped fresh red chili pepper
   or dried red pepper flakes
   to taste
¼ pound thickly sliced
   pancetta, cut into ½-inch-
   wide strips

Salt to taste
1 tablespoon unsalted butter
2 tablespoons chopped fresh
   parsley
⅓ to ½ cup freshly grated
   Parmigiano-Reggiano cheese

Prepare the gnocchi, place on a cookie sheet, and refrigerate, uncovered, for several hours or overnight, until ready to use.

Heat the oil in a large skillet over medium heat. Add the onion and chili pepper. Cook, stirring, until the onion is lightly golden, 4 to 5 minutes. Add the pancetta and cook until golden, about 2 minutes.

Bring a large pot of water to a boil. Add 1 tablespoon of salt and the gnocchi. Cook, uncovered, over high heat until the gnocchi rise to the surface of the water, 1 to 2 minutes. Remove the gnocchi with a large slotted spoon or a skimmer, draining off the excess water against the side of the pot.

Place the gnocchi in the skillet with the sauce. Season with salt, then add the butter and parsley. Mix well over low heat until gnocchi and sauce are well combined. Add some of the gnocchi cooking water if they seem a bit dry. Taste, adjust the seasoning, and serve with a sprinkling of grated Parmigiano.

POTATO GNOCCHI BAKED WITH TALEGGIO CHEESE

Gnocchi di Patate al Forno

❦

SERVES 4 TO 6

There are dishes that fit certain seasons perfectly. This is, without a doubt, a winter dish—rich, luxurious, and highly satisfying. It is also a simple dish and most of the preparation can be done ahead. If you are like me, after a portion of these gnocchi you will be happy with only a small, refreshing salad. But if you are like my husband, you will probably skip the salad in favor of a second helping of gnocchi.

1 recipe Basic Potato Gnocchi (page 316)
3 tablespoons unsalted butter
1 cup heavy cream
Small pinch of powdered saffron (page 12)

3 to 4 ounces taleggio or fontina cheese, cut into small pieces
Salt
½ cup freshly grated Parmigiano-Reggiano cheese

Prepare the gnocchi, place on a cookie sheet, and refrigerate, uncovered, for several hours or overnight until ready to use.

Heat the butter in a small skillet over medium-low heat. Add the cream, saffron, and cheese. Season lightly with salt and simmer, stirring, until cheese is melted, 1 to 2 minutes.

Preheat the oven to 400° F.

Butter a baking dish generously. Bring a large pot of water to a boil. Add 1 tablespoon of salt and the gnocchi. Cook, uncovered, over high heat until gnocchi rise to the surface of the water, 1 to 2 minutes. Remove the gnocchi with a large slotted spoon or skimmer, draining off the excess water against the side of the pot, and place in the buttered dish. Pour the sauce over the gnocchi, mix gently to coat, and sprinkle with the Parmigiano. Place the dish in the center rack of the oven and bake until gnocchi have a nice golden color, about 8 to 10 minutes. Remove from the oven, allow to settle for a minute or two, and serve.

BAKED SEMOLINA GNOCCHI WITH SMOKED MOZZARELLA

Gnocchi di Semolina con Mozzarella Affumicata al Forno

SERVES 6

Baked semolina gnocchi topped with butter and Parmigiano is known as *gnocchi alla romana.* Semolina gnocchi are made in the same way as polenta is made. The liquid, which in this case is milk, is brought to a gentle simmer, then the semolina flour is added by the handful and stirred constantly for about 15 minutes, until the yellow mass is smooth, velvety, and completely cooked. Butter, eggs, and Parmigiano are stirred into the mixture, which is then spread on a smooth surface to cool and firm up. When cooled, the semolina is cut into small rounds, placed in a buttered baking dish, topped with butter and Parmigiano—or as in this case by butter and smoked mozzarella—and baked until golden.

I can't even begin to tell you how incredibly alluring the aroma that permeates the kitchen is when this dish bakes. All of a sudden you find yourself wonderfully hungry and eager to get to the table. Soft, creamy Gorgonzola can be used instead of the smoked mozzarella.

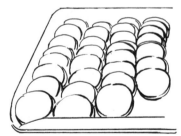

FOR THE SEMOLINA GNOCCHI

4 cups milk
1½ cups finely ground semolina
2 tablespoons unsalted butter, at room temperature
½ cup freshly grated Parmigiano-Reggiano cheese
2 egg yolks, lightly beaten in a small bowl

2 teaspoons of salt

FOR THE TOPPING

2 to 3 tablespoons unsalted butter
2 ounces smoked mozzarella, grated or diced

CONTINUED

Prepare the gnocchi: Put the milk in a heavy-bottomed, medium saucepan over medium heat. As soon as the milk begins to simmer, very slowly start pouring the semolina by the handful in a thin stream, stirring constantly with a whisk. When all the semolina has been incorporated, switch to a long-handled wooden spoon and stir constantly, making sure to reach all the way to the bottom and sides of the pan. As it cooks the mixture will become very thick and will bubble and spit back at you. Keep cooking and stirring until the batter comes away clean from the sides of the pan and forms a large, voluptuous mass, 15 to 20 minutes.

Remove the pan from the heat. Add the butter, Parmigiano, egg yolks, and salt and stir energetically and quickly until everything is thoroughly incorporated.

Moisten a smooth, cool surface with water and pour the mixture over it. Spread it out with a wet spatula to an even thickness of ½ inch. Dip the spatula into cold water as you spread it out. Let it cool completely.

Preheat the oven to 400° F. Butter a 13 by 9-inch baking dish generously.

Prepare the topping: Melt the butter over low heat. Using a 1½-inch round cookie cutter or small glass, cut the semolina into disks. Arrange the disks in the baking dish, slightly overlapping each other. Brush the melted butter over the gnocchi and sprinkle with the smoked mozzarella. (The semolina gnocchi can be completely prepared and assembled in the baking dish 2 days ahead. Refrigerate tightly covered. Allow the dish to sit at room temperature 2 hours before baking.)

Place the dish on the center rack of the oven and bake until the cheese has melted and gnocchi have a nice golden color, about 10 minutes. Remove from oven, allow to settle for a few minutes, and serve.

WASTE NOT

As you cut the cooled semolina into rounds, you will have odd pieces left over. Since nothing goes to waste in an Italian kitchen, this is how you can use them:

- *Cut them into smaller, more or less equal pieces and toss them with a light tomato sauce.*
- *Toss them with a bit of prosciutto and peas sautéed in butter and oil.*
- *Fry them, pile them on a plate, and let your kids enjoy them.*

BREAD DUMPLINGS WITH PORCINI MUSHROOMS

Gnocchi di Pane con Funghi Porcini

༄

SERVES 4 TO 6; MAKES APPROXIMATELY 20 DUMPLINGS

The cooking of the Trentino–Alto Adige region has been strongly influenced by its neighboring countries, Austria, Germany, Hungary. Canederli are large bread gnocchi quite unlike the typical Italian gnocchi. These dumplings, which are made from a few days'-old bread, are soaked in milk, combined with a variety of other savory ingredients, and shaped into large balls. The dumplings are generally cooked in broth and served either in their own broth or by themselves next to a stew. Of course, they are also wonderful dressed simply with sweet butter and Parmigiano or with any other light sauce that allows their wholesome flavor to come through.

The sauce of porcini mushrooms, fresh sage, and cream adds a delicate touch to this already wonderful dish. Take the pan with the dumplings to the table and serve them straight out of the pan.

FOR THE DUMPLINGS

½ pound stale Italian bread, crusts removed, cubed and soaked in 2 cups milk for 15 minutes
2 tablespoons unsalted butter
¼ cup finely minced yellow onion
1 garlic clove finely minced
1 large egg, lightly beaten
¾ cup freshly grated Parmigiano-Reggiano cheese
1 tablespoon chopped fresh parsley
2 ounces finely minced prosciutto
½ to ¾ cup unbleached all-purpose flour
Salt to taste

FOR THE PORCINI SAUCE

1 ounce dried porcini mushrooms, soaked in 2 cups lukewarm water for 20 minutes
3 tablespoons unsalted butter
1 garlic clove, peeled and lightly crushed
5 to 6 fresh sage leaves, shredded, or 1 tablespoon chopped fresh parsley
¾ cup heavy cream
Salt to taste
½ cup freshly grated Parmigiano-Reggiano cheese

CONTINUED

Prepare the dumplings: Heat the butter over medium heat. Add the onion and garlic and cook, stirring, until onion is pale yellow and soft, about 5 minutes.

Strain the milk through a sieve and squeeze the bread dry with your hands. Place the bread in a large bowl. Add the egg, onion, garlic, cheese, parsley, prosciutto, ½ cup flour, and salt. Mix well with your hands until well combined. If the mixture seems too sticky, add more flour. Cover the bowl loosely with a kitchen towel and refrigerate for about 1 hour to firm up the mixture.

Take a heaping tablespoon of the bread mixture and shape with your hands into a small ball about the size of a walnut. Roll lightly in flour, place on a floured cookie sheet, and refrigerate, uncovered, for a few hours or until ready to use.

Prepare the sauce: Drain the porcini and reserve the soaking liquid. Rinse the mushrooms well under cold running water, then chop them roughly. Line a strainer with 2 paper towels and strain the mushroom liquid into a bowl to get rid of the sandy deposits. Set aside.

Heat the butter in a large skillet over medium heat. Add the garlic and brown on all sides. Discard the garlic and add the mushrooms and sage. Stir for a minute or two, then add ½ cup of the reserved mushroom liquid and the cream. Season with salt. Reduce the heat to medium-low and simmer, stirring occasionally, until the sauce has a medium-thick consistency, 2 to 3 minutes.

Meanwhile, bring a large pot of water to a boil over high heat. Add 1 tablespoon of salt and the dumplings. As soon as the water comes back to a boil, reduce the heat a bit and cook the dumplings, uncovered, until they float to the surface of the water and are cooked all the way through, 10 to 12 minutes (see Note, below).

Place the dumplings in the skillet with the sauce. Add about half of the Parmigiano and stir gently over low heat, shaking the skillet to distribute the sauce evenly. Serve at once with the additional Parmigiano.

❧

NOTE

Once you have put together the mixture for the dumplings, take a small piece, form a ball, and drop it in boiling water. If the ball surfaces after 10 minutes without breaking, the mixture has the right consistency. If it breaks, a little more flour is needed.

When all the dumplings have been added to the boiling water, reduce the heat. Boil gently or the dumplings will break apart. If they seem heavy, perhaps you have added too much flour.

Polenta

Polenta—The Modern Method

Polenta—The Traditional Method

Baked Polenta with Sausage Ragù

Baked Polenta with Prosciutto and Onions

Molded Polenta with Pork Skewers

Polenta with Fontina, Butter, and Sage

Polenta with Beans

Soft Polenta with Pancetta, Garlic, and Hot Pepper

Soft Polenta with Bolognese Tomato Sauce

Small Polenta Timballos with Mixed Mushrooms

It is hard to believe that corn is not a native Italian ingredient. That's because for the past 250 years, polenta—not pasta—has been the staple of life for several northern Italian regions. In the Veneto, Lombardy, and Friuli–Venezia Giulia regions, preparing polenta is a ritual that gathered the family around the stove or fireplace where the polenta was cooked and stirred endlessly in a large unlined copper kettle called a *paiolo.*

Polenta, a wonderful dish that was once a poor's man staple, is now in fashion. Top Italian restaurants serve it in small amounts in delicious variations. *Trattorie* use it just as our grandparents did, with exuberance and joy as comfort food. It is great to see this dish back again—like recovering something precious that we thought was lost forever.

I have warm, vivid memories of the making of polenta: cold winter nights in Bologna. A humble kitchen with a large wood-burning stove. A small woman, my mother, stirs the golden polenta, reaching all the way to the bottom of the *paiolo.* A feeling of sharing, when all of us reach for the golden polenta mounded on a wooden board in the middle of the table and pile it in our dishes.

Polenta is a hard dish to categorize for it can be used in many ways. It can be an appetizer, a first course, an entrée, or a side dish. It can be served soft, straight from the pot, or sliced and fried, baked, roasted, grilled, and sautéed. It can be sliced and layered with meat sauces, then baked just like lasagne. Polenta is almost always served next to, coated with, or topped with savory ingredients. Just like pasta, the mellow flavor of polenta pairs well with myriad sauces and flavors.

Polenta can be made with coarse-grained or fine-grained cornmeal. The recipes in this book use a combination of the two, which produces a lovely medium-textured polenta.

While cooking polenta the traditional way—stirring and stirring—will enhance your appreciation of the dish, today it is possible to make very good polenta using a host of other methods. My favorite by far is the modern method, given here. That is the method for all the recipes in this chapter and that is what I suggest you use. It can be done with hardly any stirring, yet it produces a smooth, velvety, perfectly cooked polenta.

Other methods for making polenta are:

- *In an electric mixing pot.* This is fitted with a rotating arm that stirs the polenta constantly. (I have seen these pots in Italian specialty food stores.)
- *In the oven.* The cornmeal is poured into boiling water, transferred to a bowl that is sealed with foil, and baked in a preheated 400° F. oven for 1½ hours. It is stirred every half hour or so.
- *Precooked.* Polenta is sold precooked and this is ready in 10 minutes (but to this I say, no, no, no).

POLENTA—
THE MODERN METHOD

※

(SEE PAGE 357 FOR INGREDIENTS AND YIELD)

Bring the water to a boil in a medium pot over medium heat. Add the salt and reduce the heat to medium-low. As soon as the water begins to simmer, start pouring in the cornmeal by the handful in a thin, constant stream and stir constantly with a wire whisk to prevent lumps from forming. When all the cornmeal has been incorporated, pour the polenta into a large stainless steel bowl and put the bowl over a large pot containing 3 to 4 inches of simmering water. Check that the bowl does not touch the water, then cover the bowl completely with foil, sealing it well so that there is no escape of moisture, and cook 1½ hours.

Every 25 minutes or so, remove the foil and with a large spatula or wooden spoon, stir the polenta, reaching all the way to the bottom of the bowl. Make sure there is always enough simmering water in the pan. Add a bit more water if necessary. Cover the bowl with foil again after each stirring. When the polenta is done, after 1½ hours, it will be thick and appealingly smooth.

FOR SOFT POLENTA

Spoon polenta directly out of the pot into serving dishes.

FOR SOFT, CREAMY POLENTA

Add a few tablespoons of butter and some heavy cream to the polenta and stir well. Spoon it directly out of the pot into serving dishes. If the polenta is a bit too firm, stir in some additional water, chicken broth, cream, or milk.

FOR SOFT POLENTA PREPARED AHEAD

Make the polenta with the modern method and when done, keep it in the pot over very slowly simmering water. It will stay soft for 2 to 3 hours. Stir occasionally. When you are ready to serve, stir the polenta energetically with a large wooden spoon. If it is a bit too firm, stir in some water, chicken broth, or milk.

FOR FIRM POLENTA

As soon as the polenta is done, turn it onto a large board, shaping it with a large wet spatula into a mound, or spread it evenly with a wet spatula to a ½-inch thickness. Allow the polenta to firm up, about 15 minutes, before slicing it, and serve while still warm with your favorite sauce.

FOR BAKED, GRILLED, OR FRIED POLENTA

Turn the polenta onto a large board or baking sheet, and spread it evenly with a wet spatula to a ½-inch thickness. Allow the polenta to cool completely for 2 to 3 hours before using it. Polenta can also be prepared a day ahead. Keep it tightly covered in the refrigerator. Cut the polenta into manageable rectangles or squares. Bake, fry, or grill the polenta as instructed in the recipe.

POLENTA—
THE TRADITIONAL METHOD

SERVES 6 TO 8

7½ cups cold water
1 tablespoon salt

1½ cups coarsely ground
cornmeal mixed with
1 cup finely ground cornmeal

Bring the water to a boil in a heavy, medium pot over medium heat. Add the salt and reduce the heat to medium-low. As soon as the water begins to simmer, start pouring in the cornmeal by the handful in a thin, constant stream and stir constantly with a wire whisk to prevent lumps from forming. When all the cornmeal has been incorporated, keep the mixture at a constant simmer and stir the polenta constantly with a long-handled wooden spoon. Cook the polenta, stirring and checking its consistency, for about 30 to 40 minutes.

As it cooks, the polenta will thicken considerably and bubble and spit back at you. Keep stirring, crushing any lumps that form against the side of the pot. The polenta is cooked when it comes away effortlessly from the side of the pot.

BAKED POLENTA WITH
SAUSAGE RAGÙ
Polenta Pasticciata

❧

SERVES 6 TO 8

In many parts of northern Italy, especially in the cold high mountain areas of Trentino–Alto Adige and Friuli–Venezia Giulia polenta is the chosen vehicle for sauces. Here, polenta is cooled, sliced, and layered with a rich, savory sausage-porcini ragù, sprinkled generously with Parmigiano cheese, and baked. This is not a dish for timid appetites.

FOR THE SAUSAGE RAGÙ

1 ounce dried porcini mushrooms, soaked in 1 cup lukewarm water for 20 minutes

⅓ cup extra-virgin olive oil

½ cup finely minced yellow onion

1 pound mild Italian sausage, casings removed and finely chopped

2 ounces pancetta, finely minced

½ cup medium-bodied red wine

3 cups Basic Chicken Broth (page 21) or low-sodium canned chicken broth mixed with 3 tablespoons tomato paste

Salt and freshly ground black pepper to taste

1 recipe Polenta—The Modern Method (page 356), plus 2 tablespoons unsalted butter

TO COMPLETE THE DISH

1 cup freshly grated Parmigiano-Reggiano cheese

1 to 2 tablespoons unsalted butter

Prepare the ragù: Drain the porcini mushrooms and reserve the soaking water. Rinse the mushrooms well under cold running water and chop them roughly. Strain the soaking water through a few layers of paper towels over a small bowl to get rid of the sandy deposits.

Heat the oil in a large skillet over medium heat. Add the onion and cook, stirring, until it is lightly golden, 4 to 5 minutes. Raise the heat to high, add the sausage and pancetta, and cook, stirring, until sausage is lightly colored, 3 to 5 minutes. Stir in the mushrooms, cook for a minute or two, then add the wine. Stir until the wine is reduced by half, about 2 minutes. Add the reserved mushroom water and the broth with the tomato paste. Season with salt and pepper. Bring the liquid to a boil, then reduce the heat to low and simmer, uncovered, for 30 to 35 minutes, stirring occasionally, until the sauce has a medium-thick consistency. Taste, adjust the seasoning, and set aside until ready to use. (Makes approximately 4 cups sauce; only 2 cups are need for this recipe; see Note, below.)

Prepare the polenta: As soon as the polenta is cooked, add the butter and stir until it is melted. Pour the polenta onto a working surface and spread it evenly with a wet spatula to a ½-inch thickness. Allow the polenta to cool and firm up completely before using, 2 to 3 hours.

Preheat the oven to 400° F. Smear the bottom and sides of the baking dish with butter. Cut the polenta into slices to fit your baking dish. Cover the bottom of the dish with a layer of polenta, spread some meat sauce over the polenta, and sprinkle with Parmigiano. Repeat with one more final layer of polenta, meat sauce, and Parmigiano, and dot with butter.

Place the dish on the center rack of the oven and bake until the top has a nice golden color, 10 to 15 minutes. Remove from oven and allow the polenta to settle for a few minutes. Bring the dish to the table and serve.

NOTE

For this dish, you will need approximately 2 cups of sauce. Since the recipe yields 4 cups, you will have 2 cups left over. This was not a mistake on my part. It was planned so that you can freeze it and use it over rigatoni, fettuccine, or pappardelle.

BAKED POLENTA WITH
PROSCIUTTO AND ONIONS
Polenta Pasticciata al Prosciutto e Cipolle

SERVES 6 TO 8

Italians call dishes like this *pasticciati,* or "messy," because after they are baked, the layers of ingredients lose their identity and bind together in one scrumptious dish. This is a wholesome, cold-winter dish that can be modified to fit the availability of ingredients. Use boiled or baked ham if prosciutto is not available, and grated mozzarella for the Parmigiano.

1 recipe Polenta—The Modern Method (page 356)

FOR THE BÉCHAMEL

2½ cups milk
4 tablespoons unsalted butter
4 tablespoons all-purpose flour
½ teaspoon salt

TO COMPLETE THE DISH

¼ to ⅓ cup olive oil
2 large yellow onions (1½ to 2 pounds), thinly sliced
¼ pound sliced prosciutto, cut into thin strips
1 cup freshly grated Parmigiano-Reggiano cheese
1 to 2 tablespoons unsalted butter, cut into small pieces

Prepare the polenta: As soon as the polenta is cooked, pour it onto a working surface and spread it evenly, ½ inch thick, with a wet spatula. Allow the polenta to cool and firm up completely before using, 2 to 3 hours.

Prepare the béchamel: Put the milk in a small saucepan and bring short of a boil. While the milk is heating, melt the butter in another small saucepan over low heat. Raise the heat to medium-low, add the flour, and stir with a wire whisk for 2 to 3 minutes. Do not let the flour brown. Remove the pan from the heat and add about half of the hot milk. Stir quickly until the milk has been completely incorporated. Put the saucepan back on the heat and add the remaining milk. Season with salt. Cook and stir the sauce constantly until it has a dense, creamy consistency, 4 to 5 minutes. Set aside. (Makes 2¼ cups.) (For preparing the béchamel ahead, see page 113.)

Preheat the oven to 400° F. Smear some butter on the bottom and sides of the baking dish.

Heat the oil in a medium skillet over medium heat. Add the onions and cook, stirring, until very soft, almost wilted, 10 to 12 minutes.

Cut the polenta into slices to fit your baking dish. Cover the bottom of the dish with a layer of polenta. Spread a layer of onions over the polenta and top with the prosciutto. Pour in some béchamel and sprinkle with Parmigiano. Repeat with one more layer. Dot the last layer with the butter.

Place the dish on the center rack of the oven and bake until the top has a golden color, about 15 minutes. Remove from oven and allow to settle for a few minutes. Bring the dish to the table and serve (see Storing Cooked Polenta, below).

STORING COOKED POLENTA

If you are planning to keep the polenta for a day or two in the refrigerator after it is cooked, spread it on a cookie sheet with a wet spatula and allow to cool. (Dipping the spatula into cold water will smooth out polenta more evenly.) Wrap the polenta with plastic wrap and refrigerate until ready to use.

MOLDED POLENTA WITH
PORK SKEWERS
Polenta con Spiedini di Maiale

❧

SERVES 6 TO 8

Many years ago dish of this type was often available in country *trattorie* and if not, they would make it for a customer upon request. Today that is not always the case. In this preparation, the cooked polenta is poured into a bowl and allowed to firm up. Then it is unmolded over a large serving platter, brushed with garlic-scented oil, and served with grilled pork skewers.

FOR THE PORK SKEWERS

6 ounces pancetta, cut into
⅛-inch-thick slices
2 pounds center-cut boneless
pork loin, cut into 1-inch
cubes
30 fresh sage leaves
⅓ cup extra-virgin olive oil
2 to 3 tablespoons red wine
vinegar
Salt and freshly ground black
pepper to taste

1 recipe Polenta—The Modern
Method (page 356)

TO COMPLETE THE DISH

¼ cup extra-virgin olive oil
1 garlic clove, peeled and
lightly crushed
6 to 8 fresh sage leaves,
shredded
2 dried bay leaves, shredded

Prepare the skewers: Cut the pancetta into 1½-inch pieces. Thread the pork cubes, pancetta, and sage alternately on skewers. In a small bowl, combine the oil and vinegar and brush the meat with this mixture. Put the skewers in a deep dish, pour over remaining oil-vinegar mixture, season with salt and pepper, and marinate for an hour or two.

Prepare the polenta: As soon as the polenta is cooked, pour it into the buttered bowl. Smooth the polenta with a wet spatula and press it down gently, to fill the bowl completely. Leave for 10 to 15 minutes to allow the polenta to firm up.

Meanwhile preheat the grill, barbeque, or broiler and when nice and hot, add the skewers and cook 5 to 6 minutes on each side, until the meat has a nice golden color. Baste the meat with the marinade a few times

Heat the oil in a small skillet. Add the garlic, sage, and bay leaves, and cook, stirring, until the garlic begins to color, about 1 minute. Turn the heat off under the skillet and discard the garlic. Season the flavored oil lightly with salt.

Check the polenta to make sure it has firmed up, then turn the bowl onto a large, round serving platter. Pat the bowl gently to release the polenta. Brush the polenta generously with the flavored oil. Put a few skewers over the polenta top and arrange the remaining skewers all around the platter. Bring the platter to the table and serve.

MAKE A GAME PLAN

If you are well organized in the kitchen, then the cooking will move along smoothly. When I was teaching cooking classes, I wrote down a plan of action, numbering the dishes and steps I was going to do. That left me free to talk and teach, and my cooking seemed effortless.

POLENTA WITH FONTINA, BUTTER, AND SAGE
Polenta Concia

❧

SERVES 6 TO 8

This is a traditional dish of Piedmont. The polenta is enriched with locally made fontina cheese, Parmigiano, and butter, then served very soft and creamy, topped with sage-scented butter and more Parmigiano. For me this is one of the most sinful, delicious dishes.

1 recipe Polenta—The Modern
    Method (page 356)
3 tablespoons unsalted butter
½ cup freshly grated
    Parmigiano-Reggiano cheese

6 ounces fontina cheese, diced
10 to 12 fresh sage leaves,
    minced

Prepare the polenta. When done, add 1 tablespoon of the butter, about half of the Parmigiano, and the fontina and stir until cheeses are melted and are well incorporated with the polenta.

Melt the remaining 2 tablespoons butter in a small skillet. Add the sage and stir for a few seconds.

Spoon the polenta into soup bowls, pour some butter and sage over each serving, sprinkle with the remaining Parmigiano, and serve while hot and soft.

POLENTA WITH BEANS
Calzagatti

❧

SERVES 8 TO 10

In Emilia-Romagna, this polenta and beans used to be a staple of peasant and laborers. Country *trattorie* and *osterie* would serve this filling dish straight out of the cooking pot, along with homey stews or grilled sausages and ribs. Or it was fried to a crisp to accompany some locally made salami, mortadella, and prosciutto. Today's lifestyles and eating habits have banished this type of preparation. Too bad, because this is great winter food loaded with taste. Serve it in small portions, and use what is left during the week—either fried, grilled, or baked—instead of bread.

FOR THE SAUCE

½ pound dried red kidney
  beans, soaked and drained
  (page 11)
¼ cup extra-virgin olive oil
¼ pound pancetta, finely
  chopped
½ cup finely minced yellow
  onion
2 cups canned Italian plum
  tomatoes with their juice, put
  through a food mill to
  remove seeds

Salt and freshly ground black
  pepper to taste

1 recipe Polenta—The Modern
  Method (page 356)
½ cup freshly grated
  Parmigiano-Reggiano cheese

Prepare the sauce: Cook the beans, remove from the heat, and leave beans in the cooking water until ready to use.

Heat the oil in a medium saucepan over medium heat. Add the pancetta and onion and cook, stirring, until the pancetta is lightly golden and onion is soft, about 5 minutes. Add the tomatoes and season with salt and pepper. Simmer the sauce, uncovered, for 5 to 6 minutes. Drain the beans, add them to the sauce, and simmer until the sauce has a thick consistency, 10 to 12 minutes. Turn the heat off under the pan.

CONTINUED

Prepare the polenta and cook it for 1½ hours. Uncover the polenta and add the bean sauce. Stir for a minute or two until sauce is thoroughly blended with the polenta. Cover tightly with foil and cook polenta 10 to 15 minutes longer. At the end of cooking, the polenta should have a somewhat soft, but not runny, consistency. If too thick, stir in some water or chicken broth.

Spoon the polenta into individual serving bowls, sprinkle with the Parmigiano, and serve at once.

FRIED POLENTA

Pour any leftover polenta onto a baking sheet and spread it evenly ½ inch thick. Leave for a few hours to cool and firm up, then cut it into rectangles about the size of playing cards and fry in oil until crisp and golden on both sides. Serve as a rustic appetizer or to accompany a stew or braised meat.

SOFT POLENTA WITH PANCETTA, GARLIC, AND HOT PEPPER
Polenta Appetitosa

❧

SERVES 6 TO 8

This dish can be served as an appetizer, an entrée, or a side dish. The problem is that once you start eating this sensational dish, you won't be able to stop.

1 recipe Polenta—The Modern
    Method (page 356)
⅓ cup extra-virgin olive oil
¼ pound thickly sliced
    pancetta, cut into small strips
2 garlic cloves, minced
Chopped fresh red chili pepper
    or hot red pepper flakes to
    taste

Salt to taste
1 to 2 tablespoons chopped
    fresh parsley
⅓ to ½ cup freshly grated
    Parmigiano-Reggiano cheese

Prepare the polenta.

When the polenta has only a few more minutes of cooking, heat the oil in a medium skillet over medium heat. Add the pancetta and cook until it is lightly golden, about 2 minutes. Add the garlic and chili pepper, and stir briefly, making sure not to let the garlic turn brown. Turn the heat off under the skillet. Season with salt and sprinkle with the parsley.

Spoon the polenta into individual serving bowls, top with some of the sauce, sprinkle with the Parmigiano, and serve at once.

SOFT POLENTA WITH BOLOGNESE TOMATO SAUCE

Polenta con Salsa di Pomodoro alla Bolognese

❧

SERVES 6 TO 8

This is a dish that brings back a lot of wonderful memories because it was one of my mother's favorites. She made a great tomato sauce by simmering chopped ripe tomatoes with small chunks of onion, carrots, celery, and some fresh herbs, then she would puree everything through a food mill and serve the light, almost sweet sauce over freshly made tagliatelle or soft polenta. I can't even begin to tell you how immensely satisfying this rustic dish is.

1 recipe Polenta—The Modern
    Method (page 356)
⅓ cup extra-virgin olive oil
3 pounds ripe tomatoes, halved,
    seeded, and cut into ½-inch
    pieces
1 large yellow onion, thinly
    sliced
2 celery stalks, thinly sliced
2 medium carrots, thinly sliced
½ cup loosely packed fresh
    parsley, shredded

½ cup loosely packed fresh basil
    leaves, shredded
Salt to taste
3 tablespoons unsalted butter
¾ cup freshly grated
    Parmigiano-Reggiano cheese

Prepare the polenta.

While the polenta is cooking, prepare the tomato sauce. Heat the oil in a large saucepan over medium heat. Add the tomatoes, onion, celery, carrots, parsley, and basil. Season with salt. Stir well for a minute or two. Reduce the heat to medium-low, cover the pan, leaving the lid slightly askew, and cook, stirring occasionally, until the vegetables are soft, 1 to 1½ hours. Check to make sure there are enough watery juices in the pan. If not, add about ½ cup of water.

When the vegetables arc tender and soft, put them through a food mill. Return the vegetables to the pan with 1 tablespoon butter. Turn the heat up to medium and simmer the sauce for a few minutes. If sauce is too thin, cook it down until it has a medium-thick consistency. Taste and adjust the seasoning. (The sauce can be prepared several hours or a day ahead. Refrigerate tightly covered.)

When the polenta is done, add the remaining 2 tablespoons butter and ½ cup of the Parmigiano and stir until well incorporated in the polenta. Spoon the polenta into individual serving bowls, top with some of the sauce, sprinkle with the remaining Parmigiano, and serve at once.

SMALL POLENTA TIMBALLOS WITH MIXED MUSHROOMS
Timballini di Polenta Farciti

❧

MAKES 6 TIMBALES

In this preparation, polenta sheds its humble image and becomes the elegant opening of a special meal. This is a great dish for entertaining, since it can be prepared ahead of time, allowing you time to spend with your guests.

FOR THE FILLING

1 pound mixed mushrooms (white cultivated mushrooms, shiitake, cremini, chanterelles, portobello), wiped clean
⅓ to ½ cup olive oil
⅓ cup dry Marsala wine
⅓ cup heavy cream
Salt and freshly ground black pepper to taste
1 tablespoon chopped fresh parsley

1 recipe Polenta—The Modern Method (page 356)
2 tablespoons unsalted butter
½ cup freshly grated Parmigiano-Reggiano cheese

TO COMPLETE THE DISH

Several fresh sage leaves, minced
⅓ cup freshly grated Parmigiano-Reggiano cheese

Prepare the filling: Cut the mushrooms into slices and roughly dice them. Heat the oil in a large skillet over high heat. When the oil begins to smoke, add the mushrooms, making sure not to crowd the skillet, and cook until they have a nice golden color. (If necessary, cook the mushrooms in a couple of batches.) Add the wine and cook, stirring, until it is almost all reduced. Reduce the heat to medium and add the cream, then season with salt and pepper. Cook until the cream has a thick consistency and coats the mushrooms thoroughly. Add the parsley and turn the heat off under the skillet. Set aside until ready to use.

Prepare the polenta: When done, remove from the heat. Add the butter and the Parmigiano, and stir until the ingredients are well incorporated into the polenta.

Spoon the polenta three quarters of the way up the sides of six buttered 1-cup individual molds. With a wet spoon make a hollow cavity in the center of the polenta, spreading the polenta against the sides of the mold. Dip the spoon into cold water often, or the polenta will stick to the spoon. Fill the cavities with the mushroom mixture. Spoon some polenta over the mushrooms, then smooth the top of the polenta with the wet spoon, pressing it down gently. Set aside until ready to use. (The timballos can be prepared up to this point a day ahead. Keep tightly wrapped in the refrigerator.)

Preheat the oven to 400° F. Put the molds on a cookie sheet and place in the middle rack of the oven. Bake for 10 to 12 minutes. Remove molds from the oven and cool for a few minutes.

Meanwhile, heat the butter in a small skillet. Add the sage and stir a few times. Keep the butter warm over very low heat.

Turn each mold onto individual warmed serving dishes. Hold each mold with a towel (the mold is still hot), and pat it gently to release the polenta. Brush the polenta with sage-scented butter, sprinkle with the Parmigiano, and serve at once.

KEEPING SOFT POLENTA SOFT

Soft polenta will become firm if made to wait. When you are ready to spoon the soft polenta into the molds, work fast.
If the polenta is too soft, you will have a problem making the cavities.
These are my suggestions:

❧ *Fill all the molds three-quarters full. Let them sit for about 1 minute just to firm up very slightly, then make the cavities. Quickly fill each cavity with the mushrooms, top with the remaining soft polenta, and spread with the wet spoon.*

❧ *If the remaining polenta is too firm and hard to spread, add a few tablespoons of cream or milk and mix it energetically with a wooden spoon until it is soft again.*

Mail-Order Sources for Italian Specialties

Even though special Italian ingredients can be found in Italian markets, specialty food stores, and many supermarkets across the country, they are not available everywhere.

These mail-order sources will ship across the country.

Manganaro Foods
488 Ninth Avenue
New York, N.Y.   10018
(212-563-5331)

Balducci's
426 Sixth Avenue
New York, N.Y.   10011
(212-673-2600; for catalog,
    800-822-1444 or 800-247-2450)

Dean & DeLuca
560 Broadway
New York, N.Y.   10012
(800-221-7714)

Todaro Brothers
555 Second Avenue
New York, N.Y.   10016
(212-679-7766)

Convitto Italiano
11 East Chestnut Street
Chicago, Ill.   60611
(312-943-2983)

Vivande
2125 Fillmore Street
San Francisco, Calif.   94115
(415-346-4430)

Corti Brothers
5810 Folsom Boulevard
Sacramento, Calif.   95819
(800-509-3663)

Index

vegetarian sauce, 202
vinegar, balsamic, 5, 198
vodka, pasta with bresaola, cream and, 189–190

W

walnut:
  -Gorgonzola sauce, spinach-ricotta gnocchi with, 336–337
  pesto, lasagne with ricotta and, 109–110
water, from cooking of pasta, 150
white food, *mangiare in bianco*, 304
whole wheat spaghetti with smoked mussels, 235
wine:
  pasta with veal-prosciutto ragù with Marsala, 206–207
  quality of, 290
  red, risotto with sausage, beans and, 289–290
Worcestershire sauce, spaghetti with fresh tomatoes, pancetta, cream and, 222–223

Y

yellow (golden) pasta, 86
  and green noodles with mortadella, peas, and mushrooms, 122–123

Z

ziti:
  with Neapolitan pork ragù, 211–212
  with peppers and crisp bread crumbs, 209–210
  variations for, 210
ziti:
  con peperoni e pane tostato, 209–210
  con ragù alla Napoletana, 211–212
zucchini:
  bow ties with onion, cherry tomatoes and, 190–191
  and cabbage soup, 57–58
  and fresh tomato soup, 43
  and pea soup with pesto, 50–51
  risotto with timballo eggplant and, 311–312

soup, 52
spaghetti with fresh mint and, 227
tagliolini with shrimp, saffron and, 137–138
zuppa:
  di fagioli, cavolo, e riso, 30–31
  di fagioli misti, 36
  di fave alla Siciliana, 29–30
  di fave e carciofi, 70–71
  di fave e patate alla Napoletana, 28–29
  di funghi, patate, e speck, 40–41
  di funghi e fagioli, 26
  di funghi misti e pane, 27–28
  di lenticchie, 41–42
  di lenticchie e scarola, 53
  di orzo e funghi porcini, 64–65
  di scarola, 62–63
  di verza e pane al forno, 45–46
  di zucchine e pomodori, 43